BILLY NO MAPS

BILLY NO MAPS

WILL NETT

www.6epublishing.net

BILLY NO MAPS

@NettBill

ABOUT THE AUTHOR

Will Nett is an author, freelance writer and occasional gardener. His first book, My Only Boro: A Walk Through Red And White, was described variously as "mint", "class" and "a searing insight into the mind of a Northerner".

When he's not writing, he can be found travelling shambolically in either hemisphere, contributing to any number of websites/ magazines, or staring forlornly into the River Tees. He lives somewhere near Eston Hills.

ACKNOWLEDGEMENTS

Many people were complicit in the writing of this book, whether they knew it or not, but special mentions must go, in no particular order, to the following: Anthony Regan for his unstinting generosity in Las Vegas, Steven Wilson for convincing me to go in the first place, Umrish Pandya for casting an eye over the final draft, Chris Hill for full use of his uncomfortable settee, and Andrew Stebulitis for knowing anything about computers, which is far more than I do.

Mickey Zee made Los Angeles infinitely more accessible, and dangerous, and many thanks must go to Tahiti Faa'a Airport's inadvertent hospitality, Tony's Auto Wreckers in Alice Springs for getting us back on the road, and Lin Treadgold and family for food, wine and corrections.

Lastly, thanks to anyone who read one of the many early drafts, anyone whose settee/floor/lawn I slept on while writing this, and anyone who asks why they're not on this list.

CONTENTS

PROLOGUE

A few hours earlier he was in bed with Pamela Anderson. Now he was shooting craps with a bloke from Spencerbeck: me. It had been that sort of trip. One minute I'm playing dice in Caesar's Palace with an internationally famous rock star, the next I'm being kidnapped by a bunch of Fijian furniture salesmen. Twelve months ago I was about to fall off the edge of Europe and wondering how I was going to get as far as Amsterdam from the sun-bleached harbours of southern Portugal; now I'm holed up in a Harlem apartment block writing this. Forgive me if I lose track now and again; the mad Texan spinster in the room next door keeps interrupting to tell me stories about being kept awake by the incessant shagging of a household Hollywood star, and how she once worked in Manhattan's Garment District with an equally mad woman who claimed to be the wife of Jim Morrison. She didn't say they were equally mad; I deduced that for myself. After a year of relentless travelling you automatically know when someone is filling your head with tall tales. That's what I'm doing now... filling your head with tall tales.

Out of season, Faro, the southernmost tip of Portugal, is as sedate a place as it gets: a middling fishing town built on a slippery mosaic of narrow streets and cobbled courtyards that hark back to the Crusades. The Knights Templar made base at the Convento de Christo in 1162 and must have had a lot more luck than I did in finding somewhere to stay. I'm pretty sure they didn't have to ask the receptionist at the Hotel Faro for directions. I'll wager the Knights didn't ask someone directions to the RUA PSP Hostel either, then blatantly ignore them, only to bump into that same person as they headed the opposite way in a moment of awkwardness that will forever connect them. The RUA turned out to be the Scarlet Pimpernel of hostels. I'd passed it several times already and not noticed it. In hindsight, it was probably best to get a spell of hostel-hunting under my belt early in the trip as it would become a familiar routine over the coming months. That and lost luggage, ravenous hunger, varying stages of delirium, sunstroke, acute physical pain, fish head soup, cabin fever, drunkenness, dodgy customs officials and LA gang culture.

I had no set itinerary for Europe as such, except to visit someone out in the Dutch countryside just before Christmas. I'd then hook up with my friend, Tank, the following April for the business part of the trip: 38,000 miles, thirteen territories and fifteen flights that would take us through South East-Asia, Australia and New Zealand, South Pacific, and across the US. I packed my job in a few weeks before I flew to Portugal. I'd previously worked in a cinema. It was fun at the time but if you ever stopped to think about it, you were faced with the reality of having your soul destroyed slowly and systematically in an environment that smelled of popcorn – an aroma I now associate not with the magic of the silver screen, but with a combination of brain-numbing boredom and financial insolvency. So that's why I went, because of boredom. It's my greatest fear, but it's good because it keeps you moving, and now I was really moving.

"You won't last five minutes out there," was a recurring phrase as my departure date neared, so much so that I began to believe it, even though I knew how resilient I was capable of being when I had to. For example, there was the time I had to cook a lasagne in the kettle, but the less said about that the better. Previously I wouldn't have entertained the idea of travelling alone in places as far away as Bangkok, Sydney or some parts of the US, but in time I preferred to travel alone, especially after the calamitous episode of 'the fucking van', as it will be from hereon referred to. As anyone who's found themselves in a similar situation will testify, the intensity of travelling with someone, day after day, in difficult conditions, can really test a friendship.

For the time being though, I was on my own, lost in Faro, where I never really worked out the street plan, even after a few days, the way I would in other places. I struck out into the deserted town that first Saturday night, looking for something to eat and stumbled upon, because of the lethally-wet cobble stones, a seedy-looking backstreet taverner and ate like Henry VIII, laughing in the face of the imminent bill. Here it comes now: Portuguese entrecote steak, whatever that is, chick-pea and codfish brouhaha, bread and butter, and 'complimentary' carrots. Total: 23Euros, including pint. Writing about the 'complimentary' carrots, which puzzlingly cost 2Euros, reminds me of a couple of occasions dining out in South-East Asia, firstly in Singapore, then Bangkok, where I was royally fleeced in such a way that it was almost admirable. In Singapore, the bill for one meal included a $7 service charge and a $2 fee for the 'complimentary' nuts and napkins – we didn't even eat all of the napkins! – and in Bangkok, the suspiciously inexpensive lobster we'd gorged ourselves on was to be paid for by the poundage, as opposed to 300baht for the entire creature I understood it to be. My only consolation was that it suffered a slow painful death in a pan of scalding hot water, which would have been a fate too fine for the tuk-tuk driver who recommended the place. I was still travel blind at that point, the honeymoon period of the South-East Asian leg, but I would soon wise up.

First published in paperback in 2014
by Sixth Element Publishing
on behalf of Will Nett

Sixth Element Publishing
Arthur Robinson House
13-14 The Green
Billingham TS23 1EU
Tel: 01642 360253
www.6epublishing.net

© Will Nett 2014

ISBN 978-1-908299-57-4

British Library Cataloguing in Publication Data. A catalogue record for this book
is available from the British Library.

Printed in Great Britain.

Some names have been changed.

PART I: EUROPE

CHAPTER I:
PORTUGAL TO POLAND

Whereupon I become entangled in a smuggling plot,
haggle for Nazi loot and find a Da Vinci.

"I wanted to see the continent's remorseless edges, its dark corners."

On the Sunday morning, I walked around Faro harbour, where
somewhere nearby in 1917 the Virgin Mary had landed – I presume
she flew – to inform three local children of the imminent end of the
First World War, the fall of the Russian royal family, and of course
Sirhan Sirhan's assassination attempt on the Pope, that wouldn't
take place for another 64 years. She was accurate, I'll give her that,
but unfortunately for the good people of the Algarve, she didn't
leave any lottery numbers. In fact, her parting shot was much more
impressive than that; a fireball struck the site, curing blindness.
By midday, I was bored enough to go to church. If Portuguese
telly was the same as it is now, I wouldn't have thanked Mary for
restoring my eyesight. I would watch Contacto, a Richard and
Judy-style magazine show in which Richard was played by an able-
bodied Professor Xavier, followed by Belense Pura, the Portuguese
equivalent of Neighbours (I wonder if Rakelli and Abel ever got
together in the end?).

The church was conveniently located beside Faro's premier
tourist attraction: the Capela dos Ossos, or 'House of Bones'. It
was built in 1816, presumably during some sort of worldwide brick
shortage, using the skulls of 1,245 monks that now stared at me
from cloister to floorboard. A plaque above the door read: 'STOP
HERE AND THINK OF THIS FATE THAT WILL BEFALL
YOU' which at the time could have been seen as an omen for the
rest of the trip. It left little impression on me except to say that
it's the last place you would want to be in the middle of a bad acid
trip. I thought the adjoining church, the Largo do Carmo, would

provide some light relief after that, but the blinding gold-plated decor that festooned it was even more garish than 1,200 rotting monk skulls. Everything was made of gold – the walls, the altar, the priest. It was like Liberace's bedchamber. A little side room depicted statues of Christ on various stages of his road trip to Calvary: "Here's one of me with my crucifix" etc. I suddenly remembered that I too was on a journey, but without the thorny crown and incessant persecution, so I retired to the Columbus Bar to rethink my plans. It was there, surrounded by its flock wallpaper and dim lighting, that I saw a painting on the wall that carried the following inscription in Portuguese: 'WE SHOULD LISTEN TO A LITTLE BIT OF MUSIC EVERYDAY, DRINK A GOOD WINE, SEE A BEAUTIFUL PAINTING, AND SAY SOME WISE WORDS'. All this high art, convivial chat and general bonhomie on sun-kissed shores was good for tourists but bad for travellers. I wanted to see the continent's remorseless edges, its dark corners.

The next morning I flew into the frozen heart of Europe.

Nuria didn't know left from right. Not because she worked for a budget airline – their basic training isn't that basic – but because she was bored, like me. During the safety announcements, she just wafted her arms about, gesturing at nothing in particular and not bothering to keep up with the actual announcements. At no point did her facial expression change in any way, shape or form. It was totally frozen, glacial, yet retained its Portuguese sheen, the narrow brown eyes and smiling features. In it I saw the contrasts that make Europe so diverse. The mellow demeanour of the Portuguese, at odds with the austere seriousness of the northern reaches of Poland or Lithuania. The heat-baked lunacy of the Turks, alongside the admirable arrogance of the French. The precise efficiency of the Germans – well, it's true – chafing against the irredeemable awfulness of the Italians. Nuria's triangular face said it all.

The snow surrounding the airport in Krakow was six-foot deep in places but life went on as normal, unlike at home where everything grinds to a halt at the merest suggestion of winter. I hopped on a bus, any bus, thinking that it would eventually reach the city centre. I wasn't disappointed but most of the Monday morning commuters were when I whacked each and all of them dragging my backpack down the crowded aisle. I repeated the feat when the bus reached my stop at the Hotel Orbis. I blundered through the streets around the Stare Miasto looking for the digs I'd arranged to stay at after bumping into a disreputable-looking man at the airport who was attaching an advert for 'modest' accommodation to a noticeboard. He told me to see the 'witch' in room 1C and said she'd take care of everything.

"Oh, I don't know," said Victor, "it probably saved the city from something or other."

He was talking about Dzok the dog, through a cloud of duty free cigarette smoke, somewhere under the streets of Krakow's Rynek Glowny. I could just about hear him over the din of a group of Derby County-supporting stag weekenders, drawing up a mental map of the city's premier strip clubs in the adjoining room. Earlier, they'd mistaken me for a Pole and attempted to patronise me in a way that only the English can. I took it as a compliment; it reminded me that I was able to merge inconspicuously into the character of almost any nationality, in Europe at least. I think that's why Victor was opening up now, about all aspects of Polish life. He looked like a typical student, one that had 'dropped out' of society, and later he told me he'd studied at Bristol University but didn't finish the course on medicine and pharmaceuticals. He was one of the generation that fled to Western Europe after Poland joined the European Union in 2004, leaving a vacuum where skilled workers would have been.

"Have you been to Bristol?" a voice from the end of the bar asked. "Nobody ever finished anything there."

I saw a middle-aged man fall into Victor's profile. He introduced himself as Russ and immediately launched into a discourse on the pros and cons of being an Englishman living in Poland. Top of the cons list was the apparent lack of good cheese and HP sauce.

"I try and make a trip home every six to ten weeks," Russ explained, "to pick up supplies." He laughed then continued, "... and to annoy my ex-wife." He laughed again, this time joined by myself and Victor. He'd previously been the drummer in obscure punk band Anti-Pasti, and had done stints with the Egyptian Kings and a few other long-forgotten combos.

The classically-Polish barmaid interjected with the offer of more drinks. By classically-Polish I mean she was stunningly beautiful – flinty green eyes on high, wide cheekbones with mousey hair set round a deliberately skew-whiff fringe. Even if we weren't thirsty, she could have persuaded us to be. She wet her lips and turned towards the fridge, followed by three sets of eyes. Her jeans stretched impossibly tight over her thighs as she removed two bottles of Okicim lager and the remains of Russ's white wine. She flashed her teeth in the glass door before returning slowly to the bar. The drinks dispensed, she hopped back onto her stool and inspected her nails.

"Ze dog eez cute, no?" she said. "It sad story."

She looked mournful, and even more attractive, as Russ butted in. He was a 'why-should-anyone-else-talk-when-I-could-be?' type, but not in an annoying way. The barmaid rolled her eyes at me as Russ explained how the dog's owner was struck by a car on the Monte Cassino road a few miles away. After his master's death, Dzok returned to a nearby spot, at Rondo Grunwaldzkie, every day for a year to pine for the loss, and won the hearts of the city. They erected a statue of the dog in the park at Sukkienicza, not far from the scene of the accident. I'd seen it earlier that day when I was out walking. It seemed overly sentimental for as hardened a nation as Poland to commemorate a whining dog but we all pretended to be touched by the gesture simply because of the barmaid's presence.

Russ continued prattling away as I established the barmaid's name. Elsa was a student, but unlike Victor, intended to complete her graphic design course. Victor sniffed and tossed his shoulder-length brown hair into his cigarette smoke. His free time, he explained, was now divided between selling weed and terrorising any away fans that had the audacity to visit Wisla Krakow's football stadium.

"Football for idiots," Elsa added. "Wisla, they smash my friend's face with bottle," she motioned with one of my empties, "and now, he have two mouths."

I tried not to laugh at her description but Victor showed no such reservation. Elsa looked at him the way Lech Walesa used to look at General Jaruzelski.

The next morning, with a cure-proof hangover, I boarded a bus full of tourists on Krasinskiego that would take us to Oswiecim (Auschwitz). The landscape grew sparser with every closing mile as we slowly rolled through the plunging winter temperatures of southern Poland. Any reverie or chatter that had punctuated the bus journey soon vanished when we reached our destination and its familiar-looking railroad entrance. Through another ethereal snowstorm that seemed to swallow any sound, I could make out the black foundry work of the main gates: 'ARBEIT MACHT FREI'. Nobody spoke as we walked along corridors of discarded luggage and personal belongings over seventy years old, all of it destined to be eternally unclaimed. By the time we reached Carl Clambert's 'Block 16', my hangover was long gone. I was looking into a tiny brick room where prisoners were forced to stand on broken legs for 24 hour periods but I was thinking of Elsa. I was going to ask her to come to Berlin with me at the weekend. I was interrupted by a group of people noisily waving Star of David flags in the nearby communal shower blocks and it struck me as laughable that anyone would do this. It wasn't a place for celebration, whoever you were. They were like a bunch of ra-ra football fans on an annual picnic, stringing up banners and chanting from the Talmud almost a century too late. Across town at Birkenau the celebrations continued, this time at the site of what was once a human pyre. I stood in the guard tower that gave me a view of virtually all of the camp and its approaching roads, milling around with everyone else.

Descending the steps of the guard tower, I noticed a rotund middle-aged man taking a nip on an ornate hip flask. He looked like a hairy Zero Mostel, all black beard and matching monobrow hidden under heavy clothes and hat. I slowed down as I reached him then rubbed my hands together for warmth. He immediately thrust the flask towards me, sideways from his body, without turning his head. I took a big pull on the neck of the flask. It might as well have been a recently boiled kettle I was drinking out of and it was all I could do to not present to him my entire insides on the ground in front of us. I held in a massive retch as more visitors exited the guard tower. It tasted like some sort of scientific experiment into the effects of liquefied brass on the human body. The man laughed as a few concerned tourists admired my beaming face.

"Eez okay," laughed the man, "eez American."

The people ignored him but I didn't.

"I'm not American," I said.

"But you ver American shuzz," he said, looking at my feet.

I glanced down at my threadbare Converse and tried to find my voice.

"Only an Englishman would step out into an Eastern European winter wearing a pair of split Converse," I said.

"Aah, maybe," he replied, "or maybe you are Scottish."

"I'm definitely English," I said. "I like violent sports, Only Fools and Horses, and I take my tea any time I fucking well like."

He squinted into his flask, then at me, as if the contents had driven me half mental. Then he laughed loudly across the far fields, a laugh never heard at Auschwitz before or since.

"My name is Josef," he said. "I am a German, but my vife, she make me come here, alvays in ze focken vinter. Alvays."

"Come," he said, ushering me towards the car park. He struggled in the compacted snow, grumbling about everything as his cheap trouser legs rode up and let in slush. He waved the flask in the direction of his wife and shouted to her in German. It was as if he was trying to embarrass her. She looked long-suffering, even from this distance. She broke away from the group, as if to keep Josef from them and immediately began to henpeck him. She straightened his lapels and wiped his trouser legs as he gave me a sideways glance of the 'what can you do?' variety. When she returned to eye level,

I could see she would have been a real piece of work in her youth, all lost in a blizzard of botox and liposuction.

She had an over-elaborate haircut, certainly for someone visiting Auschwitz, and was awash with jewellery of every possible kind. Only her thumbs were without rings, the rest of her fingers covered with ruby and emerald-mounted gold. Beyond the hands, her wrists were covered with any amount of bangles and bracelets that clattered up and down as she tended to Josef.

"Eez Elaine," said Josef, gesturing to her. She took no notice so I just smiled.

He went on, "Elaine, eez vot ve be looking for. Englishman. Look."

She looked up from her crouched position and still managed to appear condescending.

"I think eez American though, ha ha. Look at shuzz."

"Anyone can see he's English," she said, breaking her silence. She had a cut glass British accent that reminded me of Liz Hurley, or at least her domineering Jewish mother-in-law.

"Sez vill drink tea anytime he focken like, ha ha," said Josef.

Elaine returned to her standing position. "Definitely English then," she snorted. "The only time an Englishman puts down his tea is to fire a missile. What's his name?"

Josef looked sideways once more and raised his eyebrows.

"It's Will," I said, offering a hand. She waved it away with the hankie she'd used to clean Josef's trousers.

"Aah, Vill, Villhelm… is good German name," said Josef.

"Well I should go," I said. My bus was ready to leave and I could see the understandably glum passengers boarding from across the icy car park.

"You take ride home viz us," insisted Josef. "She drive crazy though."

Elaine didn't hear him. She was striding towards the car. A dangerous trip through blizzard conditions with an avuncular pissed German and his overpowering Jewish wife would at least give me a short story, I thought. How did they know where I was going?

In the car, when he could get a word in, Josef explained.

"Everyone who come here come from Krakow. Zer is nover else. You are going there, my friend."

He was right and I sensed his self-satisfaction as the car moved away. He said little else as his wife had undergone a transformation that compelled her to talk virtually non-stop throughout the journey. She complained about the tour guides at Auschwitz, about the traffic, the weather, and anything else you can think of, but again, always to Josef. She hardly acknowledged me and she swore like no-one's business. Even Josef winced. I hadn't spoken to an English woman for almost a week, let alone got next to one, certainly not one as refined as this one and I tried to imagine what she looked like back in the day as she steered us perilously through the blizzard. Every time Josef tried to placate her, she simply cranked it up a notch.

"This fuckin' snow… will it ever stop?"

How English of her to curse the weather.

I had lots of questions but I didn't dare ask them. I was about to chance a 'what line of work are you in?' when her phone rang.

"Oh fuck, fuck, fuck," she howled, "where the fuck is my phone?"

She gestured at the glove box with a gold-encrusted hand from where the faint tinny sound of Ravel's Bolero emanated.

Josef scrabbled for it, spilling paperwork into the footwell.

"Oh, just hand me the fuckin' thing," she ordered. "It'll be fuckin' Julia, I bet."

Julia must have been quite the chatterbox as she managed to silence Elaine for a blissful ten seconds.

As if to make up for it, she suddenly exploded.

"Oh well that's fuckin' great. Give the cunt half a page in a newspaper and he thinks he owns the fuckin' world." She was paraphrasing Jeffrey Bernard if I'm not fucking mistaken. I pictured Julia holding the phone away from her head. Did Elaine work in publishing? That was my first thought; she was Jewish and talking about newspapers, a generalisation maybe. I may have landed on my feet. She cursed on and on as Josef sat quietly, all the way back to Krakow. When we reached the city centre, she pulled up on Bernadynska, in the shadow of Wawel Hill, and berated a rickshaw driver who cut across her. Then she spoke to me for the first time. I think Josef had fallen asleep.

"We'll be at Moana tonight. About nine. You can return the favour of the lift for us."

Could I? It seemed like a North London accent to me, but then anything south of the Trent sounded like London to me. I'd heard of Moana. It was a new place somewhere off the Rynek Glowny where they served warm beer that the locals wouldn't touch.

"I'll try and be there," I mumbled.

"You'll be there," she said, pursing her duckbill lips.

Josef woke up with a start when I opened the car door.

"Who'll be where?" he shouted, still half dozing.

"Will's coming to see us at Moana tonight," Elaine said impatiently.

"Oh, yes, Vill, I see you zis evening. Ze beer is varm, like English beer, no?"

"I'll see you there," I lied, closing the door. "Thanks for the lift."

Josef waved with one hand and rubbed his beard with the other as I joined the crowds of tourists and commuters in the last of the daylight. I walked up Grodzka to the main square as Josef and Elaine disappeared towards Kazimierz. It's not every day you're accosted at a concentration camp by a foul-mouthed cockney Jewess and her narcoleptic German husband.

I reached my shithole digs over the basement jazz bar on Szewska to a chorus of Polish domestic discordance from the couple next door whose daily routine seemed to consist of fuck-fight-fuck-fight-fuck-fight in precisely that sequence. They were presently on the fight section of the itinerary as I opened my dry-rotting front door onto a festival of epic cockroachery and creakiness. Every single part of the one room apartment made a noise that it wasn't supposed to. The taps sounded like they were passing a litre of gravel whenever you turned them on. The heating system, for what good it was during a Polish winter, clucked and rumbled constantly and gave little return for its trouble. The windows were nailed shut, inside and out, and the WWII-era wallpaper was permanently occupied with peeling itself from the wall. Other than that, the place was a real palace, and I was paying 35Euros a night to the spiv

I'd met at the airport for the pleasure. The neighbours switched to fuck mode as I wrote up the day's events and considered the coming evening. I'd meet with Josef and Elaine, I'd now decided, purely out of intrigue, then head round to see Elsa at the bar, and give her some patois about needing someone to show me round the city tomorrow, my last day before I headed for Berlin, or Budapest, or Bratislava, or somewhere else beginning with B. As I prepared to go out, I could hear the couple from next door arguing on the landing. Normally, being an Englishman, I'd avoid any such confrontation but it's always nice to put a face to the orgasm so out I went. They hardly noticed me as I edged past them. The girl looked like she liked her food and the man, like a large majority of Krakowians of a certain age, looked like a young Trotsky. I made a mental note never to hear them having sex again.

It was still snowing as I stepped out, swerving to avoid the jazz musicians as they ferried their instruments into the club. I'd probably be listening to them in a few hours time, if all went to plan, as I was going to invite Elsa back, even though I dreaded her seeing the apartment, but maybe I was getting ahead of myself. First I had to find the Moana bar, which was about as probable as me finding a gateway to another dimension in these conditions on the streets. I was dressed for it though; I'd done away with the Converse and now looked like a Communist dock worker – heavy duty boots, fisherman's cap, black wool coat and matching facial hair. Having mastered the art of shuffling through deep snow over the previous few days, I no longer walked as though I'd shit myself, and moved across the main square towards the restaurant on Jadlostalya that I'd discovered on my arrival. It was well hidden but it did good food cheap, essential criterion for the budget traveller. The restaurant part, which was apparently based around the theme of gothic interpretations of fairytales – Washington Irving meets Aesop – was reasonably quiet but through a partition that separated the room from the bar, there was a party going on. I saw a lean-bodied stripper grinding away in the lap of a terrified birthday boy of about twenty. By the time I finished my Pierogi, the stripper and her client were down to the bare bones, much to

16

the delight of the rest of the party, and the stripper was dictating proceedings with a length of bamboo cane. I could hear it snapping through the air and cracking bare skin in between mouthfuls of my dessert. Every couple of minutes, the sweaty chef stuck his ugly head round the kitchen door to see what was going on at the party, much to the disgust of the waitresses and the all-female bar staff. If I'd have seen him before I ordered, I'd have probably eaten elsewhere.

As the party died down, I went for a piss in the dimly lit toilet whose only form of decoration was pro-Wisla Krakow graffiti. When I went to settle the bill, I was startled to see the stripper, as naked as her own birthday but for a pair of knee length boots, having her fee for the night begrudgingly counted out by one of the barmaids. I'd seen plenty of her through the partition but it was nice to get a close up. I queued patiently behind her bony body and pretended to look everywhere else but in front of me, but I couldn't. Her whispy black hair led down to a simple tattoo on the back of her neck, a thin crucifix design, comprising just the two lines of the cross on the nape of the neck. Another barmaid came from the kitchen and thundered around behind the bar momentarily before urging me to come forward and pay. Standing beside the stripper, we both counted money that would go in opposite directions – mine for the bill, hers for services rendered. She had a little button nose and too much thick black eyeliner. I heard the swish of the kitchen curtain as the chef's head once more made an inspection of the bar, this time with more interest than usual.

I liked this post-Communist Poland, where an aspiring writer could queue patiently alongside a naked stripper who now probably earned more in an hour than her parents did in a month of toiling in shipyards and scavenging for half-edible potatoes.

At Moana Bar, the walls were sloshed with orange paint and the tables were occupied by professional types drinking and smoking. Amongst them was the motionless bulk of Josef. He saw me and became animated, waving me, and the waiter, over at the same time. He offered me a seat then said something in Polish to the waiter.

The waiter scribbled in his note pad then disappeared, only to be replaced by Elaine.

"Will, how are you?" she said. There was no time to answer; she was already saying something else, this time to Josef.

"Did you get him a drink?", then to me, before Josef could answer, "Did he get you a drink, Will... you try this warm lager they do. It's fucking awful but you have to try it."

"It's coming, it's coming," Josef explained.

I sat down beside him. He'd somehow gotten a tie around his neck, or more likely Elaine had. The waiter returned and presented me with a bubbling pint of beer with two cinnamon sticks half-submerged in it. They bobbed up and down like a couple of fingers urging me to fuck off.

I supped from the glass cautiously. Elaine looked on; even Josef moved forward awaiting my reaction.

"It tastes like the fucking Thames," I summarised.

Elaine laughed out loud, while Josef of course looked puzzled.

"I won't fuck about Will," Elaine said, "we want to offer you a job."

Josef butted in. "A favour," he said. "Ve offer you favour."

Elaine glared at him, for his bad English, and for interrupting.

"We want you to transport a prized possession of ours across Europe."

Josef came in again. "To St Petersburg, only zis far," he said, almost pleadingly.

"You're travelling around anyway, aren't you?" Elaine asked. "So you can earn some money as you go. Good money. We like you because you seem to fit your surroundings."

This much was true; I'd somehow developed a knack, not deliberately, of going unnoticed amongst locals wherever I went, especially in Eastern Europe, as the Derby fans in Elsa's bar had discovered. No matter how much Elaine appealed to this 'skill', I'd already decided I wasn't going to Russia, but I was intrigued by this so-called 'prized possession'.

I instantly thought of some form of jewellery, a diamond as big as Josef's head perhaps, but why would they entrust that with a stranger? I declined immediately and began to rush my pint, which had begun to cool down and become something drinkable.

"I can't go to Russia," I said, breaking an awkward silence. In my head, I made the decision to go to Germany as soon as I could get a bus ticket.

Josef gave Elaine an 'I told you so' look as she lit another cigarette. She didn't seem put out by my refusal as I got up to leave. My knockback seemed to signal the end of our relationship.

"I have to ask…" I said, but Elaine jumped in before I could.

"I know what you're going to say. What was it? Forget we ever met Will, and good luck."

Josef nodded, and I never saw them again.

I wasn't the only one not going where someone wanted me to. Elsa wasn't moving either. She said she couldn't go to Germany with me as her mother was ill but instead said she'd show me around Krakow the next day, as a leaving gift. We met at the bus station where I bought a ticket to Berlin for the following morning. Elsa was in my ear at the ticket window, "Vy you go to Berlin, Vill? Once I go and my mother, she not tell my grandfather. He not let me go." She pulled an inquisitive face at me.

"He probably thinks the war is still on," I said.

"You stupid, Vill, you know this? Is because you Viking… always go North."

Speaking of stupid, we shoved past a bunch of American tourists and their countless bags and walked towards Kazimierz. Elsa wanted to visit the market. I didn't. Imagine all the excitement of an English market, go on, all of it, then transplant it to the coldest square mile on Earth. That's what the Kazimierz market was like. Some of the stalls even sold old family photographs in tatty picture frames. Elsa loved this.

"You can make up your own story about these people, Vill. They could be anyone. Is nice thing."

I wasn't so sure. I sifted through the buckled brass and old carpet on one stall and came to a selection of WWII memorabilia, if Nazi jewellery can be called memorabilia. Lighters, watches, pens, and there, in the middle of the pile, an Iron Cross. With Oak Leaves. Real or not, I wanted it. I picked it up and fingered the cold black steel. It had probably been fingered the same way by a bullet-riddled Panzer Corp as he took his last breath in the frozen mud of the Ardennes. Or had been made in a nearby factory and used by re-enactment groups for the past thirty years. It was more likely the latter, as indicated by the price; the fuzzy-faced Pole behind the stall wanted 70plz for it – about £15. That was steep, even for a replica. I knocked him down to 50plz, then finally settled on 40plz. I was over the moon; imagine the stories I could make up about it. And just moments earlier, I'd mocked Elsa for saying you could create stories around the old photographs. I inspected the medal closely, the swastika in the centre, above the 1939 inscription, and the year 1813 on the reverse. Elsa glided across the snow to see what I'd bought.

"Hmm," she huffed, "you are typical boy," and gave a crooked smile.

We circled the grounds of Krakow's centrepiece tourist attraction, Wawel Castle, as yet another dusting of snow settled on our shoulders. The castle sat majestically on Wawel Hill and from its highest point would have given views far beyond the city. It would also have made a fearsome sight for potential invaders as it was packed to the rafters with every type of bludgeoning instrument or blade you could think of. I fiddled with the Iron Cross in my pocket as Elsa chatted to one of the guides. They were speaking fluent Polish but I was nodding along knowingly, trying to look like I understood. My grasp of Polish was beneath limited; aside from basic greetings, it just about covered the following few words: uwaga, pisuar, kabinar, bizety, pimo and muyka, so if anyone needed warning about the cost of warm cubicle music, I was the go-to-guy.

As Elsa yapped away, I mused on the various travel experiences I'd had and would have: bored and alone in the Portuguese sunshine, and now, just days later, standing in the grounds of a snow-blown fairytale castle with Miss Krakow 2003. You could have shrunk the entire scene, put it in a glass ball and stuck it on your nan's mantelpiece. What next, I thought… in Germany, then to Amsterdam, where I'd been several times, then across to Malaysia. I was beginning to get a bit intimidated about it all when Elsa returned.

"What were you talking about?" I asked.

"He says he sees you with the dog smugglers," she explained.

"What?" I then pulled a face so confused it was last seen worn by the vicar at Elton John's first wedding.

"At Moana. He know your friends. They travel dogs through world with drugs inside them." She looked at me sternly for clues.

"Fucking hell," I said, a bit too loud for the elderly American couple who were passing in front of us.

They'd wanted me to smuggle drugs hidden in a dog into Russia. The dog was literally a drug mule, they just needed someone to walk it.

"Is why you go to Germany with me, Vill?" Elsa enquired. It was her turn to look like Elton John's vicar.

"No. No. I'm going because I like Germany. I'm not great with dogs at the best of times, not least when I'm sneaking them past Soviet customs men. I'm just surprised to hear what they were up to. I met them at Auschwitz. An English woman and her husband. A bit weird but nice enough."

"Yes, vell, you keep away from them," she ordered.

I liked this. It was like a proper relationship; we'd known each other for a few days and she was already telling me off in public and stopping me from seeing my friends.

"Come," she said, taking me by the arm.

The guide gave me his most satisfied glare as we walked down the ramp back towards Grodzka and the main square.

"Hey, Vill. You ever been to Paris?" Elsa said, out of nowhere.

"No."

"Italy?"

"No."

"Then you must come to Czatoryski museum. See something never before."

She was right. It was something I'd never seen before.

The Czatoryskis had been one of Poland's most prominent families and the modest little museum was testament to that. It was the usual collection of portraits of jut-jawed dukes and gleaming pike staffs but its showstopper was Da Vinci's Girl With An Ermine, a well-kept secret and one of only a few of his existing works. It was displayed in a darkened room, artfully lit, behind a velvet rope. The room fell silent as I stared at it. It was like looking at a photograph. A real Da Vinci, right before my eyes, in this tiny backstreet museum in the middle of Poland. Who knew? I stared so hard my eyes began to sting.

Elsa clumsily broke the silence. "You like this, Vill? Not like his other painting." Then she lifted her fingers to the corners of her mouth and pulled a glum face, referring, I think, to the Mona Lisa. Her green eyes looked sad and her cheeks were flushed by the heat after coming indoors. I smiled and looked back at the painting. It was over five hundred years old and had a colourful provenance. It was brought by the family's Prince Adam and hidden from the rampaging Russians during their march through Europe. A hundred years later, it was ferreted away by the invading Germans, before being returned, Nazi jackboot print and all, to the museum. Elsa had seen it many times before and was looking at the empty picture frame that hung opposite it.

"A Rafael," she said, pointing at the frame.

"Must have been one of his off days," I said. Rafael's empty frame would probably go for six figures if someone had produced it today.

"Nooo," she said. "Stolen. By Germans. They everywhere in Krakow."

The Nazis might have been in the jazz bar sixty-five years earlier, looking for Resistance members. It was that sort of place – a dark cellar with an arched brick ceiling low enough in places for me to have to duck. We took seats right down the front as the combo noodled away like only jazz musicians do – convoluted and at length. They covered all the jazz clichés: child prodigy on keys who was so talented it had actually made him blind, middle-aged geography teacher on bass, swinging cat at the back on brushes, and fragile songbird on vocals. People nodded pretentiously, stroking their chins during the solos and applauding at every opportunity. I almost jumped up and demanded they play Take Five. Now this was living. During the interval, Elsa called the waiter and ordered a bottle of wine that she assured me was 'Poland's finest'. Then she crossed her legs and carefully lit a cigarette. I was sitting so close to her I could hear the fiery crackle of the tip as she inhaled. Her flat chest rippled slightly beneath her v-neck t-shirt as she blasted smoke out across the room. It curled around, following the arch of the ceiling, then came back to us.

The wine arrived. Like all good wines, it looked cheap, tasted cheaper, and got the job done.

"You coming back, Vill?" Elsa said suddenly.

The wine, the smoke and the music had me thrown. Was I coming back?

I didn't hear the couple next door fighting or fucking that night.

CHAPTER 2:
GERMANY

A run in with the IRA, an overzealous Austrian housewife
and her husband, the Reeperbahn, and Rodrigo et Gabriela.

*"I sensed a story, that was all, either that or a good kicking,
so it was an even money shot."*

The bus journey to Berlin took around eight hours, including
several stops in Poland which I was sure I recognised from TV as
a child – the grey tenement housing blocks of Wroclaw, and the
barren farmland. I'd been on the road a week or so and I'd already
fallen in love with the place. Poland, or Krakow at least, was cheap,
easy-going, and friendly. The food was great, the wine was awful,
and you could easily get a job as a dog walker, or a drug smuggler,
if you wanted, and it had an interesting history. Not as interesting
as Germany though.

Berlin's underground rail network was so efficient that even
I understood it. It was essentially a giant city-wide loop. For an
inner-city stop, you simply changed trains once on the outer line
and Gunter's your uncle. My stop happened to be on the outer
line, and unmissable in the form of the blue behemoth that is the
Generator hostel. It was overrun with German teenagers and the
kind of hostel I would grow to hate with everything on site, at
your fingertips, so you didn't have to go anywhere, or do anything.
The dining area was like the bridge of the Starship Enterprise and
the centrepiece was its futuristic circular bar. My new roommates
comprised a diverse trio of jokers made up of Umrish (proving
there is such a thing as a likeable Essex-born person under the age
of thirty), Imran from Bradford, and Colorado's latest export, Bart.
How they knew each other was unclear but they were getting along
nicely when I blundered into them. They even managed to rope
me into one of hostelling's most loathsome events: the pub crawl.

Now there's nothing I like more than heavy drinking sessions in some of Europe's capital cities but not when it's organised and directed by some incessantly chirpy clipboard-hugging tour guide. Instead I like to step off the track, maybe have a gun waved in my face, fall down some stairs, and have it all orchestrated by a volatile Macedonian cage fighter called Sasha. I was in luck then.

Fifteen of us met in the foyer on a Saturday night for Sasha's briefing. Away from the hostel, he turned into a wild man and on at least two occasions actually howled at the moon. We bludgeoned our way on to the train at Landsberger Allee and railed our way to the Oranienburg district, what Sasha called 'the sharp end'. I'd heard about the area but had somehow failed to find it during my daytime wanderings.

I could tell it would be to my liking when I discovered that most of the pubs were situated under railway bridges. It was on one of those bridges that Sasha gave his unofficial speech, considerably more colourful than the one at the hostel. He climbed up on to the railing, his hulking frame looming over the assembled Canadians and Americans who were egging him on. He was exactly the sort of leader Americans listen to – a mad-eyed ranting badly dressed idiot. The Canadians should have known better.

"We gonna be fuckin' drinkin'!" he bawled.

The Canadians roared.

"We gonna be fuckin' fuckin'!" At this, he beat his chest.

"And we gonna be fuckin' partying... awwoooooeearrghhowwwee!" That was the noise he made, I may have spelt it wrong.

A knot of late night shoppers visibly cowered as they passed the impromptu rally. Sasha leapt off the fence and his white hoodie filled out in the wind. He looked like the Angel of Death. Everyone lapped it up though, except Umrish, Imran and I. He burst through the crowd like a Tasmanian Devil, pumping his fists and shouting, and led us to our first port of call, Die Silberbisch. It was a dingy basement affair that was already overcrowded when we arrived but Sasha insisted we pile in like we owned the place, "like the Germans did in the fuckin' war" as he put it, a bit too loudly for my liking. Our group seemed to have doubled in size now, Sasha's rousing

25

call-to-arms on the bridge having recruited a few extra conscripts. It was so crowded inside that the only way to hold your drink, if you were lucky enough to get one, was high above your head. Any visiting Eskimos would have been right at home as it was virtually impossible not to touch noses with someone at some point. From the middle of the long room, I could just make out Sasha's big shoulders and stupid white woolly hat as he remonstrated with the bar staff. He'd pre-arranged a free shot for all of our party, or at least the original members, and now had to negotiate the logistical minefield of getting them into a glass and out to people's mouths, half of whom were either still outside or being crushed on the stone staircase at the entrance. It hadn't started well then. Now he was manhandling the customers around him to make space for himself, even holding one at arm's length by the throat. The scene became increasingly aggressive, and to me amusing, when 6ft 8" Bart somehow managed to hoist Umrish, who is one of the smallest, lightest, fully-formed humans I've ever met, up above his head and set him adrift over the heads of the crowd who were only too happy to pass him along. The look on his face was priceless. Every so often Umrish resurfaced, or a body part did, as he looked for somewhere to disembark. In the interim he'd have to settle for being thrown around like a bottle of piss at a rock concert forever, or until closing time, whichever came first. Bart was shouting at him to swoop down on the bar and grab a round of drinks for us. The rest of us squeezed back out onto the street and awaited further instruction. Moments later Sasha cut through the crowd.

"Fuckers," he shouted, so loudly I wondered if Elsa heard him. I assume he was referring to the bar staff. I should stop using the verb 'shouted' to describe Sasha's delivery. All you need to know is that everything was shouted.

"One guy is on the fuckin' ceiling in there!" That'll be Umrish then. "Come." He led us down a couple of nearby streets to the next drinking post, which was exactly that, or to be precise a gated courtyard surrounded by apartments. When we had to climb the gates to get in, I knew it wasn't a legitimate venue. Bart was halfway over the gates as Imran and I looked at each other with matching expressions of puzzlement. Bart came close up to the gate from his side and said, "Hey, you Limeys coming in or what? Should have wore your hiking gear, huh?" His beaming American toothpaste advert face was beginning to get up my nose but his comment did make me momentarily assess mine and Imran's attire. This would have been lost on Bart, who was kitted out in the event of an Arctic holocaust with all the latest Rocky Mountains costumery, but when you come from North Yorkshire the only protection from the elements anyone has ever troubled themselves with is a five o'clock shadow and a copy of the Evening Gazette to wear on your head if it rains. It was somewhere below zero in Berlin, in December, and I was still wearing those Converse, as usual, jeans, and an Iggy Pop t-shirt. I'd gone to the flat Iggy once shared with David Bowie – talk about the original 'odd couple' – the day before. It was up by the Mauer Park, a spartan concrete monstrosity once infested with crackheads and drug dealers but now the much more acceptable bohemian face of Berlin – all vintage clothes shops, bistros and art galleries, all set around Schonhauer Allee and hipster-only hangouts like White Trash, which seems to have cornered the market in Chinese restaurant/nightclub country and western-themed tattoo parlors.

Once over the gates, and once again joined by Umrish, who'd spent more time in the air than on the ground, we regrouped around Sasha who amazed me by quietly – or quietly by his standards at least – announcing that we would have to keep it down as we were now quite obviously trespassing and partaking in a booze-fuelled riot. Talk about calling the kettle black. Then, in direct contravention of his new rule, Sasha slammed loudly on a corrugated iron roller door behind him, which turned out to be the gateway to someone's garage. The sound reverberated through the courtyard and I noticed a few apartment lights flicker on soon after. Someone even shouted, "Who the fuck's banging a corrugated iron roller door at this time of night?" but in German, obviously.

The shutter was raised noisily from the inside by a blonde girl standing behind a trestle table, attached to which was a single makeshift beer pump that in turn was connected to a keg under the table. And that was it, apart from the tower of plastic cups that Sasha began to hand out to the bemused crowd. As pub crawls go, it was nothing if not eclectic. Where next? A hot-air balloon with mini-bar somewhere over the Danube, or down into the sewers?

To my surprise, the next venue was an actual pub, bedecked with all the trappings of communism – Soviet flags, Marxist sloganeering and rusty old weaponry from some useless war or other, all presided over by an old guard of weathered-looking soaks in fishermen's caps and heavy greatcoats. They looked like I would have if I'd stayed in Krakow for another thirty years. They eyed us suspiciously as we fanned out noisily into the wide room, most of us barely even born when the Berlin Wall round the corner fell, signifying the end of everything the patrons believed in. Most of them were nursing 'stollies', the little white soldiers of vodka lined up in front of their wizened hands as if waiting to charge. Once again Sasha was upsetting the locals and staff in his own inimitable style, which wasn't a good idea in a place where at least half of the clientele looked as though they'd shot someone at point blank range. We stood around edgily, although I eventually felt relaxed enough to strike up a conversation with a Mexican girl and her two Croatian friends that became one of the most garbled, lost-in-translation exchanges I was ever involved in, especially when Umrish and Bart got involved.

"Are you cold?" asked the Mexican girl, eyeing up my minimal attire.

"He's from England," Bart offered.

"Aaah… I see," she said.

There followed a long pause that even Umrish couldn't fill with his incessant chatter that was only broken when the Mexican girl suddenly announced, "I will have baby soon."

Nobody said anything. I just looked down at her flat stomach, wondering if she meant she wanted some help making it, or if it was already in development. It was a real tumbleweed moment, not least because the two other girls were as stunned as we were.

Sasha boomed across. "Hey, what this?" he said. "These girls Croatian, eh?" then grabbed one of them. She shoved him away as the others looked on disinterested.

Umrish leaned into my ear. "E's a cant," he said.

"He's cool," Bart said, with all the stupid naivety I've come to expect from an American in Europe, made all the worse by the Budweiser bottle he was clutching.

The whole scene became a league of nations debate when an Irishman with a severe Mohican lurched into the conversation. I'd noticed him bobbing about earlier, like Sasha but slightly more subdued. Bart soon brought him up to speed.

"She's pregnant," he said, pointing at the girl's stomach.

The girl looked down again.

"Course she feckin' is… she's feckin' gorgeous," the Irishman bellowed.

Sasha laughed out loud.

"What's her feckin' name then?" he went on, as though she wasn't there.

"What's your fuckin' name then?" I asked her, deliberately mimicking his brusqueness. It broke the ice nicely after the awkward opening and she broke into a lethal smile.

"Lucia," she said, grinning and offering a hand.

I answered with the limp-wristed shake of the Englishman as Umrish nudged me. Then I introduced her to everyone, one by one, even though I didn't know the name of the Irishman.

"Spike," he said, raising his red eyes to the tops of their sockets to acknowledge his spikey hair. He looked a handful right from the off.

"What's the baby called?" asked Bart, somewhat prematurely.

Seriously, Bart? Again she laughed, "Is not here yet."

"It's not even feckin' born yet," screeched Spike, looking genuinely offended by Bart's stupidity.

Bart continued to grin inanely into the middle-distance. Spike looked at me for a response but I just shrugged instead.

"My boyfriend is in prison," Lucia said, "in Mexico."

Well of course, who wasn't in prison in Mexico these days?

How she'd ended up in Berlin was anyone's guess.

"I've been in prison," shouted Spike, picking up on their common thread.

Sasha seemed left out by his lack of jail time and began to lose interest.

"These guys are sooo cool, huh Will?" Bart said.

"Yeah," I said, "real cool."

"I shouldn't be talking about it in front of you feckin' English pricks though," Spike added. You can be sure as night follows day that when someone says they shouldn't be talking about something, they're about to spill the whole story. "I feckin' killed a couple of fellas so ah' did." I noticed his fists clench as he said it. He let out a little snort then waited for the reaction.

Nobody did anything, then Bart said, "He did what?"

"He killed a very tall American man years ago," I whispered.

"Yer don't feckin' believe me, eh?" he said, becoming aggravated.

The mute Croatian girls hadn't batted an eyelid between them for a good five minutes now. What is it about Eastern European women and their effortless poker faces? They remained nonplussed.

"I'll feckin' show you something then," Spike boasted, but no-one took him up on it, not straightaway, then I said, "Let's see it then." I sensed a story, that was all, either that or a good kicking, so it was an even money shot.

"Feckin' come with me then," he beckoned, heading for the toilets.

"Maybe he going to kill you, Will," Lucia said, unconcerned by my imminent death.

"Hold my pint," I said to Bart.

Usually when a complete stranger invites you into a pub toilet and reaches into the waistband of his trousers, it means you've either gone to the wrong pub or you're about to be shown a gun used by an overexcited member of a terrorist splinter group. I hadn't gone to the wrong pub.

"I don't feck about, mate," he said, waving the gun around. "I'm a feckin' Republican and don't you forget it." Then he got in my face a bit, waiting for a reaction.

How original – a ranting Irishman waving a gun at an Englishman. Why didn't he pick on Umrish? He was English too.

I couldn't remember seeing a proper handgun before. It was black, and old, like the sort of thing Dempsey and Makepeace used. I looked at my reflection in the mirror, and at my t-shirt.

I wished Iggy was here. He'd know what to do.

"Yer feckin' English cunts don't like it up em', eh?"

I couldn't remember feeling more indifferent when threatened with anything before. Was it loaded? Or even real? Like all good toilets, it stunk in there, that was my next thought. After that my head was pretty much empty. I turned around and went for a piss and heard him leave as I did so.

When I got back, the others were just standing around as if nothing had happened; none of them even asked what he'd shown me. Spike had taken up a place next to an uncomfortable-looking Lucia and Bart continued to grin and stare.

"Is all okay, yes?" Lucia asked.

"Fuckin' sound," I said, even though she didn't have a clue what this meant.

We tried another few bars in the surrounding area, including one nightclub that was empty but for us and decorated almost entirely with neon kalishnikov motifs, which was right up Spike's strasse. Even I liked it and found myself almost bonding with him over the retro Electro soundtrack.

"How's them feckin' New Order these feckin' days, Will?" he asked me at one point, then broke into a bad robot dance.

Where the club wasn't lit with gun pictures, it was pitch black, and like most German nightclubs, covered in Depeche Mode posters, who came second only to the Beatles in their appeal amongst the German public, (if you discount David Hasselhoff of course).

"I'll show you round the city some time, Will, if you want?" Spike offered.

I considered his offer for all of two seconds before making an excuse about having to leave the next day, which was actually the day when I intended to do most of my sightseeing.

"No feckin' worries then, eh," he said smiling, "but if you change your mind..."

We ended the night at a truly awful nightclub called the Matrix, our group considerably depleted; in fact there was only myself and Umrish that I recognised from the original group, even though everyone was there when we were queuing to get in. I know this because they were all as surprised as I was to be tested for drunkenness by the bouncer. Umrish had shoved me and the doorman took this as my being drunk, so hatched a cunning plan to test my alcohol level.

"Are you okay?" he asked.

"Yeah." (Not 'ya' you'll note).

"Count to five then," he demanded.

I wasn't sure if he thought I was English or German, but, being the smart arse that I am, I answered him in German.

"Ein, zwei, drei, vier, funf." Schoolchildren would pay much more attention to their teachers if they knew that the most basic piece of German would be sufficient enough to gain you access to a nightclub years later.

This confused the bouncer greatly. He looked around for one of his colleagues before blurting out, "In English."

Oh, in English... the language I've spoken for over a quarter of a century? I'll have a go...

"One, two, three, four, five?" I passed. As I entered, a German girl leaned over and said, "Das vas fantastich." The club itself wasn't though – the German equivalent of the chav magnets back in England. The girl from the queue told me she was emigrating to Sydney the following week but wasn't sure if she was doing the right thing. I told her she probably was, especially as I would be there myself in around eight months time. She laughed and told me she was only going because her boyfriend worked there.

At least he wasn't going to walk in on us then.

She was only twenty and I wondered what the fuck she thought she was doing, and what the fuck I thought I was doing, and where I was going.

I walked all the way back from the club to the hostel alone.

The next morning, about three or four hours later in fact, I walked roughly the same journey, this time to the Zooligischergarten, and set about the city on foot. I'd decided to leave the next day for Hamburg and wanted to cram in as much as I could, although I'd seen a fair bit last night, whether I'd wanted to or not, and I had the hangover to prove it. What better way to start the day then than by being hassled for change by a couple of teenage neo-Nazis? It said a lot about modern German attitudes that such an activity, in the nation's capital city, went practically unnoticed, as though it was a laughable parody of a forgotten past, which I suppose it was, and everybody knew it except these two, even though they were standing in the shadow of the symbolically-unrepaired Gedachtniskirche, one of Bomber Harris's WWII bullseyes that now looks like something that's been attacked by Godzilla. From there, I walked to Grosse Stern roundabout and its centrepiece, the Berlin Victory Monument, accessed by a dark, graffiti-lathered tunnel that ran beneath the road. Naturally, the tunnel reeked of piss but it wasn't a problem as I spent much of my youth playing in urine-soaked underpasses. The park that surrounded the roundabout was home to a giant statue of General Von Bismarck, who in turn was surrounded by a tableau of seemingly unconnected characters that included a male Britannia-type entity that looked to be relaxing after slaying the lion that lay at its feet. Next to him was either Atlas or Magnus Ver Magnusson, I wasn't sure, carrying the world on his shoulders as a Sphinx-riding woman looked on unimpressed. Foraging away behind this eclectic foursome was a bloke in a skirt flattening out his sword with a 500lb hammer. All I was thinking about though was what would happen if the Bismarck statue fell on me, and the ensuing headline: 'TEESSIDER CRUSHED BY DEAD CHANCELLOR'S FIST'. There was no explanation about the statue, except for the words 'dem ertsen reichkanzler das Deutsche volk', which, to my rough interpretation means 'the chancellor of the German people'. A short distance away stood a less contemporary statue in the form of Graf Von Moltke, the first legendary German Field Marshall. I continued north then veered right onto John Foster Dulles Avenue and in no time had reached one of the most notorious sights in European history, just a stone's throw from another. The first was the Reichstag. I stood on the green field at the front steps where I liked to think Hitler had addressed thousands of stormtroopers in the 30s and 40s, although in truth the building was hardly ever used for such events, or even in an official capacity at all. The area was now populated by snap-happy tourists, children playing football and picnicking families. The old footage of those Nazi rallies that I'd imagined took place here always reminded me of something out of a sci-fi film – regimented drones programmed to kill by their megalomaniacal leader. By 1945, the Reichstag was completely gutted by the Soviet Army, giving it the appearance of a bombed-out greenhouse, but it was resurrected and turned into what we see today, a spectacular piece of modern architecture. Around the corner stood the remnants of one of Germany's post-war episodes of global revulsion, that of the Berlin Wall that divided the city through the latter half of the 20th century. One of the first sights that greeted me as I approached the Brandenburg Gate was the irrepressible Gustav Rust, one of Germany's most famous political prisoners who was still single-handedly running his protest against his treatment at the hands of Erich Honecker. Rust had set up a number of stalls along the River Spree – where numerous attempts to cross from East to West Berlin had ended in tragedy – funded mainly by public donations. The stalls included photos of all the defectors – people like Chris Geoffrey, who became the last man to be killed attempting to escape, just seven months before the wall came down, and descriptions of the punishment meted out to any like-minded escapees. There were those who had hidden in car boots, and others who'd blithely just ran for it, with varying degrees of success. One enterprising American defector had crossed over simply by walking alongside a slow-moving coach that obscured the guards' view of him. Another had shot under the barrier in a low-slung sports car, never to be seen again, prompting a number of less successful copycat attempts in Isetta cars. The most ambitious escape award though goes to the two families that got their heads together and built a hot-air balloon out of bits of nylon cloth in the spare room before floating off peacefully into West Berlin.

Rust's protest now looks to be the work of a madman: one who routinely assaults passing tourists or harangues them into inspecting his selection of handcuffs and coshes, the likes of which he was subjected to by the GDR (German Democratic Republic).

What he is trying to achieve even now – it's not like anyone has forgotten about what the Wall represented – almost twenty years after Honecker's death, is unclear. He could though be said to be one of the lucky ones; a hundred people were shot attempting to escape during the Wall's grisly thirty year tenure. Rust didn't bother me this time, he already had a small audience, so I was allowed to quietly make my way to the Brandenburg Gate that Napoleon had claimed for France in 1806. He took the Quadriga chariot, pulled by four horses and driven by Victoria, for Paris but it was returned to its original home eight years later by General Pfuel. In an almighty display of elitism, up until 1919 only the royals and members of Pfuel's family were permitted to use the gate. I passed through it and on down the now pedestrianised Pariser Platz, but was still thinking about the Wall, and how, in its original guise, it had been thrown up in a 24 hour period in 1961, in the primitive form of a barbed wire fence. I tried to imagine what it was like: you go out to work on a morning, or to school, or even next door to borrow the lawn mower, and you're not allowed home for thirty years, unless you want to risk being shot. Then when you do get home, the first thing you are greeted with is the sound of David Hasselhoff singing, and you think that maybe the Wall wasn't such a bad idea after all. I bought two postcards at a gift shop that commemorated the fall of Berlin during WWII. One was of the destroyed Reichstag I described earlier, the other the single greatest piece of Soviet propaganda ever produced – the almost mythical image of the hammer and sickle being hoisted high over the city by triumphant Russian soldiers. Yevgeny Khaldei's photo is also one of the most speculated-upon images of the entire conflict; no-one was certain of the identities of the conquerors, accessories such as watches were removed from the image so as not to infer any suggestion of looting by Soviet troops, and the flag had actually been hoisted a few days before the photo was taken but at night, which didn't allow for as dramatic an image as the one taken on the 2nd May, believed to be of a specially selected Georgian soldier in order to please Stalin back in the Kremlin. Whatever its origins, it's an indelible image of a dramatic moment.

'SIE VERLASSEN DEN AMERIKANISCHEN SECTOR' read the sign at Checkpoint Charlie: 'You are now leaving the American sector', down at the bottom of Friedrichstrasse. The actual checkpoint, one of the most famous border crossings in the world, can now be found in the Allied Museum at Clayallee. What stands today is Rainer Hildebrandt's replica, which I discovered scrawled with the simple but striking instruction to 'FUCK WAR' in huge white spray-painted letters. All around it, faux Soviet guards were offering to mock-stamp tourist's passports and pose for photographs, stony-faced in keeping with their character as passers-by cheerfully watched it all being played out. What the older generation of Berliners made of it was open to debate but the various museums dedicated to the Wall's past, like the rest of Berlin's monuments and landmarks, gave a balanced, sensible view of the city's history, regardless of its original motives, rather than sweeping everything under the carpet. The Topography of Terror and the Holocaust memorial were two such examples in central Berlin, telling the story of the Gestapo's fearful grip on the city before and during WWII, and make no attempt to desensitise or lessen the impact of the authorities' activities. On seeing the Holocaust memorial, I was unsure what to make of it, other than it was an interesting piece of alternative art in the form of hundreds of enormous blocks, varying in size, that take up an entire city block. I wandered between them, and toward the centre of the piece where the floor sloped considerably, meaning the larger blocks were positioned more centrally, to give the whole thing an appearance of equality perhaps.

As for the Wall, there are still numerous standing sections, some in much better condition than the others, dotted around Berlin, the most prominent of them being in Muhlenstrasse, and, like much of the remains, covered in graffiti. It was the smaller piece at Potsdamer Platz that I inspected though, where I discovered in a gift shop that even smaller pieces still were available to buy as mementoes in the form of key rings, although their authenticity leaves a lot to be desired, as do the prices.

On leaving Berlin, the logical thing to do was head west, bearing in mind I was on my way to the lowlands of Holland and Belgium. I must have been sub-consciously thinking of home then when I selected my next destination: an industrial port city in the far north that had been stampeded by Vikings, seen a late 19th century population boom, and was now a thriving tourist destination. Hamburg then was like a home from home.

"…and of course zer is ze Beatles," said the man on the train. I wasn't really listening. I was too busy watching my back. I'd inadvertently arrived in Hamburg on what was potentially the most violent day of the year: a Sunday teatime a few minutes after the final whistle had gone at the Hamburg-Hansa Rostock football match. The bus journey from Berlin had passed off relatively quietly – apart from the drunken Captain Haddock lookalike sat in front of me who spent the whole trip harassing the woman across the aisle. He dropped 20Euros as he departed, which I duly picked up and considered to be an 'annoyance fee' – but the spell on the underground from the bus station to my seemingly non-existent hostel was punctuated by hardcore St Pauli fans.

"Zees are all zee… outsiders in society," the man said. He was referring to the St Pauli fans who'd sworn loyalty to their team over the greatness of their rivals Hamburg. Rather than describe the teams as neighbours, it would be nearer to the truth to call themselves housemates, such is the location of St Pauli's Millerntor Stadion in central Hamburg. In 2009, the then second division St Pauli began to tug at the coat-tails of its bigger brother when it was promoted to the Bundesliga, ensuring many more days like the one on which I'd arrived.

The man continued his sociology lesson quietly despite the constant chanting of the St Pauli fans who had turned out looking for trouble despite not attending a game that day. "Most of zem vill have no jobs. Many gays support St Pauli… and ze Turks too. Lots of Turks in Hamburg. Be careful." This was all very informative, however inaccurate, but I had other things on my mind. I wanted to talk to some of the football supporters, some of which could definitely be classed as German Ultras, but they were all drunk and on the lookout for rival supporters. By the time I reached my stop at Sternschanze, most of them had departed, leaving me strolling alone through the deserted underground station and out onto the equally unattended Max Brauer Allee. It took me an hour to find the hostel, although, as in Portugal, I'd walked past it several times. Frustratingly, none of the few locals I was able to find and ask for directions knew where it was either. As I walked on, I thought about the fact that I didn't have the first clue as to the location of hostels in my home town either. It turned out to be jammed between a trendy, and of course empty, wine bar, and what else but a sauna?

The hostel was plastered with more Depeche Mode posters and flyers for a forthcoming Johnny Cash tribute night to be performed entirely in German. As big a fan of Cash as I am, I wasn't sure how his lyrics would fly in German, especially ones like: 'The first day I got me a fuel pump, and the next day I got me an engine and a trunk', which translates as the catchy: 'Der este tag habe ich mir eine kraftstoffpumpe, und am nachsten tag bekam ich mir einen motor und ein kofferaum'.

I had the run of a huge dorm for the most part. The only other guest was an Irishman who worked fourteen hours a day, six days a week, on the docks, and spent the other day in the pub. I walked in on him once to find him closely studying the monitor on his video camera. "I'm just trying to work out what the feck happened last night. She looks familiar..."

It's just as well I took in most of the city the following day as the few that followed it blurred into a lost week of the inebriation that had become an essential staple of my trip so far.

On Monday morning, I set off and walked west in what turned out to be a massive loop of the city that took me first across the Binnenalster and all the way down to the Rathaus. The area was once referred to as Free and Hanseatic Hamburg although many of the surrounding buildings were destroyed in the fire of 1842. Now it retains much of its original charm after exhaustive restoration work, and the old part sits neatly amongst the modern department stores and expensive boutiques. The city centre was bedecked with

Christmas decorations but the real Christmas Market was over on the Reeperbahn, Europe's capital of sin, if what I'd heard was to be believed. During the day, it was a different place entirely. Through the centre of the street, workers scuttled about erecting the scaffolding that would facilitate the building of the huge Christmas Market, the centrepiece of it at that early stage being what looked to be a giant ski slope. It wasn't until the next few days that I discovered the real Reeperbahn. I walked right along the edge of the Elbe, and the sprawling docks that looked like they might stretch all the way to Scandinavia, past the Fischmarkt and Baumwolle, and then all the way back along Max Brauer Allee.

When I returned, two new guests had arrived. Larry was from Strensall, in York. He had the same dress sense of a generation of Brits in their late twenties – myself included – that prompted the other new guest, Mikey, to comment, "You guys look like something out of an Oasis album." Mikey's dress code was totally different for totally different reasons. He was a fanatical acolyte of Neil Strauss's The Game. For the unacquainted, Strauss's book concerns itself with the activities of a new breed of bore: the PUA, or Pick Up Artist, a group of men so devoted to the 'art' of womanising that they make Warren Beatty look like a wallflower. No stunt was too spectacular for the PUAs, as long as it secured a phone number, or better still a date, or still better still, a 'root' as Mikey called it. The PUA lifestyle was well-suited to someone like Mikey. He was a brash Aussie with some Italian blood in him, a combination that made him super-confident with an almost pathological need for female attention. It also gave him a distinct air of insecurity that I imagine most PUAs have. He wasn't particularly striking to look at, he looked like Man Vs Food presenter Adam Richmann, but his confidence made up for any shortcomings in his appearance. As we got ready to go out one night – this consisted of Larry and I simply dragging on our shoes and Mikey going through his whole psyching-up ritual – he gave us a crash course in the fine arts.

"Okay. First thing: you've got to grab their attention. Doesn't matter how you do it. Tonight I'm going to do it like this," he said, and disappeared behind his bed. He rummaged through his bag for a moment as Larry and I sat on opposite beds swigging from a tiny bottle of corn liquor Mikey had given us. He popped back up wearing a Stetson. It was black with a red fur trim. Larry burst out laughing but I just looked at him seriously. Mikey was serious too; for him it was normal.

"I'm not finished," he said. He then proceeded to attach a silver chain choker around his neck that had an enormous-winged dragon on the front of it. Now even I couldn't keep a straight face.

"Are you fucking serious?" I enquired.

"Just wait and see," he said, knowingly.

"Yeah," I said, "I don't doubt you'll get attention. You look like Danny La Rue."

"Who's he?"

"Dame Edna," Larry offered, "you look like Dame Edna. And you sound like her."

Mikey hadn't quite finished. He put on a couple of kid's plastic rings, the sort you get in a Christmas cracker.

"Well I'm ready," he said, grabbing what was left of the corn liquor. He took a shot of it and winced. Then he held his chest as his face flushed red under the shade of that huge hat brim. We jumped in a taxi and headed for the Reeperbahn a mile or so away. The taxi driver kept looking in his rear view mirror at Mikey, then at me in the passenger seat for want of an explanation. It was much funnier not to explain it but at one point when the silence became unbearable, I jerked a thumb back over my shoulder and said, "Pimmelkopf." It was lost on Mikey but Larry laughed. He was a translator for a German courier firm and spoke the language fluently. He'd travelled around much of the country over the years while studying for his degree and had now secured his dream job. He'd even done a term of Turkish and amazed them on a two week placement in the country by speaking it fluently.

Mikey started in with the second part of the lesson: contact.

"Okay. Listen up you both," he said, "once you've got their attention, you ignore them." Then he fell silent, allowing us to process this bombshell of information, even though it's one of the most basic traits of human behavior. We didn't react so he moved on to the next stage.

"Now this is crucial," he insisted, "if you don't make physical contact within thirty seconds, you've failed. Just a light pat on the arm will do, keep it simple, and see how they react. But don't forget to ignore them as well, especially if one of them is really hot. Always ignore the hot one, she'll soon come back to you if she's interested, and she will be interested, because you'll make her interested."

The taxi dropped us at the western end of the Reeperbahn – but not before the driver had taken us on the obligatory fare-increasing tourist joyride – near the Hans Albers Platz, a foreboding concrete square surrounded by rough pubs and a huge apartment block that I was sure was a brothel. A statue of Albers himself, one of Germany's most famous entertainers, stands at the centre of it. We ducked into an empty pub, the London Bar, to begin with, and were glad of its lack of customers when you consider what Mikey was wearing. The barman's face was much the same as the taxi driver's had been, more so when I ordered the round: a lager for me, a beer for Larry, and a shot of snakebite for Mikey! A single shot. Of snakebite.

"That's not gonna last very long," I said.

"How can you drink those English beers of yours?" Mikey asked, disgustedly.

He swallowed the shot and looked like he might drop dead right there.

"Come on," he said, "we need to find some fraus." He was at least picking up the lingo. The barman grinned and reminded us that the Herbertstrasse was literally just out the back of the pub. Hamburg's red light zone, or the 'kiez' as it is known locally, revolved around Herbertstrasse and stretched right across the Reeperbahn to the Grosse Freiheit, even taking in the police station at Davidwache, where Paul McCartney was once booked for arson. The men-only Herbertstrasse is around a hundred yards long and cordoned off at either end by two huge red barriers, erected so as not to offend some of the city's less liberal residents, although this seems virtually impossible when even the main thoroughfare is a hot bed of tacky sex tourism. It still seemed more respectable than say Amsterdam for example, but I wasn't sure why. It could have been something to do with the romanticism of its musical heritage but more of that later. Tonight the street was fairly sedate as we sloped along, despite the window shopping crowds admiring the goods. Most of the women looked typically German but Mikey was awestruck all the same on his first time in Europe.

"This is what I came for," he said excitedly, gawping at an Oriental girl in a Borat-style mankini. He was a long way from rural Perth now and like a kid in a candy store, or an aquarium – one girl even admonished him for tapping on the glass.

"I think when the curtains are closed, it means they're in a meeting," I said.

"It's the ultimate challenge," he said.

"What is?" Larry said, who like me, had seen it all before.

"These… women. I want all of their numbers. I want to have them, but not like this. Away from all this."

I wasn't sure if he fully understood how prostitution worked.

"What about her?" he said, pointing at a disinterested blonde in stocking and suspenders. "I could have her."

"Well, get your hand in your pocket," Larry said.

She began to sway slowly in the window as she realised we were talking about her. Then she laughed, pointing at Mikey's hat.

"See," said Mikey, "told you it works," grinning at the girl.

"You could have a lump of dog shit on your head but if she thinks you've got money, she'll still smile at you," I said.

"I can do this," he said, to no-one in particular. "I'll take her out tomorrow night. Somewhere nice."

"I hope you like pimps and iron bars cos you'll be seeing plenty of both if you start chasing around after her," I said.

He raced off to open the negotiations as Larry and I wandered to the other end of the street and back on to the Reeperbahn where we saw the occasional prostitute illegally looking for work outside the police station. We went into the Meanie Bar, over the dungeon-like Molotov basement bar that had hosted the likes of the White Stripes just a few weeks before and took seats at the deserted bar amid the immaculate velvet drape décor and intense white lighting.

There was only a handful of people in the place but one of them was a clapped-out old Merchant Navy type from Portsmouth who sat alongside us at the bar. You could tell by looking at him that he had a few stories, and that he wouldn't mind telling you them, if he could remember them. He had a big, blotchy, boozer's face, a greasy rocker's hairstyle and arms full of maritime tattoos that could have told his life story without him saying a word. He didn't bother to introduce himself; he just started right in talking about the Beatles like they were something from Norse mythology when he overheard me telling Larry that John Lennon once performed at the Star Club with a toilet seat round his neck. The man looked like he could have been late sixties or even early seventies. I was poised ready to listen by the time he leaned his skinny arms on the marble top bar and said, without pre-amble, "First time I saw 'em was up the road at the Indra. I'd never seen a thing like it and haven't since, and I've seen 'em all playing down here." Then he took a long drag on his cigarette. "I was barely old enough to be in there. In fact George got deported for being under age at one time, but they kept coming back and we kept going to see them... at the Kaiserkeller, the Star Club, anywhere." His voice was gravelly, from fifty years of smoking and talking, but it smoothed out as he became more nostalgic. "When they were on, they were fucking ON... you couldn't look away. Shoulda seen 'em... kitted out in leathers from a tailors on Spielbudenplatz. And I'm still dressing like 'em now."

He was. I looked down at his black Cuban heels and matching jeans, this man of seventy perhaps, still decked out like his teen idols. The only thing missing was a packet of Senior Service jammed up the sleeve of his t-shirt. I had a million questions but I didn't want to interrupt him in case I triggered a bad acid relapse.

"This is where they got good," he said, "right here in Hamburg. Everything that came after was because of this."

He was right. With their various line-ups comprising Pete Best, Stu Sutcliffe and then Ringo, they once played six-hour sets for forty-eight consecutive nights. It's no wonder they turned to drugs with a schedule like that.

"They were loud, dark, and fast and the coolest bunch of cunts we'd ever seen," he continued.

Had he just affectionately called the Beatles 'a bunch of cunts'?

He was impressed when I mentioned Tony Sheridan, who at the time was established enough to call the Beatles his backing band. I'd seen his name on an old 45 that belonged to my parents: 'Tony Sheridan... and the Beatles' it read, the Fab Four almost an afterthought!

"Tony was the king bee around here back then," the man said. "As much as I loved them, I could never bring myself to get my hair cut like them." He carefully stroked his quiff. "I'd have been ripped to shreds on the boat for it." That comment made me think. Here we were, in Germany, two men of barely thirty talking to a man of seventy about a band from Liverpool that were around fifty years ago, and how revolutionary their haircuts were, who I'd probably still be talking about in another fifty years. They might be from Liverpool but they're the first thing that comes to mind when I think of Hamburg. The whole of the Grosse Freiheit that runs north off the Reeperbahn includes most of the spots where the Beatles kicked up dust: the Grosse Freiheit club itself, beckoning you with its huge neon guitar outside, and the Indra, where they made their European debut. The walls were covered with posters and handbills advertising the likes of Rory Storm and the Hurricanes – one of whom was Ringo Starr – Ten Years After and Gerry and the Pacemakers. Gerry Marsden once went to a brothel with John Lennon not far away and was presented with a girl so big that "she looked like a bus with a bra on".

The Star Club monument was the most striking of all though – a six foot black marble obelisk emblazoned in gold lettering with the names of all the acts of those lethal early years of rock'n'roll. Under the heading 'Hier Gastierten' was a roll call of American and British music of the time: Ray Charles, Little Richard and there, sandwiched between the names of Duane Eddy and Ian and the

Zodiacs, the 'killer' himself, Jerry Lee Lewis, the surviving sovereign ruler of rock'n'roll.

"I saw the Killer at the Star Club," the man at the Meanie Bar said. He paused after he said it, and looked at me, to see if I knew who he was talking about. I knew. Everybody knew.

"It was the only time I ever saw a Star Club crowd give anyone immediate respect," he explained. "By that, I mean we didn't crowd the stage the way we did for everyone else. It was like we didn't dare... especially when he came stalking along the front of the stage, in case he grabbed us and dragged us back to where he came from." He had a quick go at his drink then looked at me gravely. "I don't mean back to America," he said. "I mean back to wherever... cos that fella wasn't from this world."

I never believed anything more ridiculous in my whole life, but I believed it. He made it sound as real as the book in your hand.

Nowadays the Grosse Freiheit is relatively tourist friendly, compared with its former self at least, and attracts mainly young sightseers obsessed with the birth of rock'n'roll.

The Star Club closed on New Year's Eve 1969 but was reopened in 1978, never really managing to recapture the excitement of its early days. Along with most of the other clubs around it, the Funky Pussy, Baha, and the intriguingly named Domicile de Sade, it draws a lively student crowd in search of indie discos, which is what Larry and I were looking for. We found one in Rosi's Bar way back in the darkness of the Seilerstrasse. Like the surrounding pubs, Rosi's Bar looked unwelcoming from the outside – blacked-out windows, unsavoury ruffians loitering in the doorway and a sign depicting an anchor, which is always a mark of distinction. We drifted into the sweet sound of The Stranglers' anti-monarchy anthem Duchess, soundtracking a circus of stylish, urchin-headed students either moodily standing around nodding or scrambling all over the tiny carpeted dance floor that had been created by plonking a booze-stained turntable between a pair of old clock sprung settees – just like a typical student club then. The barfly crowd were much more reserved and classically Hamburgian: stubbly old sailors and the likes of the local drug dealer, who looked like Frank Gallagher but dressed like Iggy Pop – that man again – in skin-tight stick-of-rock jeans and string vest. He stood quietly in the corner near the toilets with a pocket full of counterfeit e's. We grabbed a few beers and hung around on the edge of the madness until Mikey returned, about ten minutes later, breathless, and thankfully jewelleryless. The cowboy hat you could just about get away with in Rosis's. He looked like he'd just had his brains fucked out, which wouldn't have taken long.

"Well?" I said.

"I've just had my brains fucked out," he said, "but I didn't get any numbers."

"You should have made contact in the first thirty seconds," I said.

"You should have ignored her," Larry added.

"Oh, I made contact alright," Mikey said, bursting into another of his big grins. And then he was off, into the maelstrom of the dance floor and its skinny jeans and mod haircuts. Larry made some small talk with the locals as I hung at the bar talking with a Venezuelan exchange student who was staying with her brother for the time being and had already blown most of her three-month budget in the pubs and clubs around the 'kiez'.

"I'm not going back to Venezuela," she said defiantly, and then cackled like a Bond villain. Another self-appointed addition then to Hamburg's rich seam of immigration. As she fumbled in her pocket for change, Iggy leaned languorously forward and said quietly, "Holz vor der hutte haben." Then he returned to his motionless position in the corner like a bug-eyed sentry guard. I later learnt that the phrase is a German colloquialism referring to breast size and translates as something like, "She's got a lot of timber in front of her house."

"Keep your hands on your wallets," someone warned, but it was so dark in Thai Oase on Paul Roosen Strasse that you'd have been hard pressed to spot any pickpockets. The warm glow emanating from the karaoke machine seemed to draw Mikey – attention seeker that he was – to the small stage in the corner, and he soon informed us that none of us would be leaving until we'd all performed. I was about to inform him that if I performed, everyone would be leaving, but he'd already gone and sat down in the middle of a bunch of complete strangers, all of them female. I blasted out Andy Williams's Can't Take My Eyes Off You, no better, or quieter, than the last time I'd performed it, which was alongside 15,000 people at a Boro match. My saving grace this time was that I dedicated it to 'alles der schonen madchen' which drew greater applause than the song itself. Fortunately somebody murdered Danny Boy immediately after, neatly sweeping my performance under the sticky carpet. I missed Mikey's turn as I was at the bar having my drinks bought by an Austrian woman whose only reference points for England were that she once saw Take That in Manchester, and soon after got lost in Blackpool, two unimaginably horrendous experiences that no visitors to the country should ever have to endure. I know of what I speak as one of them happened to me. I'll let you decide which…

"I like English boys," she said, patting my thigh. We were getting cozy now as Mikey managed to tear himself away from his newfound friends to check in with us. He exuberantly ordered several rounds of drinks, all of them shots of various kinds, then presided over their messy consumption; at least three went in the air and then back behind the bar sans glasses.

"Hey… you making mess my fuckin' pub," snapped the barmaid, a scrawny, fearsome-looking Thai woman no taller than the bar she served from. She must have said 'pub' for the benefit of Mikey and I but the Austrian woman spoke equally bad English and simply scowled back. I slid off to the toilet, via three hundred yards of unlit haunted catacombs deep beneath the bar. I wasn't even sure I'd arrived at the toilet as it was so beset with graffiti it was like walking into a magic eye exhibition. It didn't have any doors either. When I got back upstairs, the Austrian woman had been joined by a giant of a man with a hostile face. I tried to ignore him and spoke to Larry for a while. The woman was minding her own business now; she certainly wasn't broadcasting what kind of men she liked. I felt a firm tap on my arm. If you want to attract strange men in Germany all you have to do is mind your own business at a bar. It was Mikey's 'ignore them' rule played out for nutters: first the wise-cracking drug dealer at Rosi's Bar, now this mountainous crag-faced Jebediah Springfield lookalike. With the tap on my arm, the man said, "My friend... you are German?" He loomed forward slowly as he spoke.

He was getting bigger. Massive in fact. He had a Tom Selleck 'tache, like a real man. I thought if I could sweep his legs and get him on the deck, I'd be able to take him down but it didn't come to that.

"I'm English," I said.

He relaxed, dropping his shoulders. "Then we must drink," he roared, "and forget your football problems. I am Austrian."

Football problems? His country's most recent contribution to the beautiful game was Toni Polster's heart-stopping mullet.

We did just that though, at his expense, and I reminded myself to interfere with Austrian men's wives more often in the future. The bar eventually closed at 5am but we weren't quite finished, although Mikey was past himself with women and shots and headed back without us. Larry and I finally threw in the towel, appropriately enough, at German boxing legend Herbert Nurnberg's Golden Handschuh pub, a classic dockland flophouse that was once the haunt of wall-eyed barmpot and occasional serial killer Fritz Honka. After a blaze at his Ottensen apartment in 1975, firefighters found four toothless prostitute corpses who he'd killed after they'd mocked his oral sex obsession. The Handschuh had improved its clientele since then but only marginally so I wasn't surprised to see an actual pirate in there, hook-handed and eye-patched and missing only the parrot, and a woman so skint that she tried to pay for a pint with her pearl earring. She placed it carefully down in front of the perplexed barman as though it was a perfectly acceptable form of payment. I made a show of snatching the earring and theatrically biting the pearl to test its provenance and in the process probably caught a previously unrecognized strain of hepatitis, but it got a big laugh and earned me a free drink so it was worth it. It was the final gesture of a night that I would have otherwise forgotten if I hadn't pieced it all together the next morning and then written it all down. I could see now why the Irishman I'd seen on the first day was having to watch a recording of his night out to see what had happened. It was that sort of place.

I was the walking dead the next day but I forced myself out to the Dom funfair and along the Neuer Kampf-Feldstrasse, the new respectable Hamburg for the more faint-hearted. It was here, in the Heiligengeistfeld district that I learnt Romany psycho-folk loons Gogol Bordello were playing that night. I'd seen an advert in the Flakturm IV – literally Flak Tower 4 – an enormous former WWII defence post that had been converted into a giant concert hall and shopping centre. Normally the prospect of being entertained by a screaming rabble of wild zither-laden, tom-tom wielding Eastern European punk funk gypsies would seem an attractive prospect but after the previous night's exertions I plumped for the altogether more sedate and infinitely more talented Rodrigo Y Gabriela over the road at the Knust Club. I proudly purchased the tickets that afternoon in excellent German and Mikey tagged along. He was so ruined from the night before that he couldn't even remember if he'd seen the duo somewhere before; maybe he had, actually he hadn't, and then he had, and then oh, he couldn't remember and now he had a headache thinking about it. He couldn't even be bothered to go as his skirt-chasing alter-ego Stetson Mctwatnecklace. Instead he came as Mikey, the insurance salesman from Perth, but he still managed a few of his tricks. One of them was infiltrating the Swiss banking convention that had taken over the entire upper floor of the hostel.

The Knust Club was full of musing folkies and sweaty thrash heads, such was the origins of the band. They'd cut their teeth playing in various heavy metal line-ups in Mexico before hitting the busking circuit in Dublin for the hard miles before finally cracking it in the UK. Now they were bringing all kinds of influences to the party: flamenco, mariachi, Pink Floyd, Metallica, and throwing it all out there in a big ball of rapid-fire staccato percussion and barely believable fret work. The gig was beset with a few technical hitches but they were capable enough to overcome them. It was testament to their ability that despite the audio problems, they still put on a memorable show. Afterwards we went for a drink at the ominously named Ebel and Gefahrlich (Evil and Dangerous), where we met up with an equally worn out Larry. It was here that I discovered Mikey and I had at least one thing in common: we were both leaving Hamburg to meet a girl in Holland; I was assuming at that point that it wasn't the same one. When he explained that it was someone he'd met at Rosi's Bar who lived in a house near the Dutch/Germany border that had a tunnel connecting the two countries, I knew I wouldn't be bumping into him. For Larry though, Hamburg was home, as it was or had once been for as diverse a group as the Beatles, Hans Albers, Fritz Honka, thousands of Turks, the Venezuelan student, and the drug dealer. Would I go anywhere else in the next ten months that was quite as interesting?

CHAPTER 3:
BELGIUM TO AMSTERDAM

Feeling Hoorny in the Lowlands,
and a show of fine Yorkshire hospitality.

"No-one truly useful has ever come out of Belgium."

If Hamburg was the beating heart of northern Europe, then Belgium was its faulty pacemaker. I flew into rainy Charleroi one Thursday evening so exhausted that I jumped into the first taxi I saw – something I usually avoid – and demanded to be taken to the Etap hotel 'rapide', which was one of the few words of French I spoke. Actually it wasn't, I knew more, I was just holding back because the taxi driver, who was played by Rene from 'Allo 'Allo, was pretending he didn't speak English. For 20Euros he took me on a journey that I calculated cost 1Euro per second. We arrived at exactly the same time as the free shuttle bus that had set off just in front of us at the airport. I then spent a wild night in the Belgian hinterland watching a 24 hour Russian rolling news channel and wondering how long it would be before my stomach completely ate itself. I couldn't wait to get out of there and first thing the next morning I was back at the airport – this time by free shuttle bus – waiting for another bus to Brussels. As I waited I saw Rene, stuffing his fat face in the patisserie, made possible by my 20Euros, surrounded by mayo-sucking bean counters in bad suits on their way to further mutilate the economy, all in the name of European unity, or as I call it, greed. I reached Brussels' Midi Station utterly devoid of enthusiasm. The country's vapidity was slowly choking me. Through the rain, everything was grey and the only thing driving me on was the thought of that little house in the Dutch countryside. I'm probably being unfair to Belgium on the whole but hey, we've paid for it all. The bus driver had taken all the traits of his country's most remarkable man, Eddie Merckx, and decanted them into his all-or-nothing driving style. He belted through the Belgian countryside, blinded by the torrential rain, and like Le Cannibal, on two wheels for the most part. It was by far the most exciting thing I was ever likely to experience in Belgium and I was surprised to see we'd actually made it to the train station. If the train driver taking me to Amsterdam was anything like the bus driver, I'd better keep my insurance policy handy. It states that: 'This policy does not cover visits in any capacity to Iran, Afghanistan, Iraq, Libya, North Korea and Belgium'.

The train coughed its way slowly into Amsterdam Central Station late Friday morning, leaving me with a good few hours to kill before Lorna finished work at 5.30pm. Normally I'd be glad of the spare time to do a bit of sightseeing, but this being Amsterdam, I'd seen most of it on numerous assorted stag dos: the sex museum (which seems to have become so staid that on my last visit one small group of visitors spent most of the time stealthily traipsing around after a stunning Croatian girl; stealthily until one of the party was prompted to loudly announce to myself and a friend, whilst pointing at the girl's bottom, that, "that is the best fucking thing I have seen in here." Everybody nodded in agreement as the girl quietly inspected the ceramic dildo exhibit), the recklessly piloted 'bromfietsen' bikes, and the clog-centric tourist trade. This time I'd come to see something else, I wasn't sure what, as long as it wasn't anything Belgian. I took refuge in Le Pot Au Fer, in my opinion the finest reasonably-priced restaurant in the whole city. It's also the only restaurant where the waitress looks like Nicole Scherzinger, so she could have handed me a platter of fried rats droppings and I still would have smiled idiotically. I hung around for longer than I needed to solely because of this. The journey from Brussels had really caught up with me by now; that and lugging my pack into the icy wind was really wearing me down. I wasn't even sure what day it was, but I soon discovered it was Christmas Eve. Sort of. I plonked myself exhaustedly down on the floor outside the Hotel Krasnopolsky, my sub-conscious daring anyone to move me. The WWII monument in the centre of the square was lit up by the time I started to snap out of my newfound vagrancy. I squinted beyond it, through another light snowfall, at the Royal Palace, thinking about how accessible it looked, as if you could walk right in and find Beatrix with her clogs up doing her knitting. As I got back on my feet, some form of hallucinogenic delirium began to take hold, triggered by a man in robes riding a white charger through a crowd of unimpressed Christmas shoppers. What madness was this? I gave my head a shake as the Krasnopolsky concierge explained that it was only Saint Nicholas, or Sinter Klaas, as he called him, and he did this every December 5th, the night before the exchanging of gifts apparently, and three weeks before the rest of most of Europe, the impatient buggers. This wintry burst of pantomime horseplay was distracting me from the job in hand, which was probably just as well as the prospect of spending the weekend in the Dutch countryside with complete strangers, Lorna aside, was beginning to frazzle my nerves. I hadn't seen her for over a year and now I was turning up out of nowhere, well, Belgium, and relying on the hospitality of her parents, who I'd never even met. To be fair, it was Lorna's idea and it seemed like a good one over the phone a few weeks earlier.

"Oh come on, Will," she had said. She was always trying to convince me of something, even though her ideas were usually worse than mine. "You've got loads of stuff in common with my parents. Mum's a writer and Dad's… well Dad's dead dry and clever like you." Flattery, that'll do it every time.

It was half-past five now, according to my travel phone, an indestructible Nokia3210 that was the sole reason my backpack was so heavy. I circled the monument from a distance, pondering whether to run away, though eventually this option was far outweighed by the prospect of some home cooking and a decent bed, for which I would have killed a man with my bare hands by that point. Also, there was something acutely romantic about meeting a girl in a European capital city on a white Christmas Eve (their Christmas Eve, that is).

Once we got on the train, Lorna handed me a massive bar of chocolate and I instantly forgot about everything that had gone before.

"It's Fair Trade," she explained. "It's horrible. Some kids ran in the office earlier and threw it at me." I wasn't sure the Fair Trade marketing team had thought this through but then she explained that it was another of the Dutch Christmas customs: groups of kids bursting into people's places of work unannounced and pelting them with confectionery. We flopped into the seats of a deserted carriage as Lorna gave me a doom-laden account of her daily commute on the same route.

"Usually I can't move at all on this line. I just read a book or something. I'm dying for a drink tonight," she added. If she was dying for a drink, I must have already been dead.

Out of nowhere she said, "Mum can be a bit overpowering, y'know."

It was a thinly-veiled warning, the kind you give to people who've never met your immediate family before that turns out to be unnecessary as you're already fortunate enough not to be one of their children. I knew they'd be no bother, especially after a few drinks, as I wasn't anywhere as high maintenance as Lorna. On the train, I remembered the last time I'd seen her. She was dropping me off at the pub about two years earlier. I was going to get pissed, she was going to start a new life in another country. It didn't feel like that though. I knew I'd see her again, somewhere. I think we were supposed to have changed, because we were older, and because of absence, but I was still frazzled by travel, and anticipation, like I'd always been. We hopped the train somewhere on the edge of Schagen, although the station was so badly lit we could have arrived at Colonel Kurtz's compound for all I knew. We completed the journey to t'Zand in Lorna's car.

"I hate this journey," she said as she freed the handbrake with both hands. I wondered if she still left the spoon in the cup when she drank from it, so it clinked around the cup and hit her in the face every time.

As it turned out, Lin wasn't overpowering, but she was every inch the housemaker, and a hellish cook. As a home-alone housewife for the most part, she channelled her considerable energy into her twin passions: animals, in particular the conservation of Orangutans, and writing. It would be inaccurate to describe Lorna's dad Chris as 'long suffering' but he seemed to have developed an admirable passive-tolerant personality from sharing the house with Lin and his recently returned daughter.

The car pulled onto the drive around 7.30pm. I'd been on the move for almost twenty-four hours and stepping into that cozy house, with its burning radiators, beaming light, and busy kitchen was like reaching Shangri La. We squashed into the narrow passageway beside the staircase as the familiar chaos of Lorna's life began to unfold. In between greetings, Lin chirped up, "Lorna dear, there's some news about your documentation that's a bit complicated."

"Oh what is it now?" Lorna thundered, like a storm-faced teenager. It was some bureaucratic nonsense regarding her lock-stock-and-barrel move to the Netherlands that was still ongoing.

As if to placate her, Lin added, "We'll discuss it after dinner."

Chris rolled his eyes, his default gesture it would seem, when listening to Lorna, Lin, or more often than not, both of them at the same time.

"Come on… I'll show you where the beer is," he said, "but we'll probably start off on the wine."

And so we did, over dinner, the four of us, the conversation powered resolutely by Lin, with witty interjections from Chris, usually apropos of nothing, eg, "Do you know what Olympic event I'd really like to see, Will?" He was straight-faced under his grey beard. "Ski-jumping combined with clay-pigeon shooting." Then he returned to the meal, leaving me in a fit of laughter that overcomes me even now, writing about it years later. If I wasn't laughing so much at the time, I could have put forward my like-minded idea of making Formula One infinitely more exciting by the introduction of ramps. I noticed Lorna drifting off slightly, foggy from the South African wine. I made a conscious effort to slow down when I began to get light-headed, then set about interrogating Lin about her writing, much to Lorna's dismay. She proudly told me how she'd written the first draft of her latest work in three months. It takes me double that to write half as much.

"It's called The First and Last Outpost," she announced. "I've had the idea for thirty years." She said this so matter-of-factly that Lorna promptly questioned it.

"Yeah, the title," Lorna said. "You've had that for thirty years."

"No dear, the whole thing," came the reply.

The verbal jousting between mother and daughter became a staple of the weekend, and a source of great amusement, especially as it showed Lorna in a completely different light, one in which she seemed to have reverted back to childhood somewhat. I knew her as this independent girl with a proper career and everything. She rolled her eyes, just as Chris had earlier, and I thought then that she truly is her father's daughter. Chris reminded me of John Peel, not just in appearance – a modest bald patch and that beard – but his general demeanour and tonality, not least when talking about his favourite subject, the Grateful Dead.

"I think only a handful of musicians are able to match Phil Lesh's ability as a guitarist," he offered flatly, before, just like John Peel, segueing into a story about a particularly bad trip he'd once had at Wythenshawe Jazz Festival in 1971. We talked about his work as a research scientist. I'd asked Lorna about it but like most girls I know she didn't really know what her father's job entailed. "Something to do with chemicals," she'd said vaguely, and typically. His work was the reason they'd moved to Holland in the first place a few years earlier – this was Lorna's second spell – and the spare room that Lin had prepared had a shelf of books on the intricacies of all manner of chemical processes, but I won't enthral you with the details here.

"Why don't you play Trivial Pursuit while I wash up?" Lin suggested, her face still red behind her steamed glasses from her earlier exertions in the kitchen.

"I'll help you, Mum," said Lorna, springing back to life at last, as if suddenly remembering that board games like Trivial Pursuit have caused more physical human conflict than the British Expeditionary Force, Genghis Khan, and Alex Higgins combined. And that's without two bottles of red wine and a crate of beer added to the mix.

"It's alright dear. I can manage," replied Lin, clearing the table.

"I'll roll the dice for you then," said Lorna, without looking up from the dusty box.

"We'll all play," I said.

"Okay," Lorna said, "but I'll warn you, Will, this is the pre-Soviet Union collapse edition so there won't be much by way of recent events."

Nevertheless, the invention of the penknife, though not a recent development, was the first thing to trip me up. Apparently it wasn't created for uncorking wine bottles, or even less so, 'for stabbing capitalist American pigs' (it was the pre-Soviet Union collapse remember).

"The clue's in the question, Will," Lorna pointed out, a bit too smartly for my liking. I was still none the wiser, until she pointed out that it was for sharpening pencils with. It was a disastrous start that only got worse with drink. Was it really Connie Francis who was assassinated by the Red Brigade, and Aldo Moro who had a hit with Who's Sorry Now? Chris and I both patronisingly applauded Lorna when she finally decided that Old Threadneedle Street was the site of the Bank of England, though she'd been helped by his pointed clue: "Imagine your favourite place in the whole world. A place where you ask them for money, and even if you haven't got it, they give you it." Her glazed blue eyes sparkled at the thought of it. After much drama it was established that Chris needed to answer just one more question in order to procure that much sought after plastic wedge.

"Pick Arts and Entertainment," Lorna squealed. "He won't get it."

It was so easy I might as well have asked him what colour the sky was. Suicide is Painless is the theme tune to which TV programme? I'll leave it with you.

Lorna became increasingly drunk as the evening wore on and took to pestering Lin into buying her a dog, and then, during a lull in the attention directed at her, striking the matches we'd used to light some candles earlier, proclaiming that, "God, these just fuckin' explode in your face," as she frantically worked her way through the box. This potentially fatal arsonry prompted Lin to send her to bed, "before you burn the settee down", and to chide her for swearing, as she had done all night. She skulked off, leaving Chris and I to finish the booze as we watched Phil Lesh putting his Quantum 6 through its paces at the Warfield Theatre. If any Deadheads are reading this, do let me know if "actually Will, Phil wasn't using his Quantum 6 at that particular gig".

Lorna was no more enthusiastic the next morning over breakfast when Lin suggested she borrow Chris's car ("too big"), or hers ("too automatic"), although the real reason for shunning the latter was that it was too covered in Orangutans, as part of Lin's conservation drive which saw it garlanded with stickers of said primates. Lorna's car was off the road as of that morning due to its newly-illegal-in-Holland headlight tint. "I fucking hate that car," she said. "I should have stayed in England."

The four of us ended up in Chris's car, headed for Hoorn. I was glad the four of us went as there were always awkward silences between Lorna and I that we would break by talking at the same time. With Lin on board, there would be no awkward silences. She talked tirelessly about the Netherlands and its people. On the rare occasions he was able to, Chris took over as tour guide. As we walked along the canal, he explained how the plaques on the fronts of the houses explained what was stored there at the time, after it was lifted from the barges that served the town hundreds of years ago during the country's Golden Age. Most of them displayed beer kegs, or hunks of cheese, but one of them was covered with a poster for a well known brand of children's toys.

"And that's where the Playmobil was shipped in," he remarked dryly.

Hoorn was a charming typically Dutch town, with its rows of leaning houses and the cheese market, this bright Saturday morning that gave great views across the Ijsselmeer, the vast inlet of water between East and West Holland that's separated from the North Sea by the dam between the Den Oever and Bolsward areas. In a feat of superb engineering emblematic of the Dutch, it was created by building the dam in the Waddenzee area of the North Sea, in the 1920s, producing the freshwater lake that remains today. Some of it was drained to make a polder, thus adding an extra 637 square miles of land to the Dutch coastline that became Flevoland.

It was like a millpond today, skimmed by the occasional kingfisher or sailboat. The harbour was full of expensive sea-going craft of every variety, with telling names like Pathfinder, Pioneer, and Landseer, names that hark back to the legacy of Hoorn's, if not Holland's, most famous son, Jan Pieterszoon Coen. There was a statue of him in the cobbled town square gazing through the butcher's shop window, or maybe beyond to the South Sea Islands, the pioneering sailor of the Dutch Golden Age, or the bloodthirsty mutineer, depending on whose side you were on. Like Captain Cook but without the manners.

After spending much of the morning complaining about being skint, Lorna spent most of the afternoon trying on clothes and shoes and growing skinter, but at least it gave her the opportunity to exercise her hard-won black belt in shopping. I found refuge in a comic book shop that was home to an extensive collection of Tin Tin merchandise – we weren't far from Belgium, I suppose – none of it of the Teesside variety, unfortunately. For a friend of mine who's an avid fan, I bought a poster that captured all the darkness of Belgium and Holland's colonial past from a story entitled 'coke en stock', which I later discovered translated as 'coke in stock' and referred to the brutal Congolese slave trade of the first half of the 20th century.

My favourite though was the simple evolution-of-man-style drawing that showed our bequiffed hero in his various guises over the years: jungle explorer, astronaut, call centre worker and so on.

I was thinking of something a friend back home had said as I left the shop, that "no-one truly useful has ever come out of Belgium". With that he did an impression of a Belgian by simply walking purposefully with his arms planted firmly by his sides, his face frozen in a blank expression. "They're a bunch of Europe-faced cunts," he surmised. The Dutch on the other hand have given us a multitude of cultural enrichment such as Golden Earring, Big Brother and the Vengaboys.

On Sunday, Chris, Lorna and I went to Bergen, one of Northern Holland's best kept secrets, and the only place I can remember visiting with a beach next to a ski slope, the latter artificial, although the gradient was very real as we hiked to the top of it, passed the opposite way by gaggles of skiers, sledgers and snowboarders. Bergen was essentially an Alpine village transplanted to the Netherlands and around it had grown up a bohemian-style community of artists of every ilk. Beyond the ski slope was a massive expanse of woodland, thick with thriving fir trees and pine cones that littered the marked-out miles of adventure trails and mountain bike tracks. Like Faro, the town even had its own religious miracle story, this one dating back to the 1400s and concerning a treasure chest full of wafer biscuits that was washed up on the shore and was originally intended for holy communion somewhere. Then the chest improbably filled up with blood or something, which was all well and good but did it cure blindness? We dined at the Deerhunter Lodge, which to my disappointment turned out not to be affiliated in any way with the film of the same name as I really fancied a game of Russian roulette. On the way back to t'Zand, Chris told me about the Elfstedentocht, the country's annual speed skating race that takes place on 124 miles of the frozen canals that comprise the eleven cities of the Northern provinces, and the bouderais.

"I can see me living in a bouderai when I'm older," Lorna mused, gazing out of the window at one of the massive converted barns.

"I can see me paying for it," Chris replied.

Lorna continued, "They used to pile all the cattle in the middle of the barn to create warmth, and the family would live around them."

"I can't imagine their dinner parties were much fun," said Chris.

There was time for one more dinner party that Sunday night, somewhat subdued as everyone had to go back to work the next morning and I had to go and live in the airport again. I was awake for most of the night wondering what I was going to do next.

PART II: SOUTH-EAST ASIA

CHAPTER 4:
SINGAPORE

The Tank rolls in and we Singapore sling our hooks
to Bangkok to recuperate/hallucinate.

*"Even now, whenever I smell something similar, it takes me straight back to
Singapore."*

Schipol was ready for Christmas: tea lights, fake snow, and a replica
biplane hanging from the ceiling. I assume it was a replica, and
not a disastrous take-off by Louis Bleriot that had been snowed
off somewhere over Terminal One. I dipped into my pocket and
grabbed a handful of coins. It was time to tinkle the Tank.

He didn't mess about on the phone. He was about 437 times more
assertive than me.

"Can you get to Manchester airport by tomorrow night?" he
asked.

He was bringing the £1,200 tickets we'd booked a few weeks
before that would take us all the way round. In 48 hours we'd be
halfway to Singapore. In the meantime, I would live at the airport.
For thirty long hours. I'd turned up treating it like a bus station so
it was my own fault if one wasn't due until the next day. I loitered
spectacularly for the most part. Otherwise I spent time writing
up the previous few days in my journal – all the while thinking
Lorna would go mad if she ever read it – and avoiding the security
staff. Was this what it would be like for the rest of the trip: going
sleeplessly mad in the sparse surroundings of the world's generic
airports, hungry and dehydrated?
It had been Tank's idea in the first place and I happily gravitated in
his considerable orbit throughout the planning of the trip, most of
which we'd done in the pub. Then I shot off into Europe on my
own while he tied up a few business commitments. I'd deliberately

left my ticket with him for two reasons: so I wouldn't go on ahead into South-East Asia, although when we got there I'd have been a fool to have done so, and so I wouldn't lose the ticket, as I did with just about everything else I took along. I even lost that behemoth of a mobile phone on the way to Manchester.

We stepped through Changi airport's sliding doors and out into the street around sunrise. I was immediately struck by the wallop of raw sewage that seemed to permeate everything and it came and went with impressive consistency. It's said that first impressions are the most lasting and even now, whenever I smell something similar, it takes me straight back to Singapore.

'A spacious, well maintained, air-conditioned dorm' boasted the description of our Singapore accommodation in one guidebook.

'A cramped convection oven with a reckless disregard for fire safety regulations' was how it might have read. It gave a great view of the slums in the alleyway beneath us, and was just a fifteen minute drive away from the stunning Boat Quay, the Fullerton Hotel, the Hilton, and nearby Parliament House. Everywhere in between was spotless thanks to local laws that award on-the-spot public fines for littering, spitting, smoking, chewing gum and not flushing the toilet. I'm still unsure as to how they enforce the latter, or even how it came to be.

You could quite easily take a comfortable holiday in Singapore and never leave Changi airport, with its labyrinthine layout of TV lounges, interactive maps, saunas, steam rooms and cinema screens. If you did step out, you could always visit Suntec City, home of the world's biggest fountain, or the Long Bar at Raffles, where you may award yourself an extortionately-priced Singapore Sling, and in the process experience one of the world's many cultural travel must-dos, according to most travel guides. I didn't bother; if someone tells me I simply must try something travel-related, I usually just switch off and go to Bangkok or somewhere.

CHAPTER 5:
THAILAND

In which we are twice almost claimed by the sea,
riots engulf the capital, and, even more gravely,
one restaurant serves dessert before the main course.

"There'll be days when you wonder what the hell you're doing there."

Having cut short our week long stay in Singapore, we flew to Bangkok for a quiet week in order to plan our route around Thailand, but it didn't quite work out that way. After a few drinks on the first night, I went outside to make a phone call and in no time found myself a long way from my starting point on Charoen Krung Road, walking the streets, and considerably drunk, in no small part due to the head-to-head drinking session with two Danes we'd met. It wasn't helped by the barman's insistence that he could create a drink that none of us would be able to stomach, throwing down the gauntlet to Tank, who duly obliged. It was so elaborate and expensive that he could only make one, on the house to anyone who drank it, as long as it stayed down. The five of us huddled round in anticipation as he carefully began to build what looked like a plasma ball before Tank supped it as unceremoniously as if it was a cup of tea.

Outside, the streets swelled up and by midnight I found myself watching a game of 5-a-side in a car park. I returned to the hostel, and my cell-like room, where I lay for six hours, tossing and turning, hallucinating, and dehydrating with nothing but a noisy fan for company. I felt like Martin Sheen in Apocalypse Now. To stave off my thirst, I stupidly drank a can of Coke that I'd accidentally stolen (I intended to pay but the desk clerk was asleep). I was punished with a bloated stomach as I hadn't eaten properly, thus making me thirstier than I was to begin with. Early the next morning, we headed to Pattaya, in search of a decent beach more than anything else, and I began to feel violently ill.

Trapped in central Bangkok's rush hour traffic, the hallucinations continued as rioters descended on the parliament buildings. The beating sun and appalling levels of city centre pollution combined to make me feel as sick as I could ever remember being. I wanted to go home, be sick in my toilet, then return. The taxi driver who collected us from the airport two days earlier had offered to take us to Pattaya, his persistent hassling eventually paying off, but he'd changed his mind about the pre-arranged fare. I already had him down as a weasel from that previous ride. He was being too helpful. Soon enough he was doubling the fare and, in his own words, "not speaking so good English." He jabbered away through teeth that resembled a caveman's necklace, about having to pay highway tolls, par for the course in Thailand, but not mentioned in our original agreement, and how the fare quoted was per person and not for both of us.

"He's getting fuck all," raged Tank.

We eventually reached an agreement that involved bribing a traffic officer, a traditional Thai custom.

Pattaya turned out to be almost as wild as Bangkok but much more of a holiday resort, it being right on the east coast facing the Gulf of Thailand. In a place that attracts 5,000,000 visitors a year, everyone seemed to be an American, Australian or German sex tourist, including the wisecracking Eric Idle look-alike from Rochdale, who tried to sell me an apartment block for $20,000,000. He went on to explain that he spends six months of the year in Pattaya and the other half in Zambia, which he only said to impress me, I'm sure, thus paving the way for the sale of the apartment.

"He's full of shit," was Tank's accurate summation.

Pattaya as a resort took off over forty years ago when in 1961 American GIs were stationed there, as a stop-off on the way to Vietnam. The local women soon cottoned on to this and the vice trade began to flourish.

At the beach, a man waved a leaflet under my nose that explained he was deaf and collecting for related societies. Sensing another obvious swindle, I told him to fuck off using the power of mime, which he seemed to understand. I was unsurprised to later see him involved in an animated phone conversation.

The rat run from the hotel to the beach was lined with bars populated entirely by prostitutes and drunken holidaymakers. The women shouted, "Why you break my heart so?", and "Where you from?", or "Where you fraaaahhhmmm?" They tugged at clothes and bodies and rarely took no for an answer, but people rarely said no.

Still in search of that perfect beach, and unfulfilled by Pattaya, we made a mutual decision to get off the mainland and so flew out to Ko Samui from Rapong. The private beach at Tong Takian villa was surrounded by mountainous greenery and was a short drive from nearby Chaeweng. The beach was as good as any I would be on as long as I was away and where the white sand ended, the calm glass-clear water began. It contained hardly any coral so I was able to wade out for three-hundred yards without difficulty and take a closer look at the many shoals of fish that darted around my ankles.

The water was constantly warmed by midday temperatures around the forty degree mark and at any one time there would be as few as fifteen people on the entire beach. I soon fell into a comfortable daily routine that I could have carried on for a long time. I'd stroll down to the beach at 11am, just as the sun was approaching its hottest, fry for an hour or so then cool off in the sea before dinner. At 2pm, I'd head back to the room, then return to the beach in the early evening and watch the sunset. At night, Tank and I would board one of the many ramshackle open-backed taxi vans that ferried tourists around the islands and cling on for dear life like paratroopers waiting for the drop, as it bounced the entire route to Chaeweng at 40mph. If you're foolish enough to let go of the overhead handrail on the way, there's a good chance you'll be thrown straight off the back and onto the road. In Thailand, there's little margin for error on many of the roads due to the amount of traffic and the haphazard manner of the average motorist. Mopeds can often be seen grinding out an emergency stop of sorts with their back wheels high in the air and their front wheels inserted firmly up the arse of the person in front. The Thais at least have the sense to wear protective clothing of sorts though, unlike almost all tourists who opt for motorcycle rental, which is why most English visitors' bodies are covered in what the natives call 'Ko Phan skid marks' come the end of their stay. They tear around dusty unsealed roads, three to a seat, on a bike so powerful they wouldn't dream of riding one at home, wearing nothing but a pair of shorts and a bandana to alleviate skull fractures.

After a few days on Ko Samui, we took a catamaran to Ko Tao, or 'Turtle Island'. At the harbour, we were greeted by the usual throng of tour guides and taxi drivers and were soon rattling to the hotel in the back of a jeep. We had no accommodation booked and had to walk up and down the beach in the searing heat, negotiating with the various guesthouses on the beach front, which was a test of character if nothing else. By midday, we were in the sea, where I stupidly stayed for over two hours, ignoring most tour literatures' advice of fifteen minutes in the sun being more than enough for a pasty-faced westerner like myself.

For the next few days, I could hardly stand up or lie down as the heat of a thousand fires engulfed my back and neck. Most excruciating of all though was at the top of my right ear, which felt like it had been ironed; what was that about mad dogs and Englishmen? They remain by far the hottest temperatures I've endured. Ko Tao is one of Thailand's most popular diving sites, which is what attracts most of its visitors and is complemented by some excellent bars and nightclubs like The Brother, or the AC Bar, the latter situated right on the beachfront, its patio doors opening out on to the shoreline with the surrounding area lit only by flaming torches and green strobe lighting.

Lounging around on beaches allows for plenty of reading time so a good supply of books is important for the traveller who just can't be arsed. In Ko Tao, I found a copy of George Orwell's brilliant Down And Out In Paris And London which I read in one sitting and several times over the following few weeks. It put into perspective my budget lifestyle when I read his riveting account of the French capital's squalid hotel industry of the 1930s when he worked as a 'plongeur' alongside the hilariously optimistic Russian cripple Boris. One day Orwell, the next day, and the day after that, and the day after that, Tess Gerritsen, which led to a copy of her book, The Sinner, becoming a running joke. We simply couldn't get rid of it, be it in bookshops or with other travellers, and so it accompanied us right across the Outback, making sporadic cameos along the way. Tank would stuff it in the bottom of his backpack only to see it had miraculously moved to the top to stare him in the face whenever he opened the bag. We would trip over it just moments after we had stored it away in a cupboard or on a shelf. It wasn't always a hindrance though; we used it to swat flies, hammer in nails and even as a choc under the wheel of the fucking van at one point. Tragically, or triumphantly depending on how you look at it, it finally escaped us but we know not where, so if somebody out there has a battered copy, covered in mosquito brains, tyre tracks and kangaroo droppings, know that it served us well.

We fetched up on Ko Phangan two days before the island's famous Full Moon Party to find no room at the inn – as usual we hadn't bothered to arrange any accommodation. More dragging of backpacks around in the midday sun ensued, uphill mostly, until we finally found a room, approximately half a mile from the reception at the very back of the grounds and over an assortment of muddy slopes and rickety wooden bridges, one of which collapsed when we crossed it with our luggage. The room seemed closer to Bangkok than it did to Haad Rin, at the island's southern tip, where the party would be.

Located in the mountains, Haad Rin is hidden by thick jungle that houses an array of unseen chirping, squawking, chattering, screeching creatures that were particularly vociferous during early afternoon. The Full Moon Parties take place on the second Saturday of the month and regularly attract anything up to 5,000 people, although guidebooks have it closer to 10,000. One explanation might be that after a few hours partying the researcher was seeing double. On our visit, there couldn't have been more than 3,000 present. The exact origins of the party are somewhat muddled depending on who you talk to but most accounts credit the Kursakul family, owners of the Paradise bungalows, with the development to its current status. Others cite a birthday party in 1987 that, like all good parties, spiralled out of control but had begun with a handful of travellers of varying nationalities having a sing-song around a campfire.

I prepared for the impending madness of the party by sleeping on a leather settee in fifty degree heat. The early part of the evening saw everyone preoccupied by the FA Cup Final between Liverpool and West Ham, the majority being firmly on the side of the Reds. We watched from one of the many beachfront bars that charged 10baht for the privilege of urinating into a rusty sink next to twenty other people, and declaring it a toilet. Out on the sand, people wandered aimlessly and drunk, wearing all kinds of costumes or nothing at all. Pith helmets, stilts, and plumage were the most popular choices and anyone who couldn't be bothered dressing up simply daubed themselves in luminous body paint but ran the risk of being burnt by the fire or 'poi' jugglers. Angle grinders grinded angles and people jumped into the surf fully clothed waving flares above their heads – the trouser and incendiary kinds – commandeering boats moored nearby.

At the shoreline, you couldn't make out any particular music that came from the sound systems but a blur of noise mixed with cheering and shouting, until you walked by each one and discovered the better-defined noise of nosebleed Dutch techno and Goan trance. It didn't matter how it sounded though, everyone listening was deaf drunk, which is one up from blind drunk. It was hard not to be when you can buy a pail of vodka for £3. I washed one down with twelve bottles of Singha beer and found myself in a stupor alongside three street side hawkers, helping them to sell jewellery and hats to equally inebriated revellers. One of them became so deliriously excited when I bought her a can of beer from a nearby shop that she instantly ran away with it.

"For her husband," the others explained.

The casualties of the party began arriving around dinnertime the following day. Many simply collapsed on the beach and slept where they fell, right under the rising sun, before being lifted, paralysed by sunstroke, onto a trailer, and deposited outside their hotels.

That evening I ate at our usual place, where I'd become quite accustomed to some good Thai dishes, but on this occasion they struggled to get the courses in the right order, culminating in my apple pie and ice cream dessert arriving before the main.

We left Ko Phangan and rolled down the mountains to the harbour, before boarding what we had been told was a "really comfortable for sleeping in ferry" only to be confronted by a rusting hulk of a vessel that resembled a prototype Amistad.

"I like to get big tummy like you, my friend," shouted a Thai woman as we walked across a precarious gangplank to board the ferry. Tank wasn't amused and nor was I as we had both been awake for the best part of a day.

I brushed her aside.

"I've seen him eat parmos bigger than you," I said.

The boat housed around two hundred sweaty backpackers. The locals were obviously wise to the perils of such transportation and had avoided it. I was awkwardly placed, far too closely for my liking, between two Frenchmen and three Canadians, on a mattress less comfortable than the wooden floor it separated me from, meaning sleep was a distant dream, ironically. Luckily, I didn't feel any less deprived of it than at any other time in the week previous so it wasn't a problem. I wondered how many other people had slept on my mattress, and if we would even last the night without sinking or ploughing into an equally decrepit craft before floundering our way to a watery grave.

"There'll be days when you wonder what the hell you're doing there," people warned before I left England. This was one of them but I still didn't want to go home. Small consolation was that this was why I was doing it, to test myself in situations like this, however potentially dangerous they might be. That said, the boat trip was nothing compared to some of the experiences I would have in

Australia and the South Pacific. Everyone else seemed delighted to find themselves in such circumstances, contentedly playing Connect 4 and card games as we departed. I managed three hours sleep and woke as we arrived at first light in Surat Thani, on the mainland's east coast, still afloat rather than on the seabed as I'd anticipated.

From the bus station in Surat Thani, we took the two hour coach journey across the width of the mainland to meet our second ferry connection in Krabbi that would take us to Ko Pi Pi. The ferry that took us was like the QEII compared to the previous one but I was astonished to find that its seats were actually less comfortable so it didn't help my physical wellbeing when I fell asleep for ninety minutes. Leaving the ferry, I was handed a customer survey by a member of the crew asking me to describe the journey in less than ten words. I did it in eight but I wasn't going to win any prizes for, "It was like sitting on a fucking anvil." The in-sail entertainment was a video of an imperial half-child, half-pig Thai warrior that killed people with flatulence, and a plot that made Power Rangers look like Citizen Kane. After much haggling and remonstrating with tour operators, we booked into a smart, reasonably priced hotel, which provided a view of the narrow beach and surrounding mountains that formed a narrow gateway around 1,500 yards from the shoreline. At 10.37am on Boxing Day 2004, a tsunami swept through those rocky gates of Pi Pi Leh and washed away almost everything that ever meant a thing to anybody on the island. The wave that struck nearby Pi Pi Don was 18ft high. People, animals, houses, hotels, cars, boats, plants and livelihoods were swept into the sea or crushed by the force of the wave as it decimated Ton Sai village to such a degree that ten years later it has still not fully recovered. There was barely a hundred yards from beach to buildings on that side of the bay. Still untouched ruins were scattered over the surrounding area; at one spot, there was a rotting office chair and bureau where once had been a hotel.

Elsewhere memorials left by the tireless cleanup crews, touchingly consisting of scarves, banners and hand written signs, flapped around in the strong winds. As I ate at Amico's Restaurant, I noticed a picture on the far wall taken hours after the wave hit. I intended to go over for a closer look and to ask the staff of their recollections but as I finished my meal, a rowdy bunch of Americans came in, sat directly under the picture and started whooping, hollering and high-fiving each other, which is of course their national sport.

Back at the hotel, I read the Bangkok Post and taught myself some everyday Thai phrases. I then read with astonishment that Roy of the Rovers had his foot amputated in 1993 – incredible. Boredom had taken over. In my room I switched on CNN to see what was going on in the world. If it wasn't happening in Asia, it wasn't happening. A typhoon was harassing Hong Kong and the volcanic Mount Merapi was bubbling mischievously in central Java, inadvertently causing an earthquake 30km away and far too close to our next destination, Bali, for my liking. It wasn't all natural disasters though, an uprising by the Karen Liberation Army had threatened the area of Northwest Thailand, ruling out a possible visa run to Burma we were considering. We were surrounded, it seemed.

We eventually escaped from Ko Pi Pi over a tumultuous sea, the boat at times vertical in the water. Through the windows, I could see groups of children undeterred by the storms, cliff diving into the mouth of the bay. We crossed the Andaman Sea not far from North Sentinel Island, which is believed to be the home of the world's oldest known untreated civilization, for want of a better term. I did some research and was amazed at what I found. Lying west of the Andaman Islands and just south of the Bay of Bengal, lived a tribe thought to number anything between 50 and 400 people. Estimates are so vague because no-one has been able to, or dared to, approach the island, which can only be reached by boat, as two shipwrecked fishermen discovered when they were washed ashore, only to be attacked with spears and blowpipes. The very same treatment was administered to aid crews who flew helicopters over the island to drop supplies after the tsunami.

With time to kill, we spent a weekend in Phuket as the guests of Hasse Andersson at The Nice Hotel, which I can't recommend strongly enough to anyone staying in Phuket. Simply head for the much more well known Montana Grand then completely ignore it and its hopeless booking procedures, cross the street to Hasse's and pay half the price. Hasse was originally from Stockholm and had sold his agricultural machinery hire business six months earlier to fund the purchase of the hotel. After his fifth heart attack, he knew he needed an easier life so moved to Patong Beach, and with the help of his daughter, he was really making a go of it.

He looked like he'd never fully recovered from the heart attacks; even after half a year in the sun, his serious face was still as pale as the moon. He'd travelled much in his younger years and was keen to talk about it, particularly the US, knowing we would be going there in November. He excitedly traced his route using Google Earth: Baja, Hoover Dam, Memphis – specifically Graceland – and New York. He told of the eerie sense of calm and peace that overcame the spot of Elvis's grave, and how everyone fell silent at the exact same time to pay their respects.

His poignant reflection was interrupted when fork lightning shattered the fuse box opposite the hotel bar, handing us an instant power cut. I'd noticed in Bangkok the illogical Thai thinking that placed hundreds of live power lines merely a few feet above the residents' heads, which seemed somewhat reckless in a country with a monsoon period. In Phuket, the storm calmed but the power stayed off so we drank by candle light, which was the least romantic experience of my life, as winds battered the bar and shutters and bar stools tumbled past. When it was calmer, I began my usual midnight ramble through the blackout. The only other light sources came from the occasional ATM, phone box or market stall. The nightclubs were still lively though and most people took refuge inside them; anyone who didn't was wandering around in the middle of the road, like I was.

I stood and watched a passable band at the Margarita bar that was situated directly under a Muythai arena where a few hours earlier Tank and I had watched a woeful exhibition match put on exclusively for tourists who didn't have a clue about Thai boxing. It entailed four poor rounds of sparring accompanied by a soundtrack of the snake charming music they seem to be so fond of, which begs the question, how do you even begin to ascertain the musical tastes of a snake? Speaking of low musical tastes, I woke the next morning to discover that back in Europe little had changed; the Eurovision Song Contest was won by Lordi.

We checked out the following afternoon at 1.30pm for another full day of travelling, this time from Phuket to Surat Thani in torrential rain. It fell relentlessly for two hours, by which time we'd boarded the bus to Bangkok for an overnight drive north of eleven hours. National stereotypes abounded as a German girl defensively spread herself across the entire back seat in order to reserve it for her fellow compatriots whilst the entertainment consisted of back-to-back screenings of the Christian Slater caper Hard Rain, which, very slowly, killed four hours. At midnight, we stopped at a soup kitchen of sorts, where I filled up on nutritional foods like cookies and crisps, which was all I'd eaten all day. I returned to the bus and awaited the onset of rickets. We reached the capital, and the spectacular but typically gaudy royal palace, around mid-morning. Months later, it would be surrounded by the army as they craftily ousted the cabinet while the Prime Minister was on holiday in London but by then I would be far, far away.

CHAPTER 6:
BALI

An arachnid attack precedes a successful attempt at haggling,
and an ill-fated surfing venture.

*"I foolishly attempted to block one of the waves using the surf board, which is
equivalent to holding an ironing board in front of an oncoming car."*

Fortified by a highly nutritious breakfast of chicken burger
and chips at Changi airport, we flew on to Bali and landed in
Denpasar late at night. I'd never been more ready for bed in my
life after over twenty four hours of travelling. Even so, after ninety
minutes of sleep, I woke up and swung a flashlight under the bed
to look for a lost earplug and in the process found myself face to
face with a giant spider – paralysed with fear doesn't even come into
it. I could see its muscles, its eyes, and its eight big feet. I hoped it
was dead but it soon legged it, confirming its rude health in the
process. It looked to be of the species 'man-scarer' and even more
terrifyingly was nowhere to be seen the next morning so maybe it
became one of the seven spiders that supposedly crawl into your
mouth during your lifetime. Actually, I would have known if it
had because I was awake all night going slowly mad in the heat.
I straightened my head out the next morning by eating the finest
banana pancake available in the whole of South-East Asia, and I'd
eaten enough to know, in Sanur. It was there I read of Kuta, on
the opposite side of Denpasar, and thought it looked appealing,
in contrast with the much more reserved and quiet area we were
currently in, and so made some enquiries regarding taxi fares for
the following day. This was easy enough as the street was lined with
bored drivers insisting they take us somewhere. We were quoted
between 60 and 70,000rupiah so working as I now was on the basis
that anyone trying to sell me anything was doubling it, I immediately
haggled for 50,000 and agreed on that. Then I changed my mind

over dinner and, feeling confident, decided I would try for less, telling the driver I had been offered the ride for 40,000 elsewhere and would accept that instead. He held out for 45,000 but I wasn't budging and walked away.

Suddenly he called out, "Okay, okay, forty thousand."

I'd still probably paid slightly over the odds but it was a fair attempt at haggling.

The Kuta beach area was much livelier and we'd found a good deal at Satriya Cottages, where we secured a 'superior room', as no 'standard' was available, not that we'd booked anything, with a 30% discount to boot. It was near the beach and had a spectacular pool fitted out with a swim-up bar, all for a meagre £8 per night. It was a long way from the traditional backpackers' lifestyle but was too good to ignore, a sort of holiday within a holiday that we justified by telling ourselves how much we had been roughing it in Thailand. For every dodgy ferry crossing or half-day bus journey, there's a silver lining when you least expect it.

Buoyed by our good fortune, I decided to try my hand at surfing. Naturally, I went out at high tide, around 10am, the worst possible time for a first attempt. I was under the impression I would simply jump on the board and ride away. Wrong. The waves were by no means enormous but big enough to knock someone over, even my 150lb wringing wet frame. I foolishly attempted to block one of the waves using the board, which is equivalent to holding an ironing board in front of an oncoming car. I was off my feet more time than I was on them and it's anybody's guess where the board got to. It was strapped to my leg throughout but we rarely saw each other. At one point, it cracked me on the knee then disappeared as quickly as it came. The best I could manage was jumping a few waves up to about fifty yards out then have them fire me back to the shore lying face down on the board. I was basically wakeboarding on a surfboard. Surfing is an obvious metaphor for life as no matter how many times you get knocked down – in my case about fifteen – you just keep getting back on again. With this in mind, I gave in after twenty minutes.

Later that day, back around the pool, we fell into conversation with a New Zealand woman who was trying to tune the TV and mentioned we were going there in October. Knowing we were English, she said she'd just started working with a lab technician from somewhere in northern Europe.

"Now, what's it called?" she pondered, thinking of the place. "Middlesbrough," she said suddenly – another amazing coincidence.

I was badly sunburnt again as we prepared to fly to Australia; worse still, Tank had all the symptoms of malaria. Our mutual fatigue sparked an argument about who organises what parts of the trip, and how important those parts were, after I'd been unable to change our flights over the Internet due to a faulty broadband connection. Of course, he had no such trouble, the implication being that I hadn't even attempted to do it. I had, but he was probably having one of the many afternoon naps that filled his days at the time. At this point, I felt we were ready to hurt each other so what better thing to do than live in a confined space in some of the world's remotest landscape?

Leaving Bali wasn't quite as straightforward as we thought it would be thanks to a couple of overzealous immigration officials. In fairness, one was simply doing a random bag search, the first one I'd encountered, but her colleague at passport control was trying to make a quick rupiah in insisting we had overstayed when we clearly hadn't, as our passports proved. He stooped behind his desk, out of the eye line of his colleagues, and reduced his voice to a whisper. I looked him in the eye and saw the face of the taxi driver from Bangkok, a sour-faced brigand, which in my mind is now the representation of corruption the world over. If we had overstayed, I would gladly have slipped him a bribe but we hadn't and had no intention of coughing up. After five minutes of stalemate, he gave up and let us pass, mumbling about "next time".

A few hours later, we returned to Singapore for the sixth time in as many weeks for our connecting flight to Australia. At 9pm, we left South-East Asia for the final time and flew to Brisbane.

PART III: AUSTRALIA

CHAPTER 7:
BRISBANE TO TOWNSVILLE

Three go mad in a van. A fucking van.
With nothing but a Guns N' Roses LP for comfort.

"I'm living in a fucking van now you see."

We stationed ourselves in the small east Brisbane suburb of Manly, specifically, Moreton Bay, with its white picket fences, seafood restaurants, and barbecues in the seafront park. People played football, others chose to power walk round the harbour in glorious sunshine while yachts coasted through the bay. The hostel was a stone's throw from the beach and more importantly, a fifteen second walk from the pub opposite, the Manly Hotel. In the previous nine months, the owner, Dave, a well-travelled Kiwi, had completely transformed the place and now it was paying off, mainly through word of mouth of its guests.

The balance of guests was the most crucial aspect of its success as it constantly attracted a mixed crowd of obscure nationalities and ages, not just the usual backpacker staples of English, Canadian and German. I was surprised to see so many Australians staying there. It seemed odd at first that Aussies would be backpacking around their own country, but then why not? It was as fascinating to them as it was to the outsider.

Our arrival was the beginning of a new core group that I noticed manifests itself at most hostels, a dozen or so mainstays, usually working nearby and staying a long time as a result. The current group had been around for a month or so and were gradually dispersing, most of them heading off up the east coast to look for work.

We were only around for a week initially, to plan our road trip, but returned as we liked the place so much. It wasn't easy planning the road trip as we were constantly distracted by the partying that was going on and the comic interludes provided by Rusty and Roy. Despite sounding like children's entertainers, Roy was an ex-soldier from Israel doing his utmost to spend every last penny from his dad's construction business back in Lebanon, and he was excelling at it. He no longer even stayed at the hostel and was currently renting a room in nearby Cannon Hill, the address of which he somehow forgot when we went to collect some of his things one day.

If Roy was absent-minded, Rusty was completely without one of his own but he would figure prominently during our stay in Australia. That night, we drank to the Old Country with the locals until we could no more stand up, relying on the drink that fuels the entire state of Queensland, Tooheys. Rusty and Roy turned out to be what the Aussies call 'two pot screamers', and the English call 'lightweights'. Tank and I were holed up in the beer garden with Cookie and Daniel, a couple of the regulars from nearby Wynnum. Daniel was born in Australia but spent most of his childhood in France where he became fascinated by the likes of Jacques Brel and Serge Gainsbourg, and punk movements like Oi!, which had inspired him to pursue a musical career, with varying degrees of success. He was now hoping to achieve something without the interference of anyone from the music industry.

He invited me along to the weekly jam session at Wynnum after I mentioned I played the harmonica. Cookie was one of many 'True Blues' I would meet in Australia. 'True Blue' is another Aussie term, used to describe a typical Australian male.

Members of the species 'Truis Bluis' are meat-eaters, usually gathering food from a primitive source known as a 'BBQ'. Any fluid required in the diet is more often than not taken from a 'tinny', a disposable flask-like device also known as a 'can'. Such liquids are also available in glass bottles known as 'tallies,' or 'long necks'. After feeding, this natural predator will go off in search of a 'Sheila', in order to mate with. The mating ritual is a Neanderthal affair known as 'rooting' and usually begins with a display of muscle flexing exercises, followed by a series of indecipherable grunts, and finally, a 'tab'.

We were no better off for a cloudless sky in Byron Bay as the sun was nowhere to be seen either but it was still the kind of weather that would have people blowing up the paddling pools in England. I tried to relax on the beach as Roy surfed but I couldn't settle as the wind whipped sand into my face and Rusty waffled on. Whatever it was, it wasn't how a beach should be and I left disappointed, mainly because the drive there had taken so long, but not as long as the return journey as we got lost after somehow heading south from Byron Bay and ending up near Surfers Paradise. Back in Brisbane, we overshot our turn-off and got lost again, this time in the city. As someone later pointed out, "When you're a backpacker, you're never lost", but this was little consolation. We returned to the hostel around midnight to find we had been accidentally evicted, our room now populated by a girls' football team, which wouldn't have been so bad if the den mother hadn't been chaperoning them.

"What do you think you're doing coming into a room full of young girls?" she demanded, with a matronly air and an unfortunate choice of phrasing.

"Never mind that. Where's the bed I paid for this morning?" I replied.

I'd been moved across the hall to accommodate. This was the first of many room/bed hops around the hostel. There was hardly a day passed when everyone slept in the bed they had paid for.

Pete was the archetypal Aussie bloke. He was from Port Douglas, up the coast, and doing a boat captain's course in central Brisbane. He spent his spare time fighting off women with a stick, except he never once fought them off. Rugged was probably the best description of him but he was humble with it, which made him a good bloke to have around the place. His roommate at the hostel was fellow course member Carl, who was often dispensing useless bits of trivia that I was always storing at the back of my mind, most of which he found on the underside of XXXX bottle tops.

Ken Hannon was the hostel's longest-serving resident, so much so that he had his own bed, even when he wasn't staying there, which he occasionally didn't. A bona-fide, self-proclaimed, non-conformist for over half a century, he would jump on his motorbike and take off for a few days to wherever he felt like, or to wherever his job as a mental health care worker took him. He had left home in Nelson, the stoner capital of New Zealand's South Island, as a teenager, and had been on the move ever since. As an older man, he had immaculate taste in music, particularly jazz and blues, and happily tolerated my incessant questioning on the subject that went on for the best part of three months. All the ingredients were in place for a good time then, that mix of ages and nationalities I mentioned, the location (opposite the pub), and plenty of 'grog'. It would all have to wait though. We were going walkabout.

"What's wrong with you?" the woman at the rental car office asked Rusty. "I never met a bloke who can't drive and doesn't drink." She was a dungarees and sensible shoes woman.

He just looked at her big face with his stupid, blank face and offered no explanation; there was no way, or time, to explain him. I flicked a sunburnt thumb through $1,600 and slid it across the tea-stained desk. Cairns, Alice, Darwin and anywhere around: one month, three poms, two states, 2,000km and countless arguments. Rusty was going as far north as Cairns, which as it turned out was far enough, and then too far.

The previous occupants of the fucking van had thoughtfully left us with a broad range of music to choose from. I found some toxic-looking cassettes in the glove box: The Love Album, Guns N' Roses' Greatest Hits, and the third one, well it sounded like a fucking headache so it was probably another Guns N' Roses album but at least we had something to throw at Rusty. We carried out the necessary checks in the car park of the rental depot. By necessary, I mean we checked for a windscreen and a steering wheel and totally overlooked what appeared to be the boot print of a sasquatch that had crumpled the most expensive part of the vehicle, the fabled Toyota badge, that we would pay for later. Guns N' Roses soon became the soundtrack to the journey and I have terrible memories of being blasted out of bed in the morning by Axl Rose welcoming me to the jungle. "We've got fun and games," promised the long-haired tit.

Tank drove the first leg, Brisbane to Noosa, and with the entire east coast at our mercy, miles of hard top beneath us, and a full tank of fuel ready to burn, we parked up and went to the cinema. It was the first time I'd visited a cinema since I'd quit my job in one back home so I knew all the tricks.

"I'm a student," I informed the cashier.

"Where's your student card?"

"Er... at home," I protested. "But I have got one. I'm living in a fucking van now you see. It's outside with my student card in it."

She didn't bat an eyelid as she charged me full price. And I knew exactly how she felt and would have done the very same. I wanted to pay as little as possible to watch The Da Vinci Code that was all. Tank loved it, I hated it, and Rusty enjoyed his first ever visit to the cinema.

On the way to Noosa, we stopped at Mooloolaba and visited Underwater World to visit its sharks and manta rays, among other things. I snapped the obligatory photo of us standing in the replica jawbones of a prehistoric shark called a Megalodon. Impressive as it was – its mouth wide open measured 6ft between the upper and lower mandibles – it was practically dwarfed when Tank posed for a picture inside it.

I opened the 300km to Hervey Bay, a choice spot for humpback whales on their way back from their annual migration period in the Antarctic. After three hours in the box seat, I could hardly stand up after not being behind the wheel for so long.

We got into a daily routine of splitting the driving between two of us. Rusty could not be trusted with apparatus as complicated as a steering wheel, which ruled him out of driving duties. Usually one of us would do the morning leg, around 10am 'til lunch, at which point we would stop and cook primitively – one time an Aborigine approached us and told us we might consider updating our food preparation methods – then the other would drive until dusk before settling down for the night. It was always best to get off the road come nightfall, especially in the Outback, due to the distinct possibility of mowing down one of the many kangaroos that came out to feed in the last of the light. They always made a point of running across the road at the last moment, which was apparently something to do with shaking off potential predators such as the Toyota Hi Lux, and explained the amount of roadkill we saw. It wasn't such a problem on the populated coastal routes though.

We reached 1770, one of the few places on the planet to be named after a number, although it had considerably more significance than that for us, being the very place where Captain Cook, another Teessider who travelled to the other side of the world, went ashore centuries earlier after a more fruitful stop at Kurnell, in what came to be known as Botany Bay, when charting the east coast.

The town was originally called Round Hill but renamed 1770 in that year to commemorate Cook's visit. Like Cook, we were not overly impressed by what we found and didn't stay long.

Cook seemed to polarise the opinions of the white Australians I spoke to but many of them, I felt, couldn't quite grasp the magnitude of what he'd achieved in even getting there. It's difficult to comprehend such achievements I often think but the carefree Aussie attitude seemed to prevail.

"We're a nation of convicts thanks to that bugger," a man would say to me later in Sydney.

"But look at the place now," I said, looking out across the magnificent Darling Harbour.

"Could be worse," he said, "could have been a fucking chink."

Whether he knew it or not, he was referring to Zheng He's voyages of the 1420s. A carved wooden figure was discovered in Darwin in 1879 that dated back to the Ming dynasty, which could put its origin anytime between the 1360s and 1640s.

Whatever your view of the settlement dates, there's no suggestion whatsoever that any of these expeditions took place before the advent of the Aborigines.

At the 1770 museum, we poked around some of the artefacts and articles relating to Cook's voyages but there was nothing I didn't already know, except the things that were incorrect. They had his birthplace recorded as Staithes, the small fishing village not far from Whitby on the North Yorkshire coast where he began his sea-faring career, when in actual fact he was born in Marton, Middlesbrough, less than half a mile from where I'm writing this. Tank soon corrected the museum's curator.

"We only have a small budget to run the place," offered the old lady apologetically. She was appreciative of the information and delighted to see the photos Tank had taken of Staithes, where Cook spent much of his childhood. The woman excitedly made a copy of the pictures for display in the museum, which led to Tank appearing in the local newspaper. We knew we would be hearing about Cook again as we left 1770 and laid waste to the east coast, tearing through Miriam Vale, Bundaberg and Rockhampton, where we stopped for the night. By then, we'd taken to parking up in the car parks of the Australian equivalent of working men's clubs, usually called RSAs.

They were always well lit with people constantly coming and going, until midnight at least, but more importantly meant we were always near a bar, precisely when England's World Cup games took place. I was pleased to see at one such place, the Frenchville Sports Club, that procedure doesn't change despite being on the other side of the world. The entertainment consisted of a husband and wife duo of pensionable age bastardising the usual rock staples like a geriatric White Stripes as the locals drank more than they could hold and let off steam by spilling out into the car park, the safe, well lit one I described above, for a no-holds barred brawl.

The weapon of choice on this occasion was a stiletto heel as we looked on with amusement from the fucking van. The brawlers weren't the only ones concerned with footwear. We woke the next morning to find that Rusty's trainers had been stolen from underneath the fucking van, where Tank ordered he leave them because of the smell. My amusement at this was magnified by the farcical shopping trip they embarked upon when Tank had to buy him a new pair, and because for once it wasn't me who had lost something. We probably could have tracked them down by following the vapour trail but time was against us. It was the second pair of footwear we'd lost in twenty-four hours. The day before, Tank ingeniously tied one of his sandals to the 'kangaroo killers' (crash bars), on the front of the fucking van to dry it off, only to see a strong gust of wind suck it clean away somewhere near Gladstone. At 120kph I wasn't about to do a u-turn. I rattled off the 400km to Mackay and parked up at a Caltex garage forecourt where we stayed the night and generally acted like we owned the place.

Tank cooked, Rusty washed up and I had a shower and shave in the bathroom whilst my batteries charged up behind the counter. Fully stocked up on fuel, water and stolen chocolate, we rocketed up to Proserpine, and Airlie Beach. I recklessly drove another 400km to Townsville that afternoon while Rusty and Tank slept in the back. It's as well they were asleep as I almost wiped the fucking van out on two separate occasions so they would have gone quietly at least. They woke up when every bit of crockery we had threw itself out of the cupboard as I was negotiating a tricky hairpin bend on two wheels. The onset of cabin fever developed into kleptomania as I stole a Boost bar from a service station and later a 'NO DIVING' sign from the Townsville ferry terminal. Townsville was another party stop on the backpacker circuit but it had much more of an Australian crowd than a lot of the other places we had visited, mainly because it was a garrison town. The city was established in the 1860s by 'blackbirder' Robert Towns. 'Blackbirding' was the term used to describe the practice of kidnapping South Sea Islanders, or 'Kanakas' as they were known, and forcing them into hard labour in Australia. It was a bank holiday weekend when we arrived so the festivities were in full swing. After the long drive, I was too tired to do anything so didn't join Tank and Rusty at the local wet t-shirt competition, which for the record neither won. Instead I watched part of a talent contest at the Seaview Hotel then walked around the war memorial like the party animal that surely I am.

Looking for somewhere to settle up for the night, I almost knocked a policeman off his motorbike, prompting him to pull us over, which I thought was a little reactionary of him, after all I'd only nearly killed him. He let us off with a slap on the wrist when we convinced him we were just passing through. I think he sympathised with us having Rusty, who, in a blind panic created by the police presence, somehow managed to lock himself in the back of the fucking van then failed to answer the simplest of questions posed by the officer.

"Do you know it's an offence to ride in such a vehicle unless you are sitting in the front cab, sir?"

"Yes," replied Rusty,

"Then why are sitting in the back?"

"Er, no I don't," answered Rusty, backtracking brilliantly.

We felt very relieved to have avoided a $450 fine as we slept in a community centre car park in nearby Oonoomba.

By the time we got to Mission Beach the next morning, we had been in the fucking van just five days but our tempers were quicker than Usain Bolt.

Captain Cook named Mission Beach for the sheer danger his crew would have met with had they tried to come ashore over the coral. It was a rough day weather-wise as I looked out to sea and saw a trawler being tossed around like a rubber duck. There was nothing else of note there but I imagined it would be pleasant enough in the summer. We'd used all our motoring offence luck up in Townsville so it was no surprise to be fined $140 for having someone in the back again as we approached Cairns and were stopped at a police speed trap.

We joined the queue of Winnebagos and Combi vans waiting to give their details in then bickered our way north. Rusty announced that he would simply rip up the ticket "if it was me". By then I would rather a monkey drove me than him and I let him know it. Considering he'd locked himself in and out of the fucking van in a twenty-four-hour period, he was in no position to be doing anything as advanced as ripping up motoring fines.

He reminded me of an amnesiac tour-guide version of Hugh Laurie. Whenever we arrived in a new town or city, which was almost daily, out would come his repertoire of nonsensical phrases.

"It's deceptive, isn't it?" he would say, slowly stroking his chin and looking around, without saying what was deceptive.

Then he would constantly change his opinion of a place whilst staying there. Take, for example, Townsville, which, at one time or another was any of the following: wild, nice, awesome, lush, cheap, expensive, and of course, deceptive. God help anybody who ever asks him for directions as every destination seemed to be left, right and straight on, all at the same time. I was sad to see him go when he left us in Cairns, as was planned, as he inadvertently provided much amusement, but we would see plenty more of him.

Our main aim in Cairns was to get out onto the Barrier Reef but we hit some bad weather and were left twiddling our thumbs for a while waiting for the winds to die down and the seas to calm. We spent most of our time parked on the seafront in a row of camper vans, keeping an eye out for overzealous traffic wardens and council representatives who usually slapped people with a 'get-out-of-town' style eviction notice for having the audacity to stop in an area where people were plainly attempting to power walk: charging up and down the seafront, stopping only to do three hundred press-ups, or sit-ups, before marching off with a dumbbell in each hand. North Queenslanders mean business when it comes to exercise. To kill time, we drove up to Cape Tribulation, as far north as we could feasibly go in such a vehicle. There was actually a sign on the dirt track out of there that said 'NO FUCKING VANS'.

"It's Land Rover territory up there," someone warned.

The run to Cape Tribulation was treacherous but spectacular as we wound our way along the coastal route, the blue of the Coral Sea to our right, and the green of the Cape York Peninsula to our left. We stopped at many of the lookout posts along the way, most notably Henry Moss Point, up in the Tablelands just outside of Cairns, and then in Daintree at the Alexandria lookout, or wahlu-wugirra, as the Aborigines called it, where it so was overcast you couldn't see anything anyway. A display map showed plans for a nearby township from years before that was to be called Whitby but never developed, although one person is known to live at the proposed site.

Disappointingly, there were no crocodile sightings as we crossed the Daintree River, completely ignoring the signs informing us to stay away from the water's edge lest we be death rolled, drowned, and eaten, in that order. The traffic slowed going into Cape Tribulation as a proud cassowary led its young across the road, stopping only to inspect its audience. It had obviously seen digital cameras before and skulked back into the bushes by the roadside. We stayed in the car park of JP's Jungle Retreat that night and had a good drink with the locals who had turned out to watch the State of Origin football match. We played euchre, another new card game we learnt, and 'yaniv', the latter apparently all the rage amongst the Israeli army, according to Roy who'd taught us it at Moreton Bay. Our opponents were Lyneham and Richard, who were unapologetically 'true blue'.

Naturally we argued about the Ashes – "You're only giving it a polish for us," declared Lyneham – and any other Anglo-Oz traditions. Every time Lyneham made a point, he would lean forward with all his weight on one elbow, raise one blond eyebrow, Roger Moore-style, and begin his statement with, "As I understand it..." The pair were up from Cairns having a boozy couple of days staying with the backpackers. Richard was an electrical goods salesman and the more reserved foil to Lyneham's lively character. They disappeared after the match finished and were replaced by a Kiwi, Courtney, and her Bristolian pal. Courtney didn't shut up from the moment she sat down to the minute she left but I was drunk enough to humour her. I spent most of the conversation, if you can call it that, just staring into her mouth. She soon tired of my withering sarcasm, which I had to jam into the exchange over, under, sideways and down in order to make a point, which at least appealed to her friend's English sense of humour. There was little I didn't know about Courtney by the time we left. Originally from Christchurch, her father was a Scouser and apparently such a tearaway as a youngster in Birkenhead that the locals nicknamed him Barabbas. She had an appealing air of the rebellious ingénue that combined neatly with her scattergun delivery, which is a very polite way of saying she was of easy virtue. She owned a horse called something like Trotty Mctippington which was apparently named after a famous New Zealand dressage rider, and when she left Australia she was off to work in Runcorn, Cheshire, for a logistical firm, and her blood type was... well, you get the idea. A perfect storm of forked lightning, disputes over card games, and cheap vodka, brought the night to a chaotic end and forced us all to bed early.

It poured down in Cape Tribulation all the time we were there, which only gave it a more tropical feel. We attempted to drive to Cooktown but immediately turned back where the road ended and the dirt track started, and returned to Cairns to loiter on the seafront. It was a Friday and we wouldn't be able to hit the Reef until Sunday at the earliest which would leave us with eighteen days to reach the Great Victoria Desert and then turn north for Darwin. By now, we had moved from the seafront and taken residence at Cannon Park racetrack. On our first night, a man with a torch disturbed us, moving us on as there was a race meeting the next morning.

When the torch flashed through the window, two words popped into my head: axe murderer. Whenever I heard the slightest noise outside, I was alert to it straight away, sitting up and listening until it went. It was only in the cities that it concerned me. Once we reached the Outback, I felt much safer because of the lack of people around and there wasn't an animal in the whole country that I was afraid of after that Balinese spider.

Back on the Cairns seafront, I walked almost its entire length, stopping to check out the heavy artillery gun placements that were used to defend the Coral Sea from Japanese raiders during WWII, before watching England's unconvincing victory over Trinidad and Tobago at the Tradewinds Hotel.

We missed the bus to take us back to Cape Tribulation for the Reef trip as Tank's watch stopped overnight, so we had to drive there ourselves. We arrived with three minutes to spare, in such a hurry that Tank parked the fucking van on a train track. The one hour journey had taken us less than forty minutes and was followed by a rough ferry trip out to the Agincourt Reef and the Low Isles, one of a group of two thousand islands along the east coast, but after feeling initially unwell, I was raring to go when we dropped anchor. It was just as well as I saw some of the most extraordinary scenery I'd ever laid eyes on as I snorkelled around.

I was in a mild state of shock to begin with when I saw what was down there but I soon adapted to the freezing, choppy sea. It was another windy, overcast day, so visibility was nowhere near as good as it could have been but I could still see everything. I could still see the reef sharks that we attracted by 'chumming' (the process of coaxing sharks by throwing red meat overboard), that raced away as soon as we entered the water, and the giant clams, now protected by law due to their dwindling numbers. I could still swim alongside a giant turtle and handle coral baskets. Shoals of fish, which could have been of any of the two thousand species believed to occupy the Reef, and Moray eels, darted towards me then dispersed in all directions when I floated by. I nosed in caves and marvelled at my surroundings as indescribable creatures shot past within touching distance. We made another equally dazzling stop at Phil's Reef, also known as 'Barry's Bommie', named after a famously friendly turtle that had recently been eaten by a shark, where our guide Louise said she would show me "the really good stuff" by which I assume she was referring to the Reef, although I don't mind telling you I was hoping for something a little more personal. Louise had summed it up best in her briefing, pointing out that the world's largest aquarium was right beneath our feet.

The Great Barrier Reef is the world's largest living organism – if you discount that big fungus thing in Canada – stretching itself between Fraser Island and Cape Flattery, a distance of approximately 2,000km, and covering a square area of 350,000km. This includes around 3,000 separate reefs of varying types although the higher quality coral is to be found on the Outer Reef, where the water can be up to 200ft deep. Of the 2,000 islands scattered along the Reef, most are uninhabitable and only a handful allow visitors, sometimes for overnight camping, when a permit is required from the Great

Barrier Reef Marine Park Authority, which has been in effect since 1975. Their current concerns regarding the well being of the Reef are related to Northern Queensland's farmers allegedly draining off no end of poisonous fertilisers into the sea, something that doesn't seem to trouble the conscience of the majority of them.

Another threat of sorts to the Reef is the phenomenon of the crown of thorns starfish, which forty years ago began eating away at the coral to such an extent that marine biologists worried it would, years later, destroy the whole thing. It was eventually decided that it was a good thing, allowing old coral to be taken away, thus making room for fresh growth.

The return trip to the mainland was as rough as our Andaman Sea crossing in Thailand but exacerbated by the free seafood buffet and chocolate cake we had plied ourselves with. As a result, there were green faces all round when we returned to the fucking van and sped down the Bruce Highway, back to Townsville, where we would swing a right into the bush. Soon after, our faces changed from green to white when, in heavy rain and near darkness, I somehow avoided a potentially fatal accident thanks to some clever braking after the driver of an eighteen-wheeler attempted to overtake us and the car in front. About halfway through, the lorry driver changed his mind and squeezed back into the gap that was probably the length of two cars by that time. I was running out of road fast as his back trailer swung towards my driver's door and braced myself for an upside down view of the dense woodland to my left but somehow I managed to get out of his way. I didn't realise the seriousness of it until much later; it had been a long day and almost the last.

CHAPTER 8:
INTO THE RED CENTRE

Living next door to Alice, penalty shoot-out, and getting
acquainted with the natives (who subsequently rob us).

"When a camel thinks it's too hot then you know you're in serious trouble."

We spent half of our budget on fuel and food the next morning in
Townsville before pointing west and swooping over the Burdekin
River on the Barkly Highway for Charters Towers. Charters would
be the first stop on the inland leg of our journey. It was also the
place where eighty years ago, people like Frank Stubley and George
Craven made and lost what even nowadays would be considered
fortunes; in Stubley's case $100,000, after they'd arrived in the
1870s to exploit the area's rich seam of ore. Many of the buildings
appeared, from the outside at least, almost exactly as they were a
century and a half earlier. The place was rightly proud of its mining
heritage and it had a decent museum that told its story. The staff
were delighted to see a visitor although seemed slightly disappointed
when I asked for a map and directions to the next town, but they
were no less helpful for it. After eating near the ironically named
Diggers Entertainment Centre, we pressed on to Hughenden. We
were lucky to get there after our planned re-fuelling had to be
abandoned because no fuel had been delivered that week. We could
wait, and for how long nobody knew, or crack on. We mulled it over
with a couple of Cornettos, then pulled back onto the road and
spun away as our brain freeze thawed in the afternoon sun.

In between coasting, rolling, and willing ourselves on, we limped
into Hughenden at sundown, past another two exhausted petrol
stations before chugging up to the ever reliable Caltex, where we
pumped in our one hundred and twenty first dollar of the day. The
further west we went, the higher the fuel prices. We pitched up
at Hughenden show grounds beside the memorial to Frederick
Walker and William Anderson. The pair had embarked on a futile

search for explorers Burke and Wills with their camels Landa and Rajah. At one point Rajah refused to walk. When a camel thinks it's too hot then you know you're in serious trouble.

In 1861, Burke and Wills made the first crossing of Australia, a stupendous achievement, from Melbourne to the Gulf of Carpentaria, and eventually died on the return journey, this time to Adelaide, as they followed Coopers Creek to Mount Hopeless. We were not far from Coopers Creek in Hughenden but there was no danger of dying from heat stroke on a freezing cold night. The only thing in danger of over-heating was the fucking van's radiator. We constantly had to stop to allow it to cool down en route to Mount Isa, where we had it unsuccessfully diagnosed by a mechanic.

We used up ten litres of water topping up the radiator, convinced it was leaking, and had it given the once over at another garage that couldn't find much wrong with it before thundering through the desert, Avon Downs, Soudan, and anywhere around, finally crossing over into the Northern Territory just outside of Camooweal. We were getting well ahead of schedule by now and decided to slow down but found that there was nowhere on the route you would need to stay more than one day to see anything. Such a place was Barkly Homestead, out in the Tablelands, where we spent one night and met three other travellers.

They comprised a level-headed Lancastrian from Blackburn, a Canadian, and an Aussie. The Australian explained that he was on a mission to integrate non-Aussie nationals into a new society he was forming, which so far numbered one member: himself. He claimed to be a 're-revolutionary' and had even designed a new national flag, loosely based on the old one he said, but now with a kangaroo incorporated, and no doubt with the Union flag part removed. I was concerned for the others. The Canadian and the Brit confessed to being slightly worried about him as they were also travelling in a fucking van but it was the Aussie who had the machete so any disagreements were soon dealt with. Did they make it to Darwin? I reckon the Aussie did. As far as I'm aware, there has been no coup d'états since I left Australia so I assume everything turned out alright in the end.

We drank ourselves to sleep at the Saddle Creek Ranch, but not before we'd had a heated argument about something trivial that ended up with the playing cards thrown all over the bar. I woke up the next morning to find that the burnt piece of toast we'd thrown out of the fucking van the night before had what by all accounts was a human bite mark in it! I don't know why I've used an exclamation mark when it was obviously Tank who did it. I'm sure I heard him easing the lid off the peanut butter during the night. We arrived at the world's remotest t-junction, at Threeways. It's right in the middle of the Northern Territory, giving you two options (or three if you go back the way you came): left for Alice Springs, 400km, or right for Darwin, 1,055km. I stopped, looked, then looked again, allowing for traffic, before turning left onto the Stuart Highway and heading south. At Tennant Creek, the second largest town in the Red Centre, behind Alice Springs, was the first real Aboriginal community we'd encountered, the majority of whom seemed to be hanging around a petrol station forecourt we stopped at.

Tennant Creek's claim to fame is the Overland Telegraph Line station, which was built in 1874. Nothing else happened there for another half century until gold was discovered. Joe Kilgariff's delivery truck, stocked with beer mainly, broke down there, and, being the enterprising chap that he was, he opened a pub. That was when cartloads of people turned up to exploit the place, as is customary wherever mining potential is discovered anywhere in the world. Kilgariff's entrepreneurial ways got me thinking about John Vaughan, who'd virtually built Middlesbrough from scratch after discovering an ironstone seam leading up to the foot of Eston Hills in 1850 that yielded an incredible 63,000,000 tonnes of the stuff over the ensuing ninety-nine years until the lease expired. If Vaughan had been born in Australia, he might have had an even bigger field day than the one he had on Teesside. He did make one indirect contribution to modern Australia though. The steel used to construct the Sydney Harbour Bridge was mined in Eston Hills and shipped down under.

We made the 100km drive from Tennant Creek to the Davenport

Range and the geological wonder of the Devil's Marbles Conservation Reserve. The marbles are a collection of enormous boulders formed by the compression of molten lava beneath the Earth's surface 1,700,000,000 years ago. Subsequent weathering and erosion over this period revealed some of the rocks to be almost spherical. Others were cracked in half and ranging in size to anything up to 20ft high. I scrabbled between them and posed for the obligatory photos. The site was originally used by Aborigines, who called the marbles Karwe Karlwe, for spiritual ceremonies, believing that people possessing magical powers lived underground at the spot, this forming part of the extraordinary Dreamtime mythology that permeates Australian history. The local Kaytetyl tribe thought the rocks to be the eggs of the Rainbow serpent and in 1953 were outraged when one of the 'eggs' was moved to Alice Springs to commemorate the death of John Flynn, founder of the Flying Doctors. The incident caused such an uproar that it was returned shortly after.

When driving through the Outback, always make sure the radiator cap is on. This way you'll avoid breaking down 30km outside of Alice Springs and being showered in boiling hot water. Our $2,000 insurance bond was in serious jeopardy thanks to my starvation-fuelled carelessness. We'd stopped earlier to check out the engine when we noticed it was overheating every couple of hours and that's when I'd left the cap off. Soon after, steam began billowing out from the engine under my seat and eventually filled the cab. I was sure that if we kept the radiator topped up until we got to a garage we'd be all right but Tank wasn't convinced. We managed to get to Alice Springs but used almost all of our drinking water in the process. The small amount we had left we used to shower ourselves with the aid of a watering can I had the good sense to steal from Caltex, on waste ground that turned out to be private property. It was primitive but satisfying.

One day, a truck pulled up as I was drying off. A gruff-faced man leaned out of the window. "Whaadaya think yer doing?" he barked. "Yer blocking me blahddy ramp."

"You're a bit big for a BMX, aren't you?" Tank enquired.

The man huffed and puffed then gave up and drove off, leaving us to bathe in peace. We were certainly roughing it now. The bath water was from a rusty tap at the forecourt of the petrol station back in Tennant Creek but we continued to drink it throughout the journey. We also used it to wash the pots after the manual pump tap on the sink broke. Slowly but surely the fucking van was falling apart, and so were we.

As soon as we reached Alice Springs, we rushed the now critically ill fucking van to Tony's Auto Wreckers on Ghan Road. Tony had the monopoly on car trouble in the Outback. If you had any problems in a rented vehicle, you'd end up there, otherwise you were stuck in Alice Springs, and you wouldn't want to be stuck in Alice Springs.

It was intended as a stopping off point, just for one night we thought, in order to watch England's obligatory World Cup quarter-final exit against Portugal, on the way to Uluru and Kings Canyon, which would be our most westerly point.

"Radiator's cracked," diagnosed Tony the next day, in the freezing cold of the early morning. We'd certainly given it some stick, driving roughly 2,000km in seventeen days.

"We can leave it overnight, although it is our house so we might need to be in and out of it every so often," I explained.

Tony made a 'pffftt' sound with his lips as he took off his baseball cap and stroked his ginger beard.

"We'll have to get the part freighted in, could take two days at least, then another two days to fit it."

Tank and I rolled our eyes simultaneously.

"You can stay in the fucking van while it's in the work shed if you want," offered Tony, "but you'll need to be out every morning when the boys come to work around seven."

How did he know we were calling it 'the fucking van'?

We had little choice and limped it into the yard while Tony phoned for the part. So there we were, living in a broken down fucking van, in a tool shed, in the middle of a desert.

I was never colder than first thing on those four mornings in the shed, when there was a thin frost on the ground at breakfast time. By lunchtime, however, the sun would be high in the sky, prompting me to remove the fleece, thermal socks and woolly hat I'd needed earlier, only now I had nowhere to put them. The fucking van repairs at least gave us plenty of time to see Alice, the only problem being we'd seen all of it after the first day and spent the rest of the week wandering aimlessly around the town centre looking for diversions, much like the Aborigines did. Each morning we walked the mile into town, along Ghan Road, the name 'Ghan' taken from the Afghan camel trains that covered the same route.

On reaching the town centre, we'd split up, Tank usually going to the cinema and me to the library, then afterwards meet up for the long walk back. We sat outside the cinema one day watching a group of Aborigines egging on an irate wife who was thrashing her husband around the head with a palm leaf branch. After a while, he retaliated with a broken umbrella and a full on slapstick comedy routine unfolded in the supermarket car park as we sat opposite eating cheese puff sandwiches. We were skint remember.

The Alice Spring, as the Spring part suggests, refers to the waterhole on the overland telegraph route. Alice was Alice Todd, the wife of the construction boss in charge of the line laying in the 1870s. Still, there was no rail access to the town until the late 1920s and the sealed road route took even longer. It wasn't established until the 1940s.

I guessed little had changed since and spent my time walking the streets, all three of them, or so it seemed, looking in bookshops and reading the local paper. I ate at La Peps diner most days, before sneaking up the road for a shower at Melanka Backpackers, which became base camp during the World Cup, or for England's one remaining match as it turned out. The living quarters of Malenkas, or what I saw of them during one of my stealth showers, looked immaculate, unlike the bar next door.

Because of the time difference, England's game against Portugal didn't get underway until after midnight. By this time, the fucking van was fixed so we stopped in the town centre park awaiting kick-off. We killed the time drinking watered-down beer over a game of cards and being hounded by the town clown.

"I stand in the mall shouting jokes for a living," he announced proudly.

Judging by his appearance, it was a far from lucrative endeavour.

"Can you lend me a few dollars for a beer?" he asked.

"Make me laugh first then."

He reeled off some bad jokes about Aborigines and Princess Diana then cleverly paused to allow for laughter. Somewhere, out in the Simpson Desert, I heard a pin drop. An equally unimpressed crowd had gathered by now. Tank jumped in.

"Yer getting fuck all, mate," he shouted, a variation on his response to the taxi driver in Bangkok that he'd honed on countless Salvation Army collectors over the years.

"I've published two joke books," replied the man.

We didn't get anything else out of him and he shuffled off to the next table. It wasn't the end of the interruptions though. The local hospital's nursing staff night out had just crash landed. A Maori woman made a beeline for our table. I could hardly understand a word she said as she slurred away.

"Me from New Zealand, you from England," she insisted on pointing out.

I thought about pulling the table away as it was her only means of support. She insisted on calling a toast with every sip, which she ended each time by slamming the bottom of her glass onto the rim of mine. As a result, we were losing beer at an alarming rate and something had to be done. I was just thinking what that would be when a bouncer dragged her away by her belt loop.

She managed one more, "Me from New Zealand, you from England," which was drowned out by the sound of every empty glass we had produced all night hitting the floor after she took a swing at them as a parting shot.

It reminded me of an insolent child being marched out of a supermarket by an angry mother and taking a swipe at the tinned tomatoes on the way – the final gesture before it all gets a bit serious. I then took it upon myself to scribble some graffiti on the toilet wall. What with this, and my chocolate bar thieving exploits, I was fast becoming a fugitive. Tank's crime spree was rubbing off on me, I think. He'd taken to writing 'Boro boys on tour' just about everywhere we went, usually on the side of someone's bunk bed.

We entered an adjoining room of the bar, even grimmer than the first, to watch the England match. As soon as the final whistle of normal time went, I knew it would end in tears and/or penalties. It was about to get a lot worse for us though. We returned to the unlocked fucking van, which we'd temporarily abandoned at nearby Heritage Park, to find that all of our bedding, pillows and sleeping bags had been stolen, probably by the Aborigines who'd been hanging around it all day. That's not to fix the blame on anyone, but who else, on finding an unlocked vehicle containing a personal stereo, mobile phone and credit cards, would ignore them and go for the dirty linen? I sympathised with them a little as they just wanted to keep warm, so did we, but it meant we would freeze that night, and we did. We'd been drinking heavily so when we woke the next morning, or rather four hours later, we had shivered all night and as a result got little sleep but we both knew how lucky we had been for the second time in a week.

Uluru, or Ayers Rock, is still treated with a special kind of reverence by everyone who lays eyes on it and we were no different. It stands at Kata Tjuta National Park, not that you'll need an address for it; if you're driving past, you're bound to see it out of the corner of your eye from as far as 50km away, it being 1,100ft high and over 2km wide.

"Apparently, according to one theory, it's a meteorite, possibly responsible for wiping out the dinosaurs," explained Tank on the approach.

I later learned that a staggering two-thirds of its mass were actually underground, totalling almost two miles of unseen rock. If it was a meteorite, it would've loosened a few fillings when it hit the ground. Like the rock itself, the surrounding area was sacred to Aborigines but not so sacred that they couldn't charge £15 to enter the site. Shrewdly, the local Anangu people were effectively renting the area to the Australian government who in turn have made it the well-organised tourist draw that it is today simply by adding a toll-booth.

Between 1958, when the park was established, and 1985, when the rock was handed back, figuratively speaking, to the Aborigines, it was referred to as Ayers Rock, after the one-time secretary of South Australia, Sir Henry Ayers, named for him by William Gosse. We paid up and joined the ranks of visitors who had arrived just in time for the famous sunset that turns it from a glowing red and orange hue to an altogether duller shade in a matter of minutes. Afterwards, for the only time in my life, I witnessed a rock being given a round of applause. Driving the 6km around it and seeing it from different angles gave it a chameleon-like quality, its colour, size and shape seemingly changing as we saw it from different angles. Its size made it difficult to photograph or even comprehend at all so we took a much closer look and discovered some of the ancient Aboriginal art inscribed and painted on the lower west face, this area being focused on serpents, particularly Liru (snake), and Kuniya (python), a recurring theme in Aboriginal legend. On almost completing our circuit of the rock, I began to hallucinate, or so I thought. How else could you explain a handrail running up one side of the rock to the summit? A handrail! I imagined a tourist board meeting in the mid-sixties.

"Right lads, what did you come up with?"

"Runway on the top of it, boss?"

"That's as useful as tits on a bull, Jonno."

"Helipad?"

"Come off it, mate. What about a handrail up the side?"

"Brilliant, cobber."

At the last count, thirty-five lunatics had died attempting the mile high climb, most of them from heart attacks and exhaustion followed by a brisk fall. The route to the top is the same as that taken by the Mala tribesmen when attending ceremonies at the summit. Uluru wasn't the only big draw in the area. A short drive west revealed the Olgas, actually Kata Tjuta, meaning 'many heads', alluding to the various rocks there, the biggest being considerably higher than Uluru at 790ft. Also worth a visit, if slightly off the beaten track, although everywhere in the Outback is off the beaten track, is King's Canyon.

It lies just outside of Wallara and is the result of 20,000,000 years of erosion that began with a small crack in the mountaintop that is now a gorge. It still shows evidence of its origins by way of fossilisation and tide marks of a sea of some sort, thought to have existed over 400,000,000 years ago. The canyon was named by Ernest Giles in 1872 on one of his three expeditions around central Australia, subsequently becoming the first European to sight Uluru. Two years later, he named the Gibson Desert after his travel partner, lost on the same trip and never seen again, and even resorted to eating a live wallaby, he was so hungry.

"The delicious taste of that creature I shall never forget," he later wrote, in Escape From The Outback. And there we were, moaning about the lack of diversity in Pot Noodle flavours.

I walked the Cairns Crook trail, after clambering to the canyon top, which was steep enough to leave someone who hadn't done any exercise in two months, gasping for breath. From the top, I could see the biggest expanse of natural land my eyes could take as I turned in a slow circle. In the gorge itself, I stumbled over rocky terrain between the orange walls either side of me, dodging logs and streams as I went, and putting every noise I heard down to being one of the sixty species of snake living amongst the rocks. I wasn't troubled at King's Canyon though, and I also managed to avoid getting lost, but a few days before we arrived, a Korean tourist had wandered off one of the walking trails and hadn't been seen since. Stranded in the Outback. I can think of little worse – stranded in Sunderland, maybe. If you lose the main road, you're in big trouble. Thousands of miles of spinifex, red desert, and termite mounds await you. Best take plenty of water. Come night-time, the temperature plummets and there's nowhere to hide and nothing to eat. There's enough to nibble away at you though: dingoes, birds, kangaroos, lizards, spiders and of course, snakes. No matter where you are in the Outback, the nearest petrol station is always miles away. You might be lucky enough to be picked up by a kindly Ute driver who just happened to be passing through. Forget it; have you seen Wolf Creek?

On the way back from King's Canyon, we spent one more night in Alice Springs, at Heritage Park again, before making our next stop at Barrow Creek, another important place in Australia's recent history but for the wrong reasons. It was the scene of the brutal culling of many Aborigines in retaliation for the deaths of John Franks and John L Stapleton, who were attacked near the Barrow Creek Hotel, where we stopped for fuel. Years before the double murder, Aborigines had killed another man in a surprise attack.

Two graves marked the deaths of Franks and Stapleton on a small plot of land just off the Stuart Highway, which itself was named after John Macdouall Stuart who had mapped the route for the Overland Telegraph Line. The town has carried its name since 1870 and was named after Stuart's friend, JH Barrow, but was first settled by Joe Kilgariff of Tennant Creek fame, when he built the original pub in what has now become the hotel. While paying for petrol, I had a look on the wall of the bar at the hundreds of notes, cards and photographs left by satisfied customers, most of whom had been stranded there without petrol, it seemed. Someone had even left a signed guitar.

It was at the Barrow Creek Hotel that Joanne Lees sought refuge after the events that led to the disappearance of Peter Falconio at the hands of Bradley Murdoch. In 2006, after one of the most highly publicised murder cases in Australian history, Murdoch was jailed for life after the dramatic story of the night of July 14th 2001 had been unravelled in a Darwin courtroom during a trial that cost $900,000. It transpired that Murdoch, a convicted drug dealer, had shot Falconio after flagging him down at the side of the road on the pretence of having car trouble. He then bound Joanne Lees and dumped her in the back of his Ute but she later escaped and hid in the scrub. Murdoch managed to dispose of Falconio's body and to this day his whereabouts are unknown. During an extraordinary trial bursting at the seams with conflicting evidence, Lees was fingered as a possible suspect. One astonishing alibi presented by Murdoch's defence claimed that the DNA of his that was found on Lees' bloodstained clothes had been picked up inadvertently at the Red Rooster restaurant at an Alice Springs truck stop they had both visited earlier in the day. Murdoch's lawyer then produced CCTV evidence of Murdoch leaving the restaurant saying he'd stopped to buy chicken to sustain him on his journey. Sydney-based magazine, The Bulletin, later produced evidence of Murdoch's refusal to eat chicken during an earlier jail sentence because he didn't like it, something the prison board recognised in an official action that excused him from eating such food. Murdoch is currently serving a life sentence.

Barrow Creek had a definite air of eeriness to it which I felt was more to do with its remote location rather than anything that had happened there. Barrow's population of eleven was made up entirely of people who worked at the hotel in some capacity. Other than that, there were two Aboriginal tribes in the surrounding areas around 50km away.

We continued to creep north, slumped over the wheel heading for the vanishing point as the temperature rose, amassing in the process a fine collection of dead butterflies on the windscreen that on impact sounded like we were driving into a hail of golf balls. After the double disappointment of the burglary in Alice Springs and England's World Cup exit, we reached the silver lining of the Mataranka Thermal Pool, an hour south of Katherine in Elsey National Park, a small body of naturally hot water that flows from Rainbow Springs and on into the crocodile-infested Roper River. The Springs are the big draw in an area crammed with natural wonders like Katherine Gorge and Edith Falls, a gorge and a waterfall respectively, for anyone who thought they were the names of porn stars, and the Cutta Cutta caves. The area was made famous a hundred or so years ago by Jeannie Gunn in her book, We of the Never Never, an account of her life at Elsey Station, on which the Mataranka Homestead was based, and was built for a film adaptation of the book. It had been modernised somewhat, for health and safety reasons, and now incorporated a handrail, which didn't seem quite as sacrilegious as the one at Uluru, and a stairway, so it would have changed considerably since Australian soldiers stumbled upon it on a training exercise in the 1930s. Back then, it wouldn't have had a fence to keep out crocodiles either but even the threat of being eaten wouldn't have kept me out of it. For a short time, it would have been a well-kept secret, secluded as it is and surrounded by vegetation. The only way to find it would have been to follow the Roper River as even now it's not visible from the Homestead.

Under a flaming sunset, we began the last leg of the road trip and arrived in Darwin, or the 'Top End', on July 5th, twenty-eight days after leaving Brisbane.

The climate was hot and muggy, even in what passes for winter in the southern hemisphere. The night before we returned the fucking van, we deposited ourselves in a park on the esplanade, hoping to avoid the wardens for the final time. The handbrake was barely on when we were accosted by an unrelenting middle-eastern accented chatterbox. Tank was trapped in the driving seat as the man extrapolated on a series of subjects that covered everything from the cost of freight for motor repair parts to how to live rent free in the local casino, which in our current situation was worth paying attention to. I gazed out of the window at Melville Island from my hiding place in the roof of the fucking van but all the while all I could see was the man's words bouncing off Tank's head. He wasn't listening. From my vantage point, I spied the man's girlfriend slumped in a deckchair beside his car as she poured a bottle of wine down her neck. After a while, she slithered onto the hot tarmac, almost under the front wheel of the man's car. She was too drunk to sit in a deckchair.

"Oh her," the man said, "she doesn't know what she wants."

Evidently. She had, after all, just thrown herself under a car. As the man launched into a discourse on how to bum free sandwiches from the 'help the homeless' van that had recently arrived, I gazed out across the Arafura Sea. It was from the here that Cyclone Tracy bounced into Darwin on Christmas Eve 1974, causing $837,000,000 worth of damage and killing seventy-one people. Unsurprisingly, this was Australia's biggest ever natural disaster. Most of the twenty-thousand homeless that were left behind moved elsewhere and didn't return, but present day Darwin is a thriving port city.

The cyclone wasn't the first time Darwin had been savaged from the air; in February 1942, it was bombed heavily by Japanese aircraft.

We arrived at the rental office and threw ourselves on the mercy of the panel beaters when we discovered the mysterious dent I mentioned earlier on the rear of the fucking van. It neatly covered the entire badge, costing us yet more money in repairs. We honestly had no idea how it got there, putting it down to someone clipping us when we were not around, and were already up against it when we were ordered to clean it to its original standard before returning it. We raced to the nearest petrol station and frantically washed it clean of dirt and butterfly brains before returning to the depot on Daly Street to find that the cost of having the dent removed and the badge replaced would be a wallet-obliterating $500, which at the time was £240. The elation I felt about being out of the fucking van, and the thought of having my own bed again, and a kitchen that doesn't throw everything out of the cupboards when you open them, had been washed away by this development, however I suppose we got off lightly as they didn't check the roof. If they had, they would have probably noticed the damage I did in Cairns when I drove the wrong way into an underground car park and almost ripped the entire ventilation system from the roof whilst reversing out.

En route to catch our flight from Darwin airport, we told the taxi driver about the extra charge for the dent in the fucking van.

"You should just rip this day right off the calendar," he advised.

I already had. Looking in the mirror in the airport toilet, I hardly recognised myself. I'd shed over a stone but that was countered by the weight of my hair, which by now resembled an enormous brown meringue, thick with the grain of the desert. Three weeks of drinking filthy water that you wouldn't wash a dog with had taken its toll on my skin but the effect on my mental state was greater, highlighted when I broke into a hysterical fit of laughter caused by the most intrinsic of things, as is usually associated with rabid delirium. A woman with a clipboard was conducting a survey in order to ascertain the quality of five new designs of chair that had been placed in the departure lounge, one of which would eventually be the departure lounge's 'in-house' chair.

I listened in as she explained the ins and outs of the chairs' three grading categories.

"I'd like you to rate the chairs on a scale of one to five, one being the lowest, five being the highest, on the following criteria: comfort, appearance and…"

I don't recall the third one but it was definitely something like 'sitability' or some other such blue sky bullshit favoured by the morons in marketing. A group of disgruntled men took it in turns to sit in the chairs, all the while keeping one eye on the State of Origin football decider between Queensland and New South Wales that was playing out on the wall-mounted TV. Each sitter did the same thing; first they slowly rubbed their hands up and down the arms of the chair looking at each in turn, then they sat bolt upright, and then… well what else can you do after that?

The woman was carping away in the background, encouraging new sitting techniques and asking questions.

"Would you recommend this chair to a friend?"

I've never in my entire life recommended a chair to anybody.

"Is the splat supple enough for you?"

Tank and I sat amazed at the tedium of it all in our distinctly uncomfortable seats.

If I wasn't so fed up, I couldn't have resisted a go myself. We discussed our responses to the questions regardless.

"What do you think, sir?"

"Call me old fashioned but it's a bit too chairy for my tastes."

Tank offered the following no-nonsense summary, "I've tried

'em all on and they're all shit," a comment heard in Matalan stores the world over.

They were still more comfortable though than the seats on the flight that would take us back to Brisbane.

CHAPTER 9:
MORETON BAY

Gulping goon, going to Gatton, girls and galivanting.

"The days rolled by and the jam sessions,
drinking bouts and hangovers all merged into one."

We landed back in Brisbane the next day after that excruciatingly uncomfortable overnight flight, my only consolation being that I'd saved on a night's accommodation.

I was worn out, run down, hungry, dehydrated, deprived of sleep and concerned about the classic backpacker ailment, the leaky bank account, and generally feeling sorry for myself.

I'd constantly told myself to stay calm at all times, and keep an even keel when things weren't going my way but it was getting difficult now. I needed a job and fast. I'd learnt though that you never know what's around the corner and to take the rough with the smooth. Rusty had somehow made it back from Cairns in one piece, Ken was still omnipresent, which coupled with his grey goatee and advancing years had earned him the nickname Obi Wan from Rusty, who seemed to pull appropriate nicknames for people out of thin air on a regular basis. He definitely had a knack for it, although it was the only thing he did have a knack for – that, and being completely useless. I'd earned the tag Wilbuuuur that Dave had labelled me with but that didn't really stick, except with him. Thanks to Rusty, Dave subsequently became Dave Hedgehog. He later bestowed the name Sugar Cane upon me, for reasons that will become apparent on later pages, which I actually quite liked. Then there was Big Mac, Tankatron, Tankatron jnr, Dougal and countless others. One of them was Des. He'd sailed to Brisbane from his home in Port Elizabeth as part of the three-man crew that made up Team Umbaliki, stopping off at St Paul's island halfway through the sixty day journey.

"Oh Will," he exclaimed, "you wouldn't believe the fishing out there. You just drop your rod in and they come in droves, it's beautiful man, just beautiful." He had a passion for life that I found infectious. In South Africa, he'd left behind a whole other life to go to Australia. He'd been a goldsmith, a lucrative trade that he could go back to any time, but one that he hated. Previously he'd been in a successful band, Limon, and had even had a number one hit in South Africa which he performed on several occasions at my insistence, pestering and pestering him to play guitar.

What's that wiggling, wiggling in my underwear?
What's that wiggling, all you people stop and stare.
Don't get funny with me.

"It was sort of a summer holiday novelty hit," he explained.

He was up on his rock music, which provided an endless source of conversation between us, Deep Purple, Black Sabbath and Focus being among his favourites. He told me about his first guitar.

"I'd saved 800rand, 770 for the guitar and the other 30 for a taxi home. I had to walk to the guitar shop and it was a long way, man. I couldn't walk back as well. Fuck that, maaan. When I got there, the guitar I wanted was now 800rand. I handed over the money and got a lift home from the shop as part of their delivery policy that was included in the total price. Now I had no money at all, and a guitar. For two years, I sat in my room playing and playing and playing, spending what little money I ever got on milk and cigarettes. When I came out of the room, I could play anything."

I loved his story. It had everything: commitment, perseverance, talent, poverty, success, hard work and music.

A typical day at the hostel consisted of getting up at around 10am, although it was hardly worth going to bed most nights what with the comings and goings of someone or other, stealing somebody's food to make breakfast, then heading into the city or nearby Wynnum for the day. I'd return to Manly in the early evening and more often than not begin drinking right through until the early hours. It was a difficult cycle to break because everyone was having such a good time but eventually it began to take its toll, financially and physically, and I knew I had to do something about it. A group of us half-heartedly looked for a job, phoning almost every farm on the east coast to enquire about fruit picking work, another backpacker rite of passage, to find that everywhere was fully booked, so instead we returned to partying, thanks to the emergency funds that seemed to be wired through to everyone who needed them from their parents.

The hostel's layout encouraged fraternisation. The communal lounge adjoined the kitchen and dining area in one big open plan room, the centrepiece being the wide screen plasma TV that caused surprisingly few arguments, but everything seemed to happen in the back garden. A short balcony led to a steel staircase at the back of the building that wound down into a car park of sorts, covered by an awning with room enough to seat everyone. The multi-coloured table that stood there was constantly littered with wine bottles, beer cans, cigarette butts, playing cards and CDs that piled up night after night. The bottle shop over the road was doing a roaring trade as a result. We occasionally went to the Manly Hotel, next door to the bottle shop, but found it a lot easier, and cheaper, to hang out at the hostel. On the occasions that we did venture out of Manly, everyone seemed to go half-insane with booze. On our first night back in Manly, we all piled into the hostel minibus and steamed down the seafront to the Wynnum Point Hotel and its neighbour, the Nautica Bar. It was Friday night and the locals were out in force.

"We're just going for a few games of pool," said Rusty.

I recall two games of pool all night. Tank and I sat in the corner watching everyone else making complete fools of themselves. Rusty was taking the pool very seriously indeed which seriously affected his drinking; he had less than his usual three pints. I'd latched on to Katrina, the first of the German guests I met there. She'd wandered over to interrupt the political debate I was having with Maria, who had arrived in Brisbane while we were in the Outback.

My hearing was a bit fuzzy by now so I don't know what Katrina opened with but she was soon reeling off a list of her favourite German politicians, which was much more interesting than it sounds now, especially coming from those lips.

I went on to convince her that Rusty had been the model for

a Marvel Comics character called The Astonishing Tit, which in her drunken German naivety she believed, though in fairness Rusty had shown the credentials to back up such a claim. We were interrupted by another guest, Adrian, drunkenly announcing what he would like to do with Katrina when we got back to the hostel but she took it in good spirit. Unsurprisingly for him, and fortunately for her, nothing materialised, but the night summed up the good all round vibe at the hostel that remained throughout our stay.

The days rolled by and the jam sessions, drinking bouts and hangovers all merged into one lost fortnight, of which I would remember very little if I hadn't kept a journal. My already erratic sleeping patterns were further complicated by the time differences; Brisbane is nine hours ahead of GMT, which made live sporting occasions quite an event as by the time they started on Australian time, usually the early hours of the morning for Premiership football matches, everyone was drunk. It was a definite case of the devil making work for idle hands. In fact, there was so little to do that I soon became bored. I read every book I could get my hands on and was having no luck searching for a job. I needed a distraction.

"Have you seen that girl who's just arrived?" asked Rusty one afternoon. I thought nothing of his excited state as I heard this question daily and generally paid little attention to him. I soon did though. I'd heard little of her and seen less as she hardly seemed to have left her room in the few days she was around. She appeared before me in the lounge one day, which was like a zoo at feeding time by then, about 7pm, but I couldn't get a clear look at her because of the crowd of people fighting over each other's shopping in the kitchen.

Later that evening, I returned to the lounge on several occasions on the pretence of 'getting some crisps' but I still couldn't get a good look at her as she always seemed to be facing away from me, engulfed in a cloud of everyone else's testosterone. I let them get on with it and returned much later just as Des was playing his trump card.

"What's it like to have such hot legs?" he asked. She looked mildly embarrassed by the attention but Des had little to offer after that and soon disappeared.

I sat on the settee and looked at the telly, not really watching it, for about an hour, with an ear cocked to what was going on behind me. One by one, everyone else went to bed. I turned round to get a closer look at her and she hit me at a funny angle with her gaze, not physically but in my head somewhere. I took a few seconds to straighten my mind out and at the same time had this vision of us enjoying a tandem ride through a sun-kissed French meadow to a soundtrack of Sacha Distel, (Jesus, this wine's a bit strong!). I was transfixed by the whites of her eyes but I gave nothing away and we soon got to talking as she blabbed away in a thick Brummie accent that complimented her down to earth nature. She never used more words than she had to and listened intently, hardly blinking as I spoke. She had a big smile made of cool white teeth and a little mole on her left cheek. Mature beyond her twenty years, she had to be; she was travelling around Australia alone for two months before returning home to the Midlands to find out which university she would study law at, Newcastle or Chester. My pupils may have dilated when she said it would probably be the former. It remains the only time in my life when the prospect of going to Newcastle seemed an attractive one. She perched on a stool as I told her about the road trip but I wasn't listening to what I was saying, and who knows, maybe she wasn't either. I was blinded by the mirror of her perfect teeth as she laughed in all the right places but at the same time was reminded of the Benjamin Franklin quote, 'She laughs at everything you say. Why? Because she has perfect teeth'. I fancied her from the off.

I felt a bit stupid for having a pre-conceived idea of her, based entirely on the fact that she was drinking tea, but then I remembered that first impressions mean little. She originally thought I was Welsh.

"Are you around tomorrow?" I asked casually.

"I'll be back at six o'clock."

"Well, maybe I'll see you around then," I said, knowing full well I would.

I spent most of the following day in a silent fug of rage after making an overseas call in order to establish the extent of the damage done to my bank account by the road trip. All I was able to establish was that it was £5 lighter after the time I spent on hold having my password refused.

"Telephone banking made easier," they informed me in a patronising voice.

I'd calmed down considerably come early evening and sure enough, right around 7pm, Jacinta came stalking out of her room and beelined for the empty seat beside me, probably because it was the only one. She made some small talk about the boat trip she'd been on that day and I made some noises about wanting to go for a drink, in a roundabout way, as usual.

"I might go for one in a bit if I can be bothered," I said. Soon after, we were in the bar next door shielding a couple of drinks and trying to work each other out. We had the whole place to ourselves as the locals were over the road turning the Manly Hotel on its ear at the karaoke night. As they bawled their way through Midnight Oil's Beds Are Burning, I got the low down from her on a variety of subjects that included the tornado alley of Birmingham council estates, Scandinavian shopping sprees, the joys of Pepparamis, ice-cream and chilli sauce, her two sisters, her law degree, and the glitz and glamour of Sutton Coldfield. She was no chatterbox but I let her talk as I savoured her accent. Like most people, she was quick to take the piss out of my monotone drone, repeatedly mimicking certain words I used.

The bar closed early but we landed in the safety net of the bottle shop behind the Manly Hotel. The only other option was to attend Daniel's jam session at Wynnum Point Hotel where he'd invited me to play harmonica. She mentioned the previous evening that she would like to hear it but I was sure she was being polite and I had no intention of subjecting her to such terror. At the Manly Hotel, I noticed the clientele had spiralled out of all control, and way outnumbered both bouncers, as they rolled around in the beer garden.

Once inside the shop, I expected to find Jacinta in the wine aisle but instead she grabbed six stubbies and slammed them on the counter while I was still selecting long necks. We sat under the moon in a cloud of smoke, and slowly descended into a boozy stupor which led to us conversing in French and Spanish and possibly biting each other.

"J'adore le posterier," she murmured as we crash-landed on the chemically hazardous settee like naughty school children at the back of a cinema. Everyone else vanished, leaving only the sounds we made ourselves, the ticking of the clock, which always sounds magnified at night when it's otherwise almost silent, and the hum of the vending machine that sounded like it was primed for take-off. We drifted in and out of sleep and come the morning she was gone, as I knew she would be, to North Stradbroke Island, a spot ripe for whale watching, 30km off the south east coast of Brisbane. I knew I would see her again but I didn't know how or where. I eventually got in touch with her after pilfering her e-mail address from the hostel guest book when nobody was looking, and, after many frustrating failed dispatches, finally worked out that one of the characters was a '1' and not an 'I'. It took me six months to decipher this most complex of codes. I managed to contact her but not until much later, telling her I'd gone to North Stradbroke Island to look for her that day, which I blatantly had not.

After she left, I went back to lackadaisically job hunting and drinking like a dog in the sun with Des, Grant, Tank and the new arrivals of Holly, from Nova Scotia, and Damo, the token Kiwi. When we weren't drinking, we were pondering what we were going to drink next. Des was rarely without a 'monster box', or 'Manly briefcase', as Holly memorably named the two-litre boxes of wine, otherwise referred to as 'goon' in Australia, that we would drink every day. She'd travelled around South-East Asia before arriving in Australia and became a firm fixture at Moreton Bay, instigating most of the drinking sessions, and was rarely without a glass of wine in her hands, (that's not a misprint). When the two of us were unfortunate enough to find jobs in the city, we'd spend most mornings in dark glasses sleeping off hangovers on the Cleveland line train that rattled through East Brisbane. That was when we did actually go to work. I was on a ten day contract but Holly went whenever she wanted, which was about twice a week.

"They won't even notice if I go in or not," she said.

Holly had the luxury of coming to the end of her trip, if luxury is the right word. That feeling of not caring because you were going home that I wouldn't feel for another four months. When it came, I was alone in Manhattan, which made it a lot easier to leave, but when you meet a good bunch of people, as we had in Brisbane and would do again in Fiji and Rarotonga, you never want to be anywhere else.

I always fell asleep on the train on my way to work. My stop was the last on the line so someone in the carriage always gave me a nudge and I would stumble off at Bowen Hills and into the showgrounds for Brisbane's nationally famous Ekka festival, where I'd been offered a job. The Ekka, short for 'exhibition', was established in 1876 as a cattle market of sorts for local farmers to parade their finest livestock, but has now become a multi-million pound event billed as 'when the country meets the city' and contains the kind of attractions that only an Australian would find interesting. The city folk, especially those in such a cosmopolitan setting as Brisbane – I can hear Syndneysiders laughing from here – have little interest in hogs, bullocks, or the latest in agricultural technology, but the Mick Dundees from Toowoomba, Ipswich and Gatton, seemed fascinated by whatever the city had to offer. I was hidden away at the exotically-named Japanese Pearl Exhibition, selling exactly what you would expect from such a stall: handheld Sudoku machines, remote controlled cars (that played Japanese house music of course), carpet sweepers and travel cushions.

I'd stumbled upon the site a week or two earlier looking for work and wormed my way into an induction that was already in progress when I latched onto a group of backpackers listening attentively to the complex procedures that entailed running a coconut shy. As it turned out, I ended up working for Australian festival colossus Jim McLaughlin.

"You go to any show in Australia and mention Jim's name and you'll walk into a job, no worries," one colleague told me.

I'd somehow survived the rigorous interview technique of Jim's wife, Tina. This consisted of her informing me that, "You'd be good at selling stuff," and establishing whether or not I owned a smart pair of trousers. Luckily, I did, which made me fully qualified to sit on a stall for ten hours a day advising people on the best way to use a portable massage machine.

"If anyone asks, just tell them you're fully qualified," Sandra, one of my new workmates, whispered. So I was a fully-fledged reflexology consultant then. She might as well have asked me to thatch a cottage roof for all I knew about massage techniques. It was said in hushed tones around the exhibit that Tina took care of business whenever Jim was drunk, but to be fair I only saw him inebriated on two occasions: day and night. Tina was hopelessly disorganised, but when it came to financial issues, which it always did, she was tighter than a submarine door, which was also a fair description of her make-up. She reminded me of Bette Davis in Whatever Happened To Baby Jane? My co-worker was Laura, another backpacker, from Derbyshire. We were both as uncommitted to the job as each other, which immediately gave us something in common. Laura was a true English rose, and about to undertake a driving trip around the country similar to my own, so we had much to talk about when we were not inconvenienced by people wanting to buy things from us.

This was rare as we were located in the festival dead zone, next door to the asthma awareness stall and opposite the intriguingly named 'show cakes arena', which consisted of a Women's Institute-type woman guarding slices of malt loaf as if they were Christ's bloodline. I spent most of my shifts reading Paul Theroux's Happy Isles Of Oceania, and talking to some of the more interesting customers that passed by, who were few and far between, like Keith, the Buddhist monk from Manchester. I first encountered him when I overheard him talking to Gered, a budding Buddhist himself from

Austria, on the next stall, still in that thick Manc accent, even after forty years away from the place.

I'm not sure Gered was cut out for a life of enlightenment. I think it would be too much for him. He was absolutely amazed when I turned up for work one day wearing a smart, white dress shirt. He found it inconceivable that I should own such a thing.

"But you are backpacker, no?" he asked.

"Yeah, but I still occasionally exercise the right to wear a shirt," I said.

It went straight over his head but trenchant sarcasm was how I dealt with stupid questions like 'why do you own a shirt?'

We alternated between stalls throughout the day. Most of the time I was with Laura but other times I was in the main arena, giving it the hard sell, which wasn't easy when you consider the merchandise. I was working alongside Dougal from the hostel one day and looked on impressively as he demonstrated one of the carpet sweepers. It was essentially a dustpan and brush but the farming crowd were gawping at it like it was Saturn 5. Dougal was really going for it, his thick Irish burr drawing the crowd as he minced up and down in a housewife's apron.

I was doing a roaring trade in remote-controlled-cars-that-play-Japanese-house-music but I still managed to keep one eye on his performance. He was sweeping a handful of marbles into the pan, closing it, then releasing them and repeating the process. We took the marbles from the jewellery section as we didn't have anything that you would ever actually need to sweep up, like foodstuffs for example. I had a packet of Quavers that I'd gone to great lengths to procure and Dougal suggested we use those for the purpose of authenticity.

"Come on," he pleaded, "it'll look good if we use them."

"You'll be on the floor before the Quavers if you go anywhere near them," I said.

He was playing to the crowd now.

"It's very durable," he announced, holding the brush aloft. "It can withstand tremendous duress." I was impressed with his choice of words, even if most of the crowd didn't have a clue what he was talking about.

"And it complies with all health and safety criteria," he added.

He swung the brush at the wall with both hands, and considerable force. He looked like an executioner beheading someone, except he was wearing a lemon-coloured pinny. A sonic boom engulfed the immediate area. The brush shattered on impact into a disturbingly high number of pieces as cheap plastic death rained down on the audience. Dougal was doubled over with laughter so he didn't notice most of the people dispersing, even before the shards had settled. The whole thing was worth the price of my airline ticket alone. The irony was we now had nothing to sweep up the mess with.

I finished work at 8pm every day and would get the first train to Wynnum, usually for the jam session, and a few beers, which took me through to the early hours of the following morning, when I would just have time to make something to eat for that day at work. If I had time, I'd iron some clothes, before hoying myself onto my bunk for another sleepless night. This was for a number of reasons: Damo's snoring, Des throwing pistachio nuts around the room at 2 o'clock in the morning (why is it always 2 o'clock in the morning when there's some sort of disturbance? – "Who the hell's beeping their horn at two o'clock in the morning?" for example), and general comings and goings.

There was always someone checking out during the night. Every night, at the same time. I lay there listening to an infinite number of zips being engaged that sounded like a SWAT team suiting up, followed by that all time classic and one of my favourite pieces, Beethoven's Symphony for Rustling Carrier Bags in D minor. The interruptions were endless but mostly amusing and as a poor sleeper anyway I didn't mind too much.

People came crashing in drunk at 2 o'clock in the morning (there it is again), declared their love for someone they had met just that night, usually German, bounced off every wall and bed post, then collapsed on the floor in a pool of 'goon'. Twenty minutes later, they would get up and attempt to climb into bed, never their own, and more often than not Rusty's, as he was on the bottom bunk nearest the door and glad of the company most of the time. It made a change from the array of objects people placed in his bed whenever he got up in the night that included ladders, CDs, bars of soap, irons, kettles, shoes, pornographic magazines and empty beer bottles, of which we had an endless supply. Alarm clocks and mobile phones were activated constantly, Freddie's at 4.30am when he got up for work!

Outside the room in the adjoining corridor, people ran up and down from the bar next door screaming their drunken heads off. At 8am, Des would march in and round the whole circus off with a vigorous vacuuming routine that sounded like someone sawing a dustbin in half.

I left the Ekka festival on the final day with $1,000 in my pocket. It had been a successful, but mostly hilarious venture, and the first real money I'd earned in Australia. I felt good about it, especially after the Gatton farrago.

A month earlier, Grant and I were desperate for work. One Sunday, when everyone else had gone to Nimbin to get out of their minds on good drugs, we headed to Brisbane's Transit Centre on Roma Street and boarded the next bus east to the Lockyer Valley for a spell picking avocadoes. We arrived late at night in a town whose only source of lighting seemed to be 'NO VACANCY' signs. I felt like Charles Bronson in Once Upon A Time In The West, rolling into a deserted town with only a harmonica to my name. Our stay was bookended by a dull, persistent rainfall.

"It's like Toowoomba all over again," Grant muttered. He'd worked in Toowoomba, further west of Gatton, months earlier and said it was similarly desolate and soulless. We had a contact at the town's caravan park but they couldn't accommodate us at such short notice so we found ourselves in the twice as expensive Gatton View Hotel, right on the edge of town. The hotel name was misleading as what could you possibly view with no windows? We expected to start work first thing the next morning, despite having nowhere to live, however it rained overnight, so, other than shovelling chicken shit, there was nothing for us to do, which gave us an opportunity to move into Gatton Caravan Park. In their capacity as proprietors, the site was 'managed' by a couple of ex-pats from Bury, Ron and

Carol. "We give all the rooms a thorough clean when people check out," protested Ron. This was a bare-faced lie, as our caravan could testify. In fairness, Ron had enough on his plate, what with standing around in slippers a dog wouldn't chew and smoking a pipe all day. The day off gave us time to suss the place out, which didn't take long. We walked into town along a dual carriageway, as there was no adjoining path, shelled out $100 each for a week's rent, admittedly a very good price, and did some shopping.

I had my first haircut in months on the high street by a barber who had owned the shop for thirty-six years, and had worked there since he began as a trainee in the 1940s, taking over from its one other owner in 1970. The walls were covered in evocative photos of men having their hair cut as the barber casually smoked a cigar and the waiting customers read boxing magazines. I could almost smell the Brylcreem. It was probably the Brylcreem.

Walking back, I watched a man test-driving a quad bike from the local outlet, seemingly for the benefit of his unimpressed girlfriend, which ended with the man flipping it directly into the side of a parked car at high speed, causing three zillion dollars worth of damage. It was a fine display of Australian machismo gone tits up. With hours to kill and nothing at all to do around the caravan park, I finished off another Paul Theroux book, Kingdom By The Sea, that I'd been reading on and off for weeks, before starting the copy of The Rum Diary that I'd found down the back of a stereo at Moreton Bay. Ten pages in and the good Doctor was already drunk and disrupting a flight on suspicion of cruelty to old people. That man knew how to travel.

The rain fell all night long, bouncing off the thin, corrugated walls of the caravan as I lay there freezing, wearing a fleece, hat, scarf and trousers. There was no duvet and I hadn't brought a sleeping bag either so used the filthy, thin sheet that I found on the bed, and had to make do with a pillow that was actually a cushion from the settee wrapped in one of my t-shirts. I alternated daily which end of the bed I slept at, determined by where the splattered cockroach brains had landed that day.

We were living at the height of discomfort, as far as civilised accommodation goes anyway, in a town that hadn't seen a drop of rain for almost five months, but yielded four days worth during our week long stay. We managed two days out in the paddock, plucking avocadoes on both occasions, which wasn't as bad as I'd envisaged, but didn't justify us paying a week's non-refundable rent or even travelling out there in the first place. I calculated that we made a profit of around $40 after our deductions for food and accommodation. Avocado is apparently the Latin word for 'testicles'. Appropriately enough, our week had been a load of bollocks.

Before we left, we attended Carol and Ron's weekly Saturday night barbecue which happened to fall on our penultimate day in town, where Grant met Ross, against whom he used to play football in school and I met Johnny Boom Boom, from Huddersfield, who had studied at, or rather attended, Teesside University, giving us a geographical reference point of sorts.

It was the first time in a long time any of us had spoken and not had to repeat ourselves. Johnny had the blunt turn of phrase of a Yorkshireman and we hit it off immediately. The barbecue ended abruptly, and criminally early, at 9pm, but mercifully so did the karaoke that had been arranged by the huge Korean workforce. The party shifted to someone's caravan as we were joined by two German girls, Marianne and Kat, and an Irish couple, Tom and Ella. The caravan looked like a horse had rampaged through it, and I don't mean that as an Irish stereotype. The party ended as suddenly as the barbecue had when Ross's bed collapsed so again we moved, this time to Tom and Ella's caravan to watch a Tommy Tiernan DVD that unsurprisingly, completely baffled the Germans. Ross passed out somewhere along the way, as Grant threw up outside.

"I thought these Scottish lads could drink?" I said to Grant.

He just shook his head and took a swig from his bottle.

The next morning, after hunting high and low and retracing my steps around the park, I resigned myself to the fact that I'd somehow lost my camera and harmonica on the way back to our caravan, which couldn't have been fifty yards from where we were at any one time. It capped a disastrous week. Until Grant woke up that is. The one place I hadn't looked was in his sleeping bag, obviously. He clambered out of it fully clothed, and shoed, and there they were.

"Ah wondered wat the fack was sticking in mah back all night," he moaned.

As long as I knew Grant, I knew he couldn't stomach hangovers and he was in bed for most of the next day. The weather, for once, was perfect, but as it was a Sunday, there was no work, so we had a kickabout instead. We quickly formed an amalgamated UK side consisting of two Englishmen, an Irishman and a Scotchman, which reminds of a joke I once heard, to play against an all-French team.

What followed was a thrashing that even Max Mosley couldn't withstand as Les Blues went down 5-1. Somewhere along the line, I accidentally concussed their best player, Leo. It was a bizarre body check, and a genuine accident, that prompted Johnny to ask if we were playing 'prison rules', and left Leo face down on the gravel and mumbling something under his breath about 'rosbif'. It was the only good thing that came out of the whole week, apart from Grant finding a big flick-knife on the field, which in hindsight was probably a crucial piece of evidence, that we used to vandalise the caravan on our last night. Early next morning, we crossed the motorway back into town for the last time and returned to 'Bris Vegas'.

Moreton Bay was overbooked when we returned, so much so that my room contained nine beds and ten people and if you were unlucky enough to drop anything on the floor, you could forget about finding it, which might explain Rusty's disappearance. The place resembled a Chinese laundry at times, with all manner of clothing strung up anywhere there was room.

Flags representing various countries hung outside the windows, serving only to aggravate the locals in the beer garden opposite. The night I returned ,there was a drunken orgy of sorts in the room next door but was only open to Scottish guests for some reason. They all quickly disappeared the next morning, taking the Maori brothers, Tyson and Freddy, with them. It was a very mysterious episode indeed. The brothers returned a week later, however. According to the unofficial rota that existed entirely in my mind, we were expecting another German girl called Kat to arrive any day now.

This particular Kat was from Geesthacht, and I was hooked on her accent more than anything else, which wasn't typically German but almost French sounding. She had a curiosity about her that fascinated me. It was as if she'd travelled into the future and was just working out her surroundings, which doesn't say much for Geesthacht. She was amazed when I explained to her briefly the rules of Rugby Union, most of which I made up.

"They can only throw it behind them," she exclaimed, "how do they go anywhere?"

"A rugby scrum is the only time it's acceptable to stick your thumb up another man's arse too," I added.

"Harse?"

"Arse," I repeated slowly, "…bum, bottom, backside."

"Yes, I understand. My English is not so good," she explained, laughing out loud and holding up a thumb. It was better than my German of course. It was my accent she was struggling with but she soon got the hang of it.

"You can even bite your opponent's ear off," I added helpfully.

"Noooo," she protested, bursting into laughter again.

"I want to make better my English," she said, "so I listen very carefully when people are talking to me." Like me, she'd left behind a mundane job in her homeland. Intriguingly, she'd been an escalator saleswoman, but was at the beginning of her trip with it all to come.

"I need to find a job," she said one night, "but I'd rather sit around smoking weed and drinking, instead." As naïve as I'd first thought she was, after spending a little time with her, I realised this wasn't the case. She seemed to be constantly rolling a joint with her tiny hands, or at least smoking a cigarette, then speaking in hushed German to her friend when she didn't want anyone to hear what she was talking about.

"We like Goan trance music and we like to make a party. One time we go to London and only to make a party," she said of herself and her friend Sanra.

"Oh yeah. Who doesn't like Goan trance. I love it," I lied, "and don't get me started on making parties."

As untypically German as she was, one occasion stood out as a fine display of Teutonic efficiency. At a barbecue, she discarded the plastic knives and forks, which were as useless as they always are at barbecues, and produced a pocket-sized stainless steel box that unfurled itself miraculously into a knife and fork.

I eventually got round to taking a trip into central Brisbane, to King George Square and its centrepiece, the museum. I stood beside the statue of Steele Rudd opposite and took some photos. Rudd was a self-proclaimed 'bush storyteller' and author from Toowomba, most famous for his 1908 work, Dad In Politics. As a testament to his writing, most of its sentiments are still relevant today. Rudd, who today would probably be called a 'larrikin' by his fellow countrymen, had little time for politicians and probably would have turned his nose up at the museum's current exhibition.

It concerned Brisbane's corrupt government of the early 1980s at the hands of the then Premier Joh Bjelke Patterson, one of the most reviled men in Australia at the time, and his crooked crony, Chief of Police, Terry Lewis. The upheaval of the city was on a grand scale with rioting, demonstrations and marches a constant feature as the public railed against Patterson's dated views on race rights, women's lib and homosexuality, which usually ended in the police giving everyone a good beating. Soon enough, as in most cases of oppression, a revolution of sorts took place. It was spearheaded by people like Don Brady, the preacher who once removed his collar during a protest march and flattened two thugs who had heckled him, and local radio station 4ZZZ FM, who teamed up with bands like the Saints and the Parameters, and the arts crowd of the famous FOCO club on Turbot Street.

The exhibition was enormous and I took in as much as I could, making notes as I went. The women's lib section included a selection of badges worn by the protesters. One of them blurted: 'IT STARTS WHEN YOU SINK INTO HIS ARMS. IT ENDS

WITH YOUR ARMS IN HIS SINK'. I walked all the way to Brunswick Street grinning at the thought of it. Brunswick Street is where the action is in Brisbane. Drugs, prostitution, booze, gambling; Brunny ticks all the vice boxes. I stumbled upon it really. The main area is directly opposite the entrance to Brunswick Street Station in the Fortitude Valley area, and consists of a main drag of seedy, run down 'nite-spots', strip clubs and sex shops, each with a busker out front on this particular day. Stepping out of the station and turning right will take you up into Bowen Hills and past the Church of Scientology. I was mysteriously drawn in. Actually, I was interested in the nonsensical principles that had been created by its members, so it was no different to any other religion in that respect, (hello Christianity). Inside I was blinded by faction and family wall charts, statues, DVDs, sticker albums and Ron knows what other paraphernalia. A messenger tried to engage me with some propaganda but I steered him off with a few questions about its popularity in Brisbane. His hypnotic face, and the fact he either never blinked or had no eyelids, made him a perfect candidate for spreading the good word. He nodded slowly when I spoke, his face never changing, a sure sign of him not listening to a word I said.

I'd seen this demeanour in vicars and priests. He locked his fingers together and held them over his stomach. The thing that aroused most suspicion though, was that he'd fastened the top button of his three-quarter-length, powder blue shirt. This was a few years before it became fashionable to do so, to my knowledge, giving it the appearance of a kind of smock, the type of garment I'd associate with Reverend Jim Jones, or David Koresh, for example.

"Most people pop in just out of curiosity, nose around hoping to meet Tom Cruise, then ask for directions to some place," he said, fixing me with the imposing gaze of a cult leader.

"Really?" I said, followed by, "How do I get to St Paul's Terrace from here then, mate?" I moseyed out, and back onto Brunswick Street, this time taking a left past the station and into Chinatown.

After the religious intensity of Gatton, Scientology seemed fairly tame. At the community centre off the town's William Street, the local church, cunningly equating today's youth with the Internet, had offered free use of its computers in a bid to lure new members, with the added sweetener of free burgers during the sessions. Our shameless exploitation at the hands of organised religion went as far as being told the book sale outside, containing various religious tomes, 'could save us', though from what was unclear. It was too late anyway, Grant and I had already dived headlong into a representation of hell on earth by going to Gatton in the first place. The backpackers, myself included, flocked in their droves, driven by a mutual appreciation of free food, and in our excitement completely disregarded the 'message', but of course I was the one who was accosted by the shrewish, middle-aged woman running the session as I browsed the Evening Gazette website.

"Middlesbrough, that's in Yorkshire, isn't it?" she asked.

"Mmmm... yes."

"They have such strong houses there, don't they?"

"Yeah. So what?"

Waiting outside for Grant, I sifted through some of the books for sale, most of which bizarrely concerned themselves with Hitler's supposed raiding of Christian symbolism for the Third Reich. I was reading a piece on Nazi hunter Peter Malkin when the woman floated over in a way that only a representative of the church could. I glanced up, slightly startled, and there she was, looking saintly and sinister in equal measure. I thought she was about to press me on the Lord and his work but instead it was her obsession with the English weather that prevailed.

"Your winters are so cold there. That's why you have such strong houses, isn't it?"

In the end, it was Grant who saved me, not Jesus, as he helpfully interrupted the woman and we made good our escape back down William Street.

I spent almost all of my remaining time in Brisbane watching live music, mainly in Wynnum, where I attended the jam sessions regularly, and met Manny, a regular performer who worked in the area as a hairdresser. "I'm a fucking barber, mate," he would say. Originally from Manchester, hence the name, he'd maintained the coarseness of the northwest in his thick accent, sense of humour and rough face. The accent disappeared when he sang but the attitude remained.

"I only sing my own stuff," he snarled down the mic one night. "If you don't like it, you know what to do." He was a man about town and well known in the area. Despite what he said about only performing his own work, he bowed to mock pressure at the end of his sets and did a version of Dave Mason's much covered but brilliant Feelin' Alright, the words evidently meaning a lot to him. The jams were organised by Daniel, who I'd met at the Manly Hotel, and his wife. Daniel's devotion to music was tireless, performing four times a week in bars around Brisbane and jamming anywhere he could.

He would open the sessions with his bluesy take on Mary Had A Little Lamb then take a back seat and let the others step up. I was amazed by the quality of the performances.

"Some of the guys we get coming through are pretty good," he said. Pretty good? They were astonishing. Incredibly, most of them didn't even have a regular band to play in so instead showed up every Wednesday at the meeting. There was no sign of Brown Sugar though. They'd been local favourites for a while before completely imploding in a vacuum of booze, drugs and creative differences. I heard it first hand from Andy, a friend of Manny's and a dead ringer for the Charlatans' Tim Burgess, who'd been the band's lead singer. We met him when he tried throwing Tank a bit of tiling work.

"Our drummer even had his own studio and we still couldn't get it together," he said. Andy was a plasterer by trade but, like most people, loved rock'n'roll enough to do it for fun, so much so that he didn't seem overly bothered about the band falling apart, as long as he could still play. Andy's carefree attitude was typical of everyone I met in Brisbane. Nothing else really mattered, as long as the sun was shining and the pubs were open.

I had five weeks left in Australia and needed to do as much work as possible in that time in order to pay for anything I would do in New Zealand, and allow for a week in Sydney. I'd been in the country for almost one hundred days and of those I'd worked just eleven.

"I'm going north," said Aaron one day. "There's a farming town in the Burdekin called Home Hill. They have a working hostel and as much work as you can do. Three months of that and you extend your visa to a second year." He was a mainstay of Moreton Bay and knew his way around, so we tagged along, setting off three days later. Grant came too, and we roped in Rusty as comic relief.

Before we left, a bizarre episode unfolded. During one of my trips home from work at the Ekka, my mobile phone had fallen out of my pocket on the train, making it the 109th item lost so far. As it only had a total of three numbers stored in the phone book – it was for emergencies only – the finder didn't have far to look to discover my whereabouts, obviously not Tony's Auto Wreckers in the middle of Alice Springs, or Sam's Chinese Takeaway. In the time it took for me to lose it on the train and get to the hostel, which couldn't have been longer than half an hour, someone had contacted the hostel to say they had found it.

"Call this number to get your phone back," Dave said as I walked in the door.

I didn't even know I'd lost it yet and already somebody was attempting to return it. I dialled the number.

"I figured you'd want the phone back," said a voice at the other end. Then he gave some almost indecipherable name of where he was calling from, which turned out to be Indooroophilly, a reasonably local suburb that I couldn't get to anyway.

"I can arrange for my brother, Alonso, to meet you in the city some place if it's easier for you," the voice offered. It was much easier and I was soon on my way to Brisbane's spectacular business district that sits on the river at Waterfront Place. I wandered up and down Eagle Street and in and out of buildings looking for Naldham House, and specifically the office of PriceWaterhouseCoopers, where Alonzo worked. Are you paying attention? There's a test at the end. After much searching, I found Naldham House, due mainly to the enormous crowd of people standing outside, on the street and in the road, and numbering thousands. The nearby bars, coffee shops and sandwich bars were rammed to the rafters with city types, all cheerfully stuffing their faces.

As I got closer to the throng, I noticed they all looked equally happy, chattering amongst themselves in the midday sun. Then I realised why; it was a fire drill. Fire drills of course allow workers the world over a damn good fully paid skive, all on company time, so it was no wonder everyone was smiling. I held little hope of retrieving the phone then as I edged along the back of the crowd, which was a long way from the building's entrance. I was gazing up at the top of the building, which looked high enough to threaten any low flying aircraft, when a Hispanic-looking man bumped into me.

"Oh, I'm sorry," I said.

"No worries, mate," he replied.

"What's going on?" I asked, although I had an inkling.

"Fire evac, mate, nothing serious. You're English, eh?"

"Oh aye," I said, speaking solid Northern. "How long you reckon you'll be out here for then?" I asked.

"All day, hopefully," he said, with an optimistic grin.

"It's certainly the weather for it," I replied. Do the English ever shut up about the weather, I wondered to myself?

"Oh aye," he said, deliberately mocking my accent.

I didn't laugh and instead exhaled dejectedly, the way a mechanic does when he has just discovered hundreds of pounds worth of life-threatening damage under your bonnet but wants to appear sympathetic when you ask how bad it is.

"What's wrong, mate?" he asked.

"I'm supposed to meet a guy who works for Price WaterhouseCoopers in there to pick up a mobile phone."

It was his turn to pull a funny face, but I didn't really pay it much attention. I was watching him reach into his pocket. He took out my phone.

We exchanged incredulous looks.

"Alonzo?" I chanced.

He nodded.

I gave him a good quality Cuban cigar as a thank you. We spent a moment or two calculating the odds of what had just happened then went our separate ways, both slightly speechless.

CHAPTER 10:
HOME HILL

Caning it with a German police officer and
the most profane man in the Southern Hemisphere.

"You can ram 'em up your knackers."

My separate way was Rainbow Beach, a battery charging stop off
on the way to North Queensland that allowed for a couple of days
rest and relaxation – like we hadn't had enough already – before
getting our hands dirty on the farms of the Burdekin. It was exactly
as it said on the tin; the multi-coloured sand, although mainly black,
gives the place its name. Rusty and I stayed at Dingo's Backpackers
on Spectrum Street and found little to do as we waited for Grant
and Aaron to catch us up, as they would a couple of days later. As
with all the other towns in Queensland, Rainbow Beach consisted
of a main drag that was home to a few shops and cafes, a library and
a hardware store. They did have the added luxury of a basketball
court though, where we spent many a minute kicking a football
around.

Rusty was beginning to wear Grant down with the endless torrent
of nonsense that came out of his mouth, and his Bermuda shorts
were making me violently ill, when we boarded the coach for the
eighteen hour final leg of the journey to Home Hill. We made a
series of stops on the way but you couldn't tell one from the other:
petrol station, a bit of grass, a couple of Utes and not much else
to hold your attention. At the end of our first day in Home Hill,
I'd been awake for thirty-four hours when I was informed in the
bar of the Crown Hotel that I would be starting work at 7.15am
the next morning, which by then was only eight hours away. I was
wondering what I'd let myself in for.

Rusty had been in town for less than an hour – and paid a week's
rent in advance – when suddenly he could take no more and got
on the next train back to Brisbane. I could see the terror in his

face when he realised he would have to work in a strange town with people he didn't know, just like a real grown up. The working arrangements in Home Hill suited us well. Anyone staying at the hostel, or its overflow holding, the Crown, as I was, would be named on the work sheet made available at around 8 o'clock every evening. The work sheet would state which farm you would be working on, at what time, with whom, and how you would get there.

Shelley and Nugget ran the hostel and had the monopoly on all the farms in the area, as far away as Bowen and Ayr some of them, and would contract the work, usually picking fruit and vegetables, out to the backpackers, of which more and more came and went daily. We arrived on a Sunday and Shelley and Nugget were nowhere to be seen, so we hung around in the house that would soon become our home. That feeling of not knowing anyone in a new place was stronger than ever but at least there were four of us from Brisbane now that Mai had joined us. I'd seen her hovering around at Moreton Bay but had never really spoken to her.

I let her have the last bed at Shelley's and lugged my stuff across the street to the Crown, where the landlady, Patty, introduced me to the already tightly knit group staying there. It consisted mainly of travellers around my age from the south of England, a small group of Koreans, a handful of German and French backpackers, and Rob, the resident nut job, from Adelaide. I was a bit unsure about living above the pub instead of at the hostel but after I spent five minutes in Grant and Aaron's room at Shelley's, I knew they wouldn't be getting much sleep. The communal area was a huge room that combined the kitchen and the TV cabinet, which were located directly outside Grant and Aaron's room. The only thing separating people's beds from the idiot box was a very thin wall that even the set designers of Prisoner Cell Block H would have rejected for being unstable. There was a constant chorus of announcements over the loudspeakers, clattering cutlery, and cacophonous chatter bouncing off the bare stone floor and underneath the dormitory doors. It was actually quieter over at the pub, the reason being that the only people who spent any time in the bar were the people who lived above it, so if everyone was in the bar then nobody was in bed, and vice versa.

Home Hill lies an hour or so south of Townsville and 1,200km north from Brisbane. Its population numbers 2,907, not including long-term backpackers, most of whom never stay for more than three months. As the old joke goes, it's the kind of place where the population never changes because when somebody gets pregnant, somebody else leaves town. It was originally part of the Inkerman Downs cattle station and a major producer of sugar cane but the process has slowed considerably over the years. Interestingly, there was a degree of dispute about how it came to be known as Home Hill, or at least its spelling.

Most accounts point to the Crimean war hero Colonel Home but I prefer the inebriated sign writer story. After a heavy night on the 'turps', he incorrectly spelt in spectacular fashion, leaving out an l from the word 'Holme', adding a space between words as he felt the need to, and stuffing an extra capital h in for good measure. It did the trick and he was back in the boozer by lunchtime. Home Hill had three pubs, the Crown, the Commercial and the Malpass, and I was lucky enough to sample all three at one time or another. Beyond that, you had to travel to Ayr for a good time.

Rising early to go to work during an English winter is not a desirable experience; more often than not it's raining, when it's not snowing that is, and it's grey. In Australia, it's a different experience altogether. North Queensland's winter temperatures peak at around thirty at noon but at first light they plummet to seventeen, weather sufficient enough in England to have people driving to work topless. First light was at 6.20am. That's when I would stumble around the room getting dressed and doing everything I should've done the night before. I wasn't even the first one out most days. Everyone would head round to Shelley's and pile into the designated vehicles before stuttering off to their respective farms. The motorcade was a sight to behold and provided much consternation, but mainly hilarity. Lining the road outside the house was a variety of clapped out, decrepit contraptions that wouldn't have looked out of place in the Wacky Races. The fleet consisted of three minibuses, two cars and a van. Between them, they had a dazzling array of defects that included the following: bald tyres, cracked windscreens, dented doors, backfiring engines, crunched gearboxes, loose bumpers, torn seats, missing seats, smashed bulbs, rusty panels, (DEEP BREATH), holes in the floor, half a steering wheel, no ceilings, tights for fan belts, bullet holes in the radiator, axe in the bonnet, body in the boot, flooding, rising damp, malaria, involuntary window, engine cramp, and oil rejection. The main cause of the damage was the backpackers themselves, screeching up and down the highways at breakneck speeds, usually in the wrong gear, and all without a licence or insurance.

I once drove at 90kph in third gear for the best part of 50km in Nugget's minibus because the gear stick wasn't working properly and I didn't really know how to use it anyway. It made an interesting noise though, something akin to an air raid by the Luftwaffe. A few days later, after Aaron and I had both run it into the ground, someone else was doing something similar to it when the gear box exploded in a cloud of blue smoke and red hot metal, coincidentally the exact effect created by throwing a grenade into the cab. Nobody was hurt and everyone laughed, especially the mechanic.

When we actually got to work, we found ourselves lumping pumpkins onto a boom arm attached to Gino's tractor. Like most of the farmers in the area, Gino was an irascible old Italian with a face like a burnt sandal who nobody paid a blind bit of notice to. He'd owned that particular farm for over thirty years but recently sold it to Ken Duncan, who joined us in the paddock everyday as we dodged snakes and spiders in order to pick eight tonnes of his precious mother lode. It was physical work I hadn't done in a long time and it was hard going in the heat but we kept on and it got easier, but never less tedious. The pumpkins were actually named 'Ken Specials' after Ken himself, and were sold all around Queensland.

At the end of each day, we knew we'd been in a job. Covered in dirt, dust and thorns, we'd all pile back into the van and head back

137

to Home Hill, and on the journey attempt to replace some of the bodily fluid we'd sweated by drinking the two litres of water we should have drunk throughout the day. I was dozing off on one of these journeys one day when Aaron announced that Steve Irwin had been killed by a stingray up at Cape Tribulation. We waited in vain for a punchline.

At the time of his death, Irwin, still more iconic in some places than even the kangaroo, was in the process of a pioneering project that mapped the routes of crocodiles through rainforests, much of which was unknown to the public, and at a time when some commentators were suggesting that he did nothing but harm to these creatures. Even as a casual observer and not a particularly big fan, I watched the memorial service the following week with a tear in my eye.

Folk singer John Williamson sang True Blue in front of a worldwide TV audience and capacity crowd at Australia Zoo as Steve-o embarked upon his final journey in that unmistakable symbol of Australian nationalism, the Ute. There were Princess Diana levels of grief throughout Queensland and the Courier Mail was taken over by all things Irwin for almost a fortnight as stingrays became public enemy number one and tributes poured in from all over the world.

Another day, another farm, another vegetable. Chillies this time then, which is no way to spend a Sunday morning.

"I can pay you by the hour, or on commission. Eight bucks for every full bucket of chillies, or an hourly rate for picking egg plants," barked Vito.

The chillies were tiny and the bucket was wider than Jordan's arsehole so I opted for the latter.

"I'll be picking fuck all so you can pay me by the hour," I said.

An hour, and eight bucks later, and he was stomping around the paddock, and all over the egg plants, shouting at everyone for slacking off, especially me.

He was livid; more so when I calmly pointed out that, "You're stamping all over the gear there, kidda." I can think of nothing more patronising than someone considerably younger than you calling you 'kidda', especially when you're already fuming. There's just something about it; maybe it's a Boro thing.

"Come with me, Pom; you're on fuckin' chillies," he ordered.

I jumped into the back of the Ute with a few others for the bumpy ride back to the shed. By the time he pulled up, I'd hopped off, and into the minibus, and was heading back to Home Hill.

"What about the bloody veg?" he bawled, through the cloud of dust coming from the tyres.

"You can ram 'em up your knackers," I shouted over my shoulder.

To this day, I'm still unsure as to whether I was fired, which would have been the only time in my life I was, or whether I walked out, which would have been the only time in my life I have. At the same time, I was wondering exactly how I was going to see out another fortnight of this. I spent the rest of the day frying in Shelley's back yard and working my way through a couple of bottles of red wine with Julie. Julie was the town hostel's femme fatale. I'd worked with her on a melon patch a few days earlier and looked on entranced as she burnt to a crisp in the sun. She was French. You could tell by looking at her. Her eyes were Lapis Lazulis that looked like they had broken a thousand hearts into a million pieces and her hair was as gold as the sun, so that's the obligatory poetic description of a Frenchwoman out of the way then. She even smoked in French, carefully making a selection from her Betty Boop cigarette case then lighting up methodically. She seemed never to take a drag, preferring instead to just hold it in front of her face, like a smokescreen to hide something.

"I cannot take much more of zis, Vill," she moaned one day, talking about Home Hill in general. She'd worked as a waitress in Perth and was thinking of returning there, but at home in Cherbourg had been a fashion designer, with little success, although I took that to mean she worked in a clothes shop. Not one man in the whole town saw her and didn't have a comment to make about her. She 'escaped' town in a hurry after just five days. I felt pretty pleased with myself by that point, sitting in the sun with a mademoiselle and a good drop of wine, like Yves Montand or someone. I say good drop, it was probably brewed in Shelley's sink.

A lot of the time, I hung out with Mikey, and his girlfriend Claudia, who were from Berlin and had no desire to go back so were really getting stuck in and getting out to work every day in order to extend their visas. When they weren't at work, they were sitting in the garden totally exhausted along with everyone else. After work, everyone's priority was a cold beer, usually on the veranda outside my room where you could hardly see over the balcony for bottles, not that there was much to see anyway, unless you're really into derelict railway stations.

I hit it off immediately with Mikey and Claudia and spent most of my time chatting with them about anything and everything, but mainly music. Claudia had recently seen Bob Dylan, The White Stripes, and the latest incarnation of the Beach Boys, featuring none of the original line-up, all in the US. If it's musical legends you want though, then consider that she worked in an office next door to 'him out of Milli Vanilli', Rob or Fabrice, who knows, aren't they the same person? Mikey and Claudia had the luxury of sleeping in a tent in Shelley's garden – only in Home Hill could sleeping in a tent be considered a luxury – and so got to hear everything that went on in the area, from the ring pull 'tsssk' of Nugget's cans, to the noise from the nearby door-slamming factory. Shelley looked like she'd been a really attractive girl in her younger years, the popular leader at school, full of attitude and fun; and then she settled down with Nugget. As addled as he was, he at least knew a good thing when he saw one and somehow managed to keep hold of her, although it appeared they'd had their fair share of ups and downs. Shelley found solstice in the weekly karaoke nights around town and Nugget found his in his beer. It was the perfect depiction of small town Australian life.

Claudia helped me to perfect a number of obscene German phrases that were actually translations of typical Australian sayings, 'finster vie ein nonnenloch' for example, which translates as 'darker than a nun's nasty' or 'so nutzlich wie brustwarzen on einem stier' which is 'as useful as tits on a bull' and many more equally useless ones of a similar ilk. More often than not, the language lessons were interrupted by one of Nugget's drunken announcements over the loud speaker, that were of no service at all, except to inadvertently make us laugh. Instead of a supermarket-style 'bing bong' to get everyone's attention, this system used an ear-splitting screech of feedback, the type favoured in films when someone with no experience of broadcasting approaches a microphone.

The announcements always began as follows: 'Backpackers... the luggage room is now open'. It was all very Big Brother. Everyone's luggage was stored in a shed at the bottom of the garden in order to minimise the amount of places bugs could form and access was only permitted at certain times.

Nobody paid any attention to the announcements as they were all watching the comedy triple-bill of The Simpsons, Family Guy and Arrested Development that packed the TV area every night at the same time. As soon as they finished, everyone would ask the person next to them, "What did Nugget say earlier?" Nobody ever knew or cared. Even if they were off work the next day, everybody was up and about at first light and 'on standby' in case somebody didn't turn up, which happened every day and was how I ended up to my neck in sugar cane.

Some days you wonder why you get out of bed. It's the safest place in the world, and the most comfortable. Why then, would you leave it in order to have hundreds of blunt pieces of wood rammed into your body at high speed whilst being bawled at by a stoned pensioner and a former German anti-riot policeman? I had no idea what I was in for that morning when Shelley's battered Land Rover skidded to a halt in front of me, almost catapulting her through the already dangerously cracked windscreen.

"Wiiaalll," she cried, perfectly executing the North Queensland pronunciation of my name, "get in, we need a planter."

"What the fuck's a pla..." It was too late, I was in, jammed between Eddie and Rob. Eddie was a local, as rough as a man gets and madder than a cut snake. He was around 5ft 6" with a trace of Aborigine in his weathered brown face and a tidy grey goatee under his foul mouth. He was a short ball of muscle and had been pulling cane, on and off, for over thirty years, giving him the kind of steel-veined cast iron grip that produced around 550 brake horse power.

He never spoke, only shouted, as we all did over the din of the tractor, but I suspected he was like that all the time. He was erratic, calm at times, explosive at others; hysterical ranting and raving was followed seconds later by quiet introspection, and sometimes almost tears, that I later discovered were caused by the recent death of a close friend.

"The piss got 'im," he lamented, referring to his alcohol consumption. Judging by his chest condition, he didn't have long himself. He was never without a smoke, or a 'cone' as he called them, of some sort, usually weed, that he would roll casually as the tractor threw us around the paddock. He had the intelligence of a man of age though, an intelligence that comes from just living and being around, and Eddie had been around. Alongside Ratso Ball, he'd held the Burdekin record for cane planting, laying down an incredible ninety-two acres in a week. By comparison, the three of us planted a still impressive sixty-two acres of appalling cane – "The worst there is," according to Eddie – in six days.

For the uninitiated then, we had to plant the cane that was being hacked down elsewhere on the farm and delivered to the paddock on trailers throughout the day. For ten hours a day, the three of us rode unsteadily up and down the paddock at the front of the trailer, jostling for position in an area of 8 sq. ft. with only the strength in our backs stopping us from being impaled by the tonnes of cane behind us. We took turns to yank handfuls of cane onto our shoulders before shoving it in the maw of the crusher attached to the back of the tractor. It was then mixed with fertiliser and rammed into the Queensland dirt.

As long as the tractor was moving, there had to be cane being fed in, all week long. I'm certain the whole adventure wasn't covered by my travel insurance policy. By the end of the first run down the paddock, I was so bamboozled I could hardly see straight and motion sickness had soon set in. I was an inch from packing in right there but firstly, I had no way of getting home, and secondly, I remembered that nobody likes their first day in a new job, unfamiliar surroundings, strange people and all, so I gritted my mud-stained teeth, and dug in. I never wanted to do anything less in my whole life but I kept thinking of the money, which would be more than I'd ever earned in one week, and the joy at planting that last acre a week later. I knew I was lucky to have the job. I replaced a local who'd fallen over drunk and put his back out. When word spread that work was starting on Louie Pensini's paddock, we'd already planted a day's worth of cane and the people beating a path to Eddie's door looking for work were turned away. The second day turned out to be an even bigger test thanks to the injuries I'd sustained. I'd partly severed my thumb as a piece of split cane was sucked out of my bare hands and into the thresher, been lashed around the face, arms and neck, had my clothes torn, and my ear drum near perforated by Eddie's ranting, and believe me, Eddie could rant for the Commonwealth. I was unprepared to say the least. The next day, with every muscle stretched to snapping point, I pulled on a respirator, glasses, gloves – I would go through three pairs in the next five days – and hat, and clambered back onto the trailer for more punishment.

Like most things, it became much easier if you stayed calm at all times, which wasn't easy in such a frantic environment. At dinner time, we'd jump in the back of the Ute and drive to a less windy spot, and there wasn't many, shovel our sandwiches in, and spend the next hour asleep under a tree like three Huckleberry Finns. When I woke up, I felt revitalised and it really helped me through the day. We'd shake our boots out for spiders and snakes and get back on the trailer, planting until the sun had seen enough and began to disappear. It was all I could do when I got home to wash, cook, write in my journal, then crawl into bed at 9 o'clock, completely exhausted, before repeating the whole thing nine hours later.

Throughout the week, I'd developed an impressive cummerbund, collar and cuffs combination of brown dirt that was constantly blown into us by the crosswinds. I also had a hairdo so fortified by mud that it could've been a crash helmet and a thousand scratches all over my body from the sharp stick ends that took weeks to heal, especially the stigmata-like wounds all over my wrists. These were always a talking point and always led to a discussion on self-harm related issues. Despite the poor quality cane, we were well ahead of schedule thanks to the ten hour days we put in and there was a more relaxed air as we neared the end. Occasionally there was a 'miss' – an unplanted area – which prompted Eddie to roar obscenities, first at the seemingly deaf tractor driver, then at the actual cane, (which was primarily just grass and thus not responsive to speech).

The type of cane made it very difficult to force into the processer as it simply collapsed in your hand and/or was blown away in the wind. This grassy part of the cane was known as the 'suckers' and was a constant source of agitation for Rob, who raged not quite as much as Eddie, and with slightly less vehemence, but in German: "Schlamper!", "Hurensohn!", "Arschlocher!" My stay in Home Hill had sent my German expletive quota through the roof.

Rob, who looked like an Eastern European version of Owen Wilson, had been a police officer in Berlin but had left to travel and wasn't sure where he was going next. I asked him how he felt about leaving behind what most people would consider a good career.

"I did it for a long time and it was boring, unless we were beating up football fans," he said.

If all this wasn't enough to contend with, there was also the small matter of snake attacks. The three of us returned from the paddock one day to find the tractor driver triumphantly wielding a machete above his head and inspecting the writhing body of a black snake as it reared up, with a considerable length of body missing. The actually black, 'brown snake', or 'brown skin' as it is more commonly known, is a prolific attacker and is almost always in an agitated state, and this occasion was no different. Its bites are not always venomous but when they are, you will be lucky to last an hour.

It had been coiled up under the water tank where we spent most of our break times, choosing to reveal itself, luckily for us, when we were not around, which indicated to me that it wasn't looking for trouble. It had found it though in the shape of Bruce, our driver, who leapt from his tractor and took a big swing, big enough to lop its head clean off. It bounced clear of the angry body but it was still staring at us with its teeth showing. I picked up what was left of it below the neck and held it aloft, the midday sun reflecting off its scaly black body as it still wriggled around. I wanted to keep the head; it would have made a really smart key ring.

"As much as I love this country, there's a lot of nasty little buggers crawling around," said one of my co-workers, as he emptied out his boots one day, common practice when working in farm environments, or anywhere else for that matter, in rural Australia. On a neighbouring farm, I'd seen a sign in the toilet that in England, if there was ever the threat of a snake coming through the u-bend in the British Isles, might have read:

'WILL PATRONS PLEASE BE REMINDED THAT ANYONE LEAVING THE TOILET SEAT IN AN UPRIGHT POSITION IS ENCOURAGING SERPENTINE ACTIVITY OF THE UTMOST.'

The one at the farm read:

'SHUT THE DUNNY OR BE BITTEN BY SNAKES.'

Succinct and well worth heeding.

From time to time, the work went on hold as other farmers from around the area stopped by to see how we were getting on. Knowing it was a big job, they would offer us cold beers to boost morale, when in fact it was a sweetener for us to go and work for them after we had finished the job in hand. They were a welcome distraction all the same. One of them even tipped us off on the actual size of the paddock – which was useful as we were being paid by the acre – explaining that it had been mapped using a satellite navigation system to the exact size, rather than the farmer's rough estimations that put the area anywhere between fifty and sixty acres. Whatever it was, it was better than picking egg plants. As we planted the final acre, any excitement we had about finishing was replaced by relief and exhaustion, save for a few whoops and shouts as we collapsed onto the back of the trailer and rode back to the fuel stop at the top of the paddock.

We started the last push at our usual start time of 6.30am but as there was little to plant we were done by 7.30am and retired to Louie's shed for a few coldies borrowed from his fridge. It was the earliest I could remember having a drink but it was well earned. Eddie came prepared that morning. He was dressed in his 'going out' gear despite the hour of planting we still had ahead of us. He wore jeans and a shirt, socks and sandals, and had brought a crate of beer to drink on the way to the pub, this at 8 o'clock in the morning. With a cheque for $1,000 in his pocket, he was king of the world for a day. Rob and I hitched a ride home in a passing Ute and I never saw him or Eddie again.

Before I left Home Hill, I had to sample the nightlife and did so on my last Friday in town. It was karaoke night at the Crown and all the locals turned out to prove beyond any doubt that no matter where in the world you happen to be, karaoke is the last refuge of the talentless. When I arrived, Shelley was doing an almost passable version of The Night Chicago Died, but was soon relieved by English George suffocating Wham's I'm Your Man and dancing in a manner that suggested he'd recently had his spine removed. The Crown was the main backpackers' bar, because most of us lived there, but later on we wobbled uptown to the Malpass for another dose of karaoke, this one actually more excruciating than the first, something I hadn't thought possible. It was hard to say why, as all the performers were the people who had been at the Crown. The real entertainment was outside where we got into a scuffle with a couple of shit-kickers who had waved a palm frond in our faces, surely the softest cause of a fight ever. Once we had placated Big Irish, we thought it best to leave, and ended up drinking through until first light in Shelley's garden. Big Irish wouldn't have it any other way as him and his sidekick Marty were leaving the next day. I'd met them through Grant, who had worked with them that week, at a barbecue at the start of the night that was being held by some of the Koreans. It wasn't much of a barbecue though and most people, myself included, only went because Julie was going.

It was high noon on Saturday when I left Home Hill, and Queensland, for the last time. It was also the last time I was sad to leave somewhere behind on my trip and I felt quite emotional when I boarded the Greyhound bus that would take me down to Proserpine for my flight later that night, although my melancholy mood may have had more to do with my hangover than anything else. Only Grant and Aaron remained from the original Moreton Bay crew that had left Brisbane and there would be much more fun and games still to come in Home Hill, but not for me. I was going to a place that former governor Lachlan Macquarie said of it, "There's only two kinds of people from New South Wales. Those who have been convicted of a crime and those who ought to have been."

CHAPTER 11:
SYDNEY

Bridging the gap between here and there, and a rendezvous with Tank.

"I wasn't leaving until I'd found some reference to Middlesbrough."

I was a bit apprehensive about arriving in Sydney late at night as it has a reputation of sorts, but I felt at ease as I walked down Kent Street among the Saturday night crowds. I was still chuckling to myself about an incident that happened on the train earlier. Travelling from Kingsford Smith airport to the city's Town Hall station, I shared a carriage with a group of teenage girls on their way to a boozy night out in the Haymarket area. After the compulsory accent-related banter, an undercover police officer came aboard and fined two of them $400 each for drinking on public transport. One of them was so incredulous as a result, and already so drunk, that she threw up all over the carriage. In the ensuing drunken exodus, one of them left her purse behind.

I planned to spend my first full day in Sydney relaxing at the hostel, recovering from Saturday's long trip, and only venturing out for food shopping, but soon found myself rambling around Darling Harbour. My first impressions of the city, on and around Liverpool and Bathurst Streets anyway, were as I felt in Bangkok a few months earlier: hot, grimy and polluted, but not quite as much. This was soon remedied by the gale blowing across the Pyrmont Bridge that in one particular gust swept most of the pavement artists' materials into the harbour. Most of the artwork made up part of a homage to one of Sydney's favourite sons, Arthur Stace. Illiterate Stace was born in the city's Balmain slums in 1884 and was inspired by the preaching of Reverend RBS Hammond in later life, so much so that from the early 1930s up to his death in 1967, Stace scrawled the word 'ETERNITY!' in large chalk letters all over Sydney an astonishing 50,000 times.

The majority of his work no longer exists but one of his more interesting efforts can be seen on the bell of the GPO Clock Tower at Martin Place. Interesting because nobody to this day can work out how he gained access to the enclosed part of the tower from where the bell is hung. Stace's gravestone stands in Waverley cemetery and I don't need to tell you what it says on it. The monstrous IMAX cinema overlooking the harbour was closed so I walked to Tumbalong Park behind it where a huge Brazilian festival was taking place; one thousand women having their pubic hair removed in public, in actual fact some sort of martial arts dancing display accompanied by traditional instruments that I later learnt is called Capoiera. I returned to the hostel on Kent Street, knowing I had plenty of time to see everything over the following week.

Sydney marked the first of half a dozen or so occasions on the remainder of the trip that I would stay at Base Backpackers, a hugely popular chain of hostels throughout Australia and New Zealand. All of them were immaculately maintained and very secure, which in Sydney is crucial, but they all seem to suffer from a distinct lack of atmosphere. Maybe it was because of the size – the Kent Street building had six floors – or just because of the clientele, which consisted almost entirely of Germans when I arrived, with maybe ten English guests. Or perhaps I'd been spoilt by the good times I had elsewhere and was still using Moreton Bay as the unsurpassable yardstick. Luckily in Sydney, there was enough to see and do to keep me occupied during my stay but a week later in Christchurch, again at a Base hostel, there were considerably fewer distractions and boredom soon set in.

Sydney's maritime museum contained little I hadn't already heard of New South Wales' aquatic heritage. Roughly three thousand Aborigines of various tribes occupied the area of what we know today as Sydney by the time Cook arrived but the area had been charted by Dutchman Abel Tasman, who as a result named it New Holland.

In 1786, British Home Secretary Lord Sydney thought Botany

Bay to be a most suitable place for the rock breaking exploits of Britain's convicted criminals.

Under Captain Arthur Phillip, who insisted that the First Fleet venture further north of Botany Bay, Sydney was settled and declared to be, "the finest harbour in the world," by Phillip himself. It turned out to be the world's biggest natural harbour and over one thousand convicts, sailors, marines and animals were marched ashore at what became Sydney Cove. Its beginnings were as hard as you'd expect in such an environment and it was over two years later when 'emergency' supplies arrived from England, along with another 740 convicts. The First Fleet had exhausted the 747,000 strong supply of nails, which they presumably lugged around in one of the forty wheelbarrows that were taken. Soon after, in true English style, everyone started getting a bit lairy and things got so out of control that William Bligh, fully recovered from his disastrous Bounty excursion, was appointed to restore order.

This also ended in tears with the event of the Rum Rebellion. Farmers were paid with the stuff in order to up the work rate but it all went pear-shaped, as is usually the case when the English are given copious amounts of alcohol, a trait Australians centuries later often display. In 1809, Lieutenant Colonel Lachlan Macquarie was dispatched to give the colony a damn good kick up the arse, which was exactly what he did; one man was given a thousand lashes for stealing potatoes, and Sydney began to prosper. It expanded with the implementation of Macquarie's housing programmes and the opportunities he gave convicts he felt had skills that could be made use of. Convicts like Francis Greenway, the forger-cum-architect who designed many of the buildings that remain today along Macquarie Street and the Windsor area, most notably Hyde Park Barracks, which in its early days contained a sign directing you to the 'office of the master of lunacy' on the top floor, which is now a museum. Many people felt Macquarie had simply paved the way for a bunch of convicts to prosper, with the offspring of most of them making the city, for better or worse, what it is today, and he was returned to England in 1821.

By 1840, there were over 83,000 convicts in Sydney.

Almost two hundred years later and Sydney's population numbers over 4,000,000 people, almost a third of whom are from overseas. I was deliberately saving my visit to the Circular Quay area, home of the Opera House and Harbour Bridge, until later in the week, and in the meantime walked through Hyde Park, past the Pool Of Reflection, and on down William Street towards the Kings Cross area, swinging left at Victoria Street beneath its enormous Coca-Cola sign. Kings Cross was originally called Queens Cross but later renamed for Edward VII, and soon became a byword in Sydney for excessive behaviour, encouraged by the controversial self-styled 'Boss of the Cross', Abe Saffron, who died just months before I visited. Today it's not quite the centre of bohemian creativity it was fifty years ago but the legacy survives, and in fact is immortalised underfoot in the history lesson written on various paving stones. Europeans, mostly German, had fled there to escape the Nazis and a thriving arty community of painters, poets and musicians had grown out of it. One inscription read: 'THE YOUNG ARE SO HARSH, SO VILE AND SO RIGHT'. A junkie lunged at me as I read it, mumbled something inaudible in my face before singing at a passing car, then wandering off. Incidentally, Kings Cross was home to Australia's first ever legal drug injection room, just outside Kings Cross Station. I watched a thin man outside Kings Café clutching a bottle wrapped in a brown paper bag and holding court to some equally defeated souls before I wandered into a bookshop on Orwell Street. I looked around for twenty minutes before the sign writer up the ladder outside informed me that the shop was closed. On the way back to William Street, a hatchet-faced tart, egged on by her cockney pimp, tried to entice me into his 'gentleman's club'. The rest of the day I spent around Macquarie Street, in particular the still active Parliament House, built in 1810, part of which housed the first ever Royal Mint to be opened outside of London, and the enormous New South Wales State Library, home to Captain Bligh's Bounty journals.

Later I was overcome by that pre-landmark-seeing excitement as I walked down Macquarie Street and reached the junction of the

Cahill Expressway. From there, I could just make out the distinctive shape of the Opera House roof and soon enough I was at the foot of the steps that lead to the building itself. It was spectacular at first glance, and in need of a good clean, but my attention by now had been drawn across Circular Quay to the 'old coat hanger'. The Harbour Bridge left the most lasting effect of any man-made structure I'd seen so far. It got stronger and stronger and appeared more formidable as I approached it along the winding Hickson Road from where I had an excellent view of its underside. I took some photos from the Dawes Point side then climbed Pylon Point up to the Bradfield Expressway that connects north Sydney to south, across the harbour's narrowest part. I crossed the bridge at road level, passing on the option of climbing a further 100ft to the arch. I could see everything I needed to from where I stood, albeit through the anti-suicide grill that had been thoughtfully erected. I could see Fort Denison, or Pinchgut Island, right in the centre of the mouth of the harbour, which was formerly a solitary confinement area for unruly convicts.

The bridge itself couldn't have been forged anywhere but on Teesside. Immovable and unimpressed with all it surveyed, it stood triumphantly, trafficking thousands of cars back and forth every day. I wasn't leaving until I'd found some reference to Middlesbrough up there and as I reached the north side, I found an iron plaque pinned to the wall by four of the 6,000,000 hand-driven rivets that held it all together. It credited John Burnett & Partners - the architectural company, Ralph Freeman - consulting and design engineer, and Lawrence Ennis OBE - director of construction for Dorman Long and co., Middlesbrough's finest, and most famous, steel producer. The man beside me struck up a conversation. Some small talk ensued about the harbour before he asked where I was from.

"I'm from Boro, mate."

"I don't know it," he replied, looking puzzled.

"Yer fucking standing on it, mate," I said.

He looked away, but he knew. He just knew.

The bridge was famously 'opened' twice in 1932. The official ceremony saw New South Wales Premier Jack Lang, as he prepared to cut the ribbon, upstaged by Captain Francis De Groot of the Irish Hussars, who charged forward on his horse Mick and severed the tape with his ceremonial sword in protest at the Governor General not being invited. De Groot was quickly disarmed and removed, which led to a huge fuss concerning the law stating that no regimental officer shall have his weapon removed when not in battle, an issue further inflated by the interference of the press and the ensuing courtroom confusion. Shortly after his interruption, De Groot was taken away from the scene and the bridge was re-opened by Lang in front 750,000 people. It took nine years to build at a cost of AU$20,000,000, which was not fully paid until as recently as 1988. Before you ask, it takes ten years to paint. The bridge provides the best views of the harbour that the rest of the world recognises immediately, and of the Opera House, far away enough to see it as you would in postcards without the off-white, off-putting discolouration. Most likely, the council puts all its manpower into painting the bridge instead.

The Opera House cost an astronomical AU$102,000,000 to build and wasn't completed until 1973, after fourteen years of work and countless arguments about what should go where and who should do this, that, and the other. Jorn Utzon, its original architect, didn't bother to stick around for the finish and returned to his native Denmark after seven years. Ironically the opening performance was Prokofiev's War and Peace. I stuck my nose in but there was little going on that Tuesday afternoon so I kept on and made my way back to the city centre via the Royal Botanic Gardens and the Conservatorium of Music, another of Francis Greenway's masterpieces.

On the Opera House steps, I met up with Tank for the first time in five weeks and we discussed a rough plan for making our way around New Zealand a week later. It was good to catch up and find out what had been going on at Moreton Bay while I was in Home Hill but I was really enjoying travelling alone and wasn't particularly looking forward to the cold climate of the South Island of New Zealand after the warmth of Queensland as my wallet grew ever thinner.

"We'll need a car," he said.

He was right.

"I know," I replied.

By now I was wondering how I would see out the rest of the trip still with Fiji, Rarotonga and the US ahead. One consolation was the size of New Zealand, tiny in comparison with the distances we had been driving in Australia. It was the weather though that was putting me off; it would remind me of home and that was the last thing I wanted.

With a couple of days left in Sydney, I concentrated on the areas around George and Pitt Street, and the Star City complex across Darling Harbour in Pyrmont, beginning with a few drinks in the hostel's adjoining bar, the Scary Canary. I wouldn't have bothered but I'd crashed out of the poker game I found in a bar on Clarence Street and had nothing else to do. The Norwegians from my room turned up and over a few drinks, I tried to work out what their story was. From what I could ascertain, Hyurveg was either sleeping with the two girls, unlikely I thought after speaking to him for a short time, or Agnetta and Trina were lesbians, though this was probably wishful thinking on my part. On my final full day in Australia, I took one last walk down Pitt Street, stopping outside the Sydney Tower to watch a contortionist called Bendy Em jam herself into a glass box the size of a Rubik's Cube. I met Tank again shortly after he'd visited the top of the tower, which was exactly the kind of tourist attraction I hated, and asked him how it was.

"Shite," he declared confidently. "I'll see you in Christchurch."

I went to Star City to buy some supplies for the New Zealand trip and felt pretty smug when I stumbled upon a 'dollar everything store' but in my excitement ended up paying $6 for a tube of toothpaste after I'd gracefully smashed an ornament with one swing of my

154

rucksack. I stood calmly as everyone in the store waited to see if I would be charged for the pleasure; I would, the cashier ruthlessly enforcing the 'you break it, you pay for it' rule that he'd just made up without a flicker of compassion. To be fair, he looked like he'd had the day from hell, selling undisputed amounts of utter shit to the scum that make up the general public – I'd had many days like it myself – in the hot sun, as an unrelenting looped tape instructed us to 'buy, buy, buy'. The ornament broken was so hideous I could hardly tell what it was, although it resembled one of those expensive glass blocks that are so in demand. I imagined the scene.

"Merry Christmas."

"Thanks. What is it?"

"It's a block of glass. What does it look like, you ungrateful twat?"

"Thanks. I've always wanted one."

The man behind bought three as I left mine on the counter. In pieces.

That night, I attempted to sneak into the IMAX theatre to watch polar exploration documentary Shackleton, but the shift manager, who I will call Ms Wakebell for the purpose of this story, was at the top of her game. I couldn't face the indignity of being asked to leave for not having a ticket whilst wearing 3-D glasses so I scooted across the Pyrmont bridge to the huge, seemingly Styrofoam monstrosity that is Star City, the only legal casino in New South Wales. I joined the escalator that rose between two waterfalls and was deposited into a maze of coffee and sandwich franchises. I soon found my way to the casino. It was the last place I should have been but I couldn't resist, not having been in one, or even having a proper bet, since I left England. I was surprised to be let in at all, dressed as I was. I did a few laps of the place but could feel the $20 note in my pocket heating up so I broke it down at a roulette table, slid a cool $3 minimum stake on the 9/12 split, trousered the even cooler $52.50 return, and retired to the bar. Sydney's passion for gambling goes hand in hand with all the other vices that made the city one of the roughest, most feral places in the world in the 1880s, especially the Rocks district over at Sydney Cove.

It was overrun with ramblers, gamblers, jailers, sailors, robbers, bastards and thieves, all jostling for space, rows deep, at places like the Shakespeare Tavern, with its electrically-charged bar, operated at will by the landlord when things were getting a bit tame. One god-fearing soul even resorted to dumping booze into the harbour as a protest at the hedonism he'd witnessed. It's probably still down there.

I put half of my Star City winnings over the bar of Paddy Maguire's and watched local favourites Singled Out going through a slick rendition of every song they'd ever learnt. As a result, the crowd wouldn't let them leave and they played right through until gone 3am. I returned to the hostel at 4am, wrote yet another letter that to this day has not arrived at its intended address, packed my bags and noisily checked out just three hours later, all the time wondering just how much more sleep I could deprive myself of. I was by then unstoppable when it came to moving from one place to another, be it by boat, train or plane and regardless of how long it took. This time, I caught an 8am train from Town Hall Station, on the way passing a few barefoot casualties of Sydney's Saturday to hail a taxi, before leaving Australia for the four hour hop to New Zealand's South Island.

PART IV: THE SOUTH PACIFIC

CHAPTER 12:
NEW ZEALAND

A home from home as I gatecrash an awards ceremony
and make my busking debut.

"It felt like we'd been transported to some epic historical film set."

I flew out of Australia, over the Illawara coastline and the Tasman
Sea on a Sunday afternoon, happy to leave but knowing I'd return
someday. It was one of the few places I could say that of. I was
heading for a strange place, Aotearoa, the 'land of the long white
cloud', New Zealand.

I found Christchurch painfully dull, a tiny piece of England
transplanted across the world. Give it a chance, I told myself, it was
a Sunday evening after all. Maybe it wasn't always this cold, grey,
and boring, but it was; every day. People drearily shopped and went
about their business in a quiet sort of way. It was a land of extremes,
from the genteel sleepy towns to the might of its natural scenery
just a short drive away, and its people reflected the contrast: the
reserved Kiwi and the boorish Maoris. There was no in-between.

We spent a couple of days hanging around Christchurch planning
our route around the island, which effectively took on the shape
of a rhombus when we traced it over the map, and covered most
of the lower part of the South Island. Christchurch is the lower
island's capital and sits on the east coast of the Canterbury region
that looks out to the Pacific Ocean. Tank and I were staying at
Cathedral Square, again at Base, which looked out into the main
diamond in the centre of town, where the locals played street chess
outside the tiny police station and dodged the trams that rattled by.
Based on cave paintings found in the area, the city as a settlement
dates back as far as 1250 but was 'rediscovered' by European
visitors in 1840. Its current population is around 350,000, and

includes the self-styled 'Wizard of Christchurch' among its number. The 'wizard' was actually borealocentric Londoner Ian Brackenbury Channell, who now lives in Oamaru, and had became well known for his oratorical exploits in the square, where he would give regular speeches on a variety of subjects dressed in full regalia. A borealocentric is someone who believes that the earth is the opposite way round, a theory which would put the Wizard's beloved Christchurch somewhere in the region of Greenland. Alternately, the UK would be situated somewhere near the South Pacific, and would probably still be as cold.

The only entertainment I saw in the square came in the form of barefoot local singer/songwriter Craig Russell. I was reminded of James Taylor as he performed his paean to the demise of the golliwog, simply called Golliwog. He'd optimistically prepared an album for purchase, at $15 a shot, but, through no fault of his own, could hardly rouse the passers-by from their mundane chores and zombie-like stupor, although more recently they've been preoccupied with the aftermath of an earthquake that measured 6.3 on the Richter scale.

One thing to shake the place from its slumber would be a repeat of Ernie 'the crocodile' Rutherford's atom-splitting exploits. They actually took place at Manchester University but the man himself was from Nelson and one of New Zealand's most famous sons, spending many of his learning years in Christchurch. The city is now home to various scientific institutes and houses of education that are named after him. For a closer look at Rutherford, try and get your hands on a New Zealand $100 bill, something I couldn't do while I was there.

At the hostel, I divided my time between looking for the holy grail of kitchen implements, the tin opener, and loitering with intent in the improbably named Saints & Sinners bar. It was dingy to say the least, just how I liked it, and one night, as Tank and I were commencing with our customary piss up, we bumped into Mo Zaniel. As a child, he'd lived around the corner from us in Middlesbrough – not that we knew it at the time – and had just finished work on director

Roland Emmerich's latest blockbuster, 10,000 YEARS BC. As the title suggests, it's a caveman epic, featuring Mo himself alongside no less a legend than Omar Sharif. Mo had done all the necessary weapons and physical training that the role called for, followed by four months of filming, and was now taking it easy and heading north to Nelson before peddling his latest co-written screenplay off Broadway. Naturally this called for a drink so we ensconced ourselves in the corner of the bar and surrounded ourselves with a battery of Jagerbombs. As the band Softcore tuned up – and I have to name check them after I joined them for an impromptu harmonica cameo the following week – we were joined by a group of cockneys who between them supported West Ham, Millwall, Spurs and Brentford, and spent most of the night arguing amongst themselves about which club had the least silverwear.

Mikey was the Millwall fan and invited me down to a match when we got back to England.

"If only to expose you as the Scouser you really are to my mates," he said.

The accent monster had reared its head again. The pot was stirred by the arrival of Ross, who I'd worked with in Gatton, and was amazed to see, unmissable in his trademark green and white hooped t-shirt, which was how I recognised him in the first place. Like most of the other guests, his stay was part of the New Zealand Experience, a package tour of sorts that takes backpackers on a coach tour of the islands, with night stops at various Base hostels. Ross and I had a lot to talk about, mainly how our experiences in Gatton had scarred us for life, but we soon got talking to a couple of local girls, Carla and Marie. We both jostled for Marie, who was having none of it from either of us, which we put down to her not drinking as she was chauffeuring Carla around in her car. Carla was gooseberrying a bit and then went to pieces when she heard my English accent as I asked Marie what she did for a living. The band drowned her out and as far as I could make out she was a 'door-stop'. Carla saw my puzzled expression.

"Body Shop," she yelled. "We work in the Body Shop."

Ross looked at me puzzled. "Car repairs?"

Oh, right. The Body Shop. Got it.

Carla had composed herself by now. I'd mentioned earlier that I liked live music and gambling.

"I'll make Marie drive us to the casino, then to Mickey Finn's, where I'll sing John Cougar Mellencamp's Hurt So Good with the band."

By Mickey Finn's, I think she was referring to a local club, as opposed to the house of the former T-Rex percussionist, and, as an itinerary, it was eclectic enough, but I declined. It was so cold outside that if you inhaled, you would die. Instead, Ross and I sabotaged the lift in order to buy vital seconds of chat-up time with the American and Norwegian exchange students we'd met in the bar. They were over on a term-break from studying engineering in Newcastle, NSW.

Rhianna was originally from Kansas City so I feigned interest in the progress of the Chiefs, her local American football team, and in particular star player Trent Green, and she soon ran away with the conversation, which mainly consisted of her telling me that everything was "so like yeah". Ross was chipping away at the Norwegian; I overhead their mutual appreciation of Ole Gunnar Solskjaer, and things were going well in Mo's room when we were interrupted by the obligatory mouthy Essex girl that had attached herself to Mikey. She appeared from nowhere insisting that we all go out onto the balcony. Nobody wanted to but we all did, and got very cold, very quickly.

I was hung over, deliriously hungry and without sleep when we picked up the hire car the next day and drove into the mists of doom around Arthur's Pass. The sky was still overcast and grey, which only added to the scene of snow capped peaks and numerous waterfalls as we wound our way through the stunning mountain area that was named for Arthur Dobson, officially recognised as the first man to successfully lead an exploration party to the Southern Alps in 1864. The Maoris were there first, of course, hunting for food, and how hostile an area it must have been. It began to rain torrentially on this October day, making the roads treacherous, but there was little traffic and we reached the Greymouth region on the west coast without difficulty. We stayed the night at Gordon Wells' jade carving enterprise, which was actually his house on Revell Street, so Tank could fuel his jewellery-making aspirations. I spent almost the entire time in bed, or sleeping on the settee in front of Gordon's blazing fireplace like a skinny white cat, and the next morning we reached the spectacular Franz Jozsef Glacier. I took some impressive photos and learnt that it was moving at a distance of 1½ metres per day, which is some speed when you consider that natural landmarks don't really move very quickly at all. German geologist Julius Von Haast claimed the glacier for the Austrian emperor Franz Jozsef in 1865.

I walked the long approach path, which made the glacier appear deceptively close, in the biting icy winds that whipped off the Waiho River and inspected the gleaming facade with amazement. The glacier is 12km long and 200 metres above sea level, and as I watched people climbing various parts, its gargantuan form was put into perspective by the miniscule black dot of a helicopter flying overhead. Leaving Westland National Park, I knew I'd seen something special but there was more to come at the Fox Glacier and especially Lake Matheson, which reflects beautifully the bona fide king of the Southern Alps, Aoraki Mount Cook, 12km away. Aoraki is of course the Maori name, which means 'cloud piercer' and perfectly sums up the 3,724 metre peak. It was a clear day and so we had the best view of its western face, the side that Tom Fyfe, George Graham and Jack Clarke scaled on Christmas Day 1894 to complete its first successful ascent. The Southern Alps, which include the slightly smaller Mount Aspiring and Mount Earnslaw, were used as a training ground of sorts for Sir Edmund Hilary, in preparation for his assault on Mount Everest, which itself is almost three times the height of Mount Cook. The drive to the wonderfully serene town of Haast was a joy amongst such scenery. It was like leafing through a photo album of postcard scenes, of enormous crystal clear lakes protectively surrounded by dense mountainside forests.

We made for Queenstown, the South Island's extreme sports capital, and passed through the Gates of Haast, presumably modelled on the Gates of Hell, such was the prevailing sense of foreboding that overcame me. On the route south, we stopped at another tourist attraction, this time man-made, in the form of Stuart Landsborough's Puzzling World in Wanaka. It was home to many famous optical illusions but most intriguing of all was the display in the foyer that explained the challenge thrown down by Landsborough to any self-proclaimed psychics. They, or any member of the public for that matter, are invited to find a substantial amount of money hidden within a 100 metre radius of the sign I was reading, in exchange for a $10,000 fee that Landsborough, or rather his daughter Heidi and husband Duncan, who were now in charge, would donate to charity. So far Landsborough's money is safe and the charities are doing well too. In other words, no 'psychics' had been successful. As publicity stunts go, it's not bad, is it? It was also the site of the world's first ever 3-D maze.

Landsborough and his wife Jan had set the ball rolling in 1973 with the building of a fairly conventional maze but the attraction was now pulling in 160,000 visitors a year.

Queenstown's Shotover Street provided yet more stunning views, especially from the kitchen of our immaculate YHA hostel. It looked out onto Lake Wakatipu, which was swarming with water skiers, power boaters and kayakers, and was all presided over by more mountainous territory. I was planning to kayak around the lake but decided to wait until we got to Milford Sound the next day. This was an insane idea as the water was almost too rough for the boat to go out, let alone a virgin kayaker.

We coasted past Bowen Falls, Mount Kimberley and through the 'gates' that were accidentally discovered by Welshman John Grenholm when his ship was blown the 15km inland from the open sea and then through them in a storm. He was about to turn back and when we got further out to sea I could see why. Its dark rock formation gave the impression of a solid wall all the way round. Grenholm named it for his homeland's Milford Haven as he thought it a safe enough place to land, reckoning without the natives that is. It felt like we'd been transported to some epic historical film set so it was no surprise when the guide explained that Peter Jackson had filmed some parts of the Lord Of The Rings trilogy not far south of where we were. Returning to the dock, we coasted by the lighthouse at the mouth of the entrance to the Tasman Sea where some of the cliffs were as high as 1,200 metres and so close we could barely see the top of them.

We were lucky enough for the clouds to lift as we sailed by, but they did so slowly, making the photos all the more dramatic as they formed a perfect ring, like a giant hoopla around the mountains, before drifting away. Milford Sound was a five hour round trip from Te Anau, where we were staying, but even that turned out to be a pleasure as it took us through mountain underpasses and across New Zealand's highest motorway.

Our last stop on the return leg to Christchurch was in Oamaru, a pleasant enough seaside town on the east coast, complete with 'Penguin Crossing' signs. One of Oamaru's more famous, or infamous residents, as well as the aforementioned 'Wizard' was Shiner Eddie, a 'swagger', or tramp basically, who would wander the area, covering some 50km a day, looking for work and telling stories. He is apparently remembered fondly today as an intelligent gentle giant, 6ft 5' in fact, but I bet in the 1930s he wasn't so popular if his photo was anything to go by. He looked every inch the hobo. The photo hung in the room of Swaggers Backpackers, another house stay that we had to ourselves.

We made it back to Christchurch and returned the car with ten minutes to spare. We'd covered around 1,000km, minus our cross-country journeys, of New Zealand's 15,000km of coastal road, in five days. I was glad to be out of the car but not so glad to be back in Christchurch, where we spent another few days before flying to Auckland.

Sydney is everything Auckland is not. It has a better bridge, better harbour, better sky tower, better weather, better Queen Street, and a better casino. Auckland ploughs on nonetheless. Another city, another

Base hostel, this time on Fort Street, which backed onto Waitemata harbour, but everywhere else seemed to be uphill from there. Auckland, called Tamaki Makau Rau by the Maoris, which means 'maiden with a hundred lovers' and refers to the abundance in food and materials that were constantly fought over by their forefathers, rests calmly on volcanic rock, in the centre of which is Mount Eden. The hostel contained the luxury of a spa on the roof, which made for an unusual experience as I sat in it, surrounded by skyscrapers as the sun began to set. It was there I thought about something Marcha, a Dutch girl, had said over breakfast that morning.

"I see all these huge buildings but I don't see the people to match them," she mused. I knew what she meant. Everyone seemed to be bustling around the place but never really getting anything done.

Tank took off to Rotorua for a few days, the real Hell's Gate according to George Bernard Shaw, who visited in 1906, but I hung around the capital, having lost the impetus to do anything but lie in the sun all day, which I would do a week later in Fiji. In the meantime I walked around Auckland, and out to the Harbour Bridge, through the affluent suburbs of St Mary's Bay, which the bridge, opened in 1959, links to the city's Northern Shore district. With the bright sun out, I could have been back in Australia, although not one of Auckland's 1.3 million residents would thank me for the comparison, given the rivalry of the two nations. Those 1.3 million people, most of whom are part of the Polynesian population, make up as much as a quarter of New Zealand's entire population, despite the country being around the size of the UK. The country's big draw is extreme sports; Auckland is home to AJ Hackett's Harbour Bridge Bungee Experience, which means for a reasonable fee you can be thrown off the bridge from a height of 130ft. Hackett is as close to a modern day national hero in New Zealand as you're likely to get and his craze, started officially back in the 1980s from Queenstown's Kawarau Bridge, has since taken off across the globe and spawned no end of extreme pursuits. For the more reserved, mountain bikes were available from most hotels and hostels should you fancy a good old-fashioned pedal. Queen Street was a hotbed of street performers and on any storefront you could see a wealth of musicians performing with a variety of instruments, always in their own designated spot. Luke Hurley for example, the undisputed king of Auckland's buskers would always be outside either Starbucks, on the corner of Victoria Street East, or on the opposite side of the road at the Westpac building. Luke was so well known that he even received an invite to the 41st Annual New Zealand Music Awards that took place in Aotea Square, where he got as good a reception as anyone, and that includes the hugely popular Fat Freddie's Drop, who also turned out for the occasion. I watched all the comings and goings of the awards ceremony from the square as the red carpet was rolled out and the guests began to arrive in the late afternoon.

The showpiece occasion had opened with a performance from Boyband, who were presumably a spoof, judging by the reception they received. By their own admission, there was a 'fat one', a 'gay one', a 'baby-faced one' etc; and all the criteria were met. Even more in keeping with manufactured boy bands, they couldn't sing a note, proved beyond doubt during a soul-blunting asphyxiation of Def Leppard's Pour Some Sugar On Me, and neither could they dance, especially 'baby face' who appeared to have his brain in back to front. Everyone enjoyed themselves though, especially the dance troupe of teenage girls, who were much more watchable than the main attraction.

As at all good award ceremonies, there was an endless supply of free coke – of the canned variety – and chocolate. With such hospitality in mind, I considered blagging my way in to the main hall but wasn't dressed for the occasion so instead stood outside watching limousines, and one hovercraft, dispensing 'celebrity' guests one after another. With the exception of Fat Freddie's Drop, I hadn't heard of any of the performers, the majority being the US style hip-hop entourages that are so popular with the youth of New Zealand, and that scourge of shopping centres the world over: emo bands. Hordes of kids had descended on Aotea Square and they'd all brought along their miserable emotive baggage. It's not that them being downbeat bothers me, these words come from the pen of a Smiths fan after all, it's just that they're so damn ugly, and this lot were wearing jeans so tight you could see the faces of their unborn children. By now the crowd had taken it upon themselves to provide their own entertainment. This involved one youth, who had one foot in the emo camp and one in a Ramones tribute band, shouting the name of his band into the presenter's microphone every time she passed, which pissed her off no end as the whole thing was being broadcast live on local radio. All I could gather from his distorted howling was that his band were called something like Rapists Of The Undead and were available for weddings, funerals and bar mitzvahs.

I went to the Globe bar for the free sausage sizzle – which I correctly assumed was a BBQ – advertised at the CCB Backpackers but I was fifteen minutes late, which meant there was nothing left. I slumped in the corner with a pair of pints feeling sorry for myself. I'd spent up and was run down but managed to slip into the Base bar for the pool competition, losing in the final just to confirm my luck wasn't about to change. In the first round, I played a South African girl called Kim who worked as a receptionist on Queen Street, despite her friend trying to put me off my shots as only a woman could. Over a drink afterwards, Kim, who I'd already noticed was wearing an engagement ring and drinking from two bottles at once, told me that her fiancé in Cape Town was a pearl diver who couldn't speak a word of English. Not so unusual at first look but she didn't speak a word of Afrikaan.

"It's greeaaat," she said. "It means we can say what we like when we argue, yaar."

She was far gone from the booze and so excited/drunk she required sedating/sectioning.

"I sleep with a knife under my pillow," she warned in all seriousness, pointing one of her bottles in my face. "You wanna' know why, ey?"

She answered before I could. "Because I'm from Cape Town. If anyone tries to rape me in my sleep, and you know the kind of people I mean in Cape Town, eh?"

I did.

"I cut their fucking balls off if they come near my family. That is why I live here, not just for work but because it is safer. But soon I will go back, because of my fiancé. Otherwise I stay here in Auckland. And you?" she asked, smiling again.

On my last day in Auckland, I walked to the Victoria Park Markets and found nothing of interest but an art gallery and a walk of fame: hand and footprints of notable New Zealanders like those gallant Knights of the Empire, Edmund Hilary and Richard Hadlee. The gallery was exhibiting the work of Aidan Law and one piece caught my eye. It was an image of around thirty identical cowboys on identical horses all waving lariats and heading in the same direction on a backdrop of stars, but it was the title that got my attention. It was called Stronger Than Batman, Superman And The Incredible Hulk Combined: a snip at $1,200.

I popped into MIANZ (Musical Institute Of Auckland New Zealand) and procured a pair of free earplugs, which were for artists only apparently, after telling the receptionist that I was "with the band in studio two downstairs". She handed them over without interrogation and I continued my trespassing at Auckland's Technical Institute, in search of free Internet use. I soon found it in the library, where a lesson was taking place, and went undetected, despite being a) the only person in the class not Chinese, b) more tellingly I thought, the only person in the class not wearing a school uniform, and c) 6ft 2', and therefore twice as tall as my new classmates.

It was late when I left as I walked back down Queen Street and I couldn't resist a snoop round the Sky Tower Casino complex on the corner of Hobson and Victoria Streets. I stood in on a big stakes poker tournament before getting comfortable at a 'pokie', where I won $31 from my initial $3 stake but was distracted by a Sri Lankan woman trying to sell me an 'action card'. Her sales pitch completely fell apart when she heard my accent and was punctuated by schoolgirl giggles thereafter but I wasn't having an 'action card' whatever happened. After she left, she kept peeping round the sides of the fruit machines at me. On the way out, I laid $5 on black on a roulette table that had produced six reds on the spin; then seven.

Back on the street, I bumped into another busker, this time playing harmonica.

I introduced myself and sat down beside Eric as he rested his lungs. We sat outside Burger King, him figuring he might appeal to the hungry Kiwis. It hadn't worked so far. He'd made about $5.

"Not so bad in a half hour," he said defensively, "…enough for something to eat."

He was down on his luck and wore a grubby, burgundy tracksuit, and a pair of scuffed leather moccasins. Above his strained face sat a grey pencil-sharpener haircut. He carried the air of a man with a life of self-inflicted hardship.

The $5 sat apologetically in a little plastic bucket, in the bottom of which he'd written, rather lamely I thought: 'THE STATE HAS MY DAUGHTER'. He'd been a music teacher and played various instruments he said, but his present venture involved him obtaining the land rights of a disused quarry and turning it into a concert hall. I blew out an improvised Scottish reel type song on my harmonica as he took a break. As I began to run out of steam, he threw a coin at my feet. I still have it. It proves I once earned a living as a busker.

At one point, Eric produced from his inside pocket, as one might a biro, a giant biro. It was one of those enormous luminous pink and green plastic ones, about a foot high, that only a child would be entertained by.

"What's that?" I asked, somewhat amazed, but not entertained. I knew what it was, I just had to make sure a grown man was using one.

"It's my pen," he said, and began to write.

I fled to the safe haven of O'Connors, the Irish bar on Vulcan Avenue, for some slightly more accomplished live music and extortionately-priced Guinness, all accompanied by a bunch of Germans dancing themselves into a state of semi-consciousness.

I woke up the next morning just ten minutes before check-out time, frantically stuffed everything into my bag and ran down to reception so as not to incur a fine as 'late fees apply'. I checked out just in time and then sneaked back up for breakfast and a shower, which wasn't easy as I now had no room key and had to take my backpack into the shower with me! The cubicle was just big enough though for me to be able to leave it in the corner out of water's way but showering with luggage is never convenient. On the way out, I snatched a handful of leaflets on Fijian accommodation. I didn't bother booking any accommodation in Fiji. I preferred turning up unannounced and Fiji was the best place to do it. There would be no stuffy desk clerks or jobsworth security guards, just smiling, brown-skinned women, with frangipani in their hair.

CHAPTER 13:
FIJI

A violent altercation with some furniture salesmen
and threatened with a cricket bat – how very English –
in the most relaxed community on earth.

"When I saw three burly Fijians appear, I knew I was in trouble."

A month before I left England, I took a look at some of my intended destinations using Google Earth. After I'd looked for my house and local pub, I typed in Nadi, which, until I planned my itinerary, I'd never even heard of. The globe rotated slowly, adding to my trepidation. It stopped directly above what turned out to be Suva, Fiji, before closing in on Nadi itself. It was barely there, but still more so than my next two destinations, Rarotonga in the Cook Islands and Papeete in Tahiti. All were miniscule specks in the island minefield of the Pacific Ocean and soon I would find myself amongst them. It was unnerving to think that I would be that remote, but more exciting than anything else. Even now, some of the places still maintain an almost mythical status amongst people who have never visited them. The South Pacific is home to the Enewetak and Bikini Atolls of the Marshall Islands, which the American government of the 1950s deemed the perfect place for a nuclear explosion drill. It includes Micronesia, home to the Mariana trench, at 11,022 metres the lowest known point on earth, and further east Hawaii, resting place of Captain Cook and site of Mauna Kea, technically the tallest mountain on the planet at 33,480ft, with 13,796ft of it underwater. Hawaii also boasts the world's largest volcano, Mauna Loa, and the most active, Kilauea. Southeast of Hawaii sits Pitcairn Island, but that's a whole other book.

The dull Fijian skyways, combined with the jetlag, left us feeling somewhat downcast on arrival, but we could still feel the heat of the sun, even if we couldn't see the thing itself.

"The sun is shining in Suva. Is capital city. I take you there. Only ten minutes," offered our enterprising taxi driver.

"Suvas a hundred kilometres away, mate. What are we gonna do, teleport?" I asked.

"Okay. Okay, twenty minutes to get there," he reasoned.

"We're goin' 'ere, mate. Alright?" I said, jabbing at one of the leaflets I'd picked up in Auckland.

On it was a picture of the Wailoaloa Beach area, a haven for backpackers as it contained seven hotels or hostels within a quarter mile radius. All of them were inexpensive, especially with the exchange rate at FJD 3.12 to the English pound. The first place I tried was fully booked until the next day so we tried the Escape Resort around the corner based on nothing else but the friendliness of the staff, which is a staple of all Fijian hospitality.

We were greeted at the gate by Arko, the landlady, who in true Fijian style was in no hurry to take money from us, instead simply gesturing towards our rooms with that familiar Fijian wave we would come to know so well, accompanied by the only phrase you may ever need out there, 'sega na lega', 'no worries'. I had a room and the best part of the guesthouse to myself, including the non-existent cooking facilities advertised on the leaflet. I hardly saw Barbara, the Tahitian fashion designer/tattoo artist who I was sharing with, as she was usually coming in just as I was going out and vice versa.

It was ideal, with just a handful of guests and Freddie, the waiter, running around introducing everyone to each other. It was Freddie who introduced us to Wayne, another tattoo artist, from Dublin. It was his second visit, having done the backpacker circuit a couple of years earlier. He followed almost the same route as us and was killing time before moving on to the US a few days later. Like every Irishman I've ever met, he didn't need a second invitation to join us for a drink on our first night piss up, and also to celebrate Diwali.

Wayne had some great Irish drinking stories: being thrown out of a party at Colin Farrell's house, his scrapes with the IRA, and spying on Robbie Williams and Andrea Corr at his local delicatessen, which is not a drinking story at all, more a stalking story. He gave us a bottle of 58% proof headache-flavoured rum that someone else had palmed off on him during his stay and that had been given to them in the first place, like some sort of liquid heirloom. We broke with tradition and regrettably drank it. It was that new time-saving alcohol developed by scientists that does away with the making a complete tit of yourself part – which we did anyway – and cuts straight to the hangover.

Luckily we'd thought ahead and already fortified ourselves with fourteen bottles of Fijian lager and a steak dinner, which put us in good stead to go and watch the bonfire on the beach that never materialised. Every day of our stay we were promised a bonfire. "It's for Diwali," someone said, but we never saw one. At Smugglers Cove, the party was jumping thanks to the NSW Coonamble Cockerels football team. If you've ever been lucky enough to be invited backstage at a Motley Crue gig you can easily picture the scene. The assistant coach, Silky, was leading by example by jumping fully clothed into the swimming pool and dragging in a couple of equally dressed girls who may or may not have minded.

It was too late of course, they were in there with nothing to keep them afloat but a crate of XXXX. By now I'd turned my attention to a group of girls sitting on the beach, as had Chris, another guest over from Escape. It was a weird scene, with maybe a dozen pretty girls all sitting in a circle in the moonlight with glitter in their hair and stars on their faces. Returning from the bar, and looking from a distance, it looked like a scene from The Wicker Man, but with a Dutch porn star, Chris, in the Edward Woodward role. We made some small talk with the girls, who turned out to be from Adelaide, while a man sitting on a log not far away kept a watch on proceedings. Every so often I caught him in my eye line. I thought Chris might have established a mean age for the girls by now but not so, so we were all the more surprised when one of them announced that they were having a lovely time on their school trip but their teacher, who was sitting on a log not far away, said they had to go.

Chris and I looked at each other then stood up at the same time, wiping sand from our clothes. Then we edged away slowly.

Later on at the bar, an exasperated woman came marching out of a room in her nightgown and asked me if I could keep the noise down as people were trying to sleep. The crucial thing to remember here is we were in a bar. At that point, the barman leaned over to tell me that the room she came from was actually one of the dorms, which opened directly into the bar! There had to have been a major misunderstanding amongst the architects. Why the girl had singled me out, I've no idea. Did I look, or sound, like a motorised dinghy, or a firework, or a rugby coach jumping into a swimming pool?

Silky went on to threaten a police car with a cricket bat we'd all autographed earlier in the night, thus inadvertently incriminating us all, before making good his escape by commandeering the aforementioned dinghy that was moored just off the beach. Naked.

Tank had been buttonholed by an older local woman who was banging on about her Scottish heritage, and I by a couple of local girls, Peko, the dark-eyed denizen of Nadi bay, and her friend Sani, who were high on Kava. Peko reminded me of Jacinta: wide eyes, sable skin, and an inability to comprehend my accent. She managed to explain that she was from Fongafale, which is one of the islands that make up Tuvalu. We sat on the beach chatting in broken English, although I found it hard to concentrate as I was using every last ounce of my brainpower in willing Sani to disappear, which seemed to work as a few minutes later she simply keeled over on the sand. Peko didn't flinch; apparently it's a regular occurrence, and probably Kava related.

I suspected it wasn't the done thing for local girls to be seen mixing socially with foreign visitors so I had half a mind to get off the beach. Earlier in the day, I'd noticed a pontoon somewhere along the shoreline, with a battered old skiff bumping against it on the gentle Pacific waves. I could just make it out now from my position on the beach, as it was lit by a dim string of bulbs from the pontoon. I made a quick check over my shoulder to see if anyone was around – the resort was considerably quieter since Silky had been hit with a tranquiliser dart, and probably an autographed cricket bat – then leaned forward and whispered in her ear.

"Do you like sailing?" I asked. As ridiculous as it sounded, I was feeling pretty pleased with myself at how corny it was, especially as there was a boat conveniently bobbing just behind her, and allowed myself a little smile. I imagined Leslie Phillips using a similar line. I subtly cocked my head towards the pontoon, which was a fair stroll away, and at the same time thought about the effects of the Kava on Sani. She was still flat out but we were near the bar so she was in safe hands. I think.

Peko was smiling as she stood up and took a few steps towards the boat, leaving a trail of little Tuvaluan footprints that eventually intermingled, and then became lost, in my big English ones.

I enjoyed my time in Fiji but could never fully relax as I was always thinking about my financial situation, which was dire, despite the exchange rate. I thought about it a lot as I lay on the beach, surrounded by crabs that scuttled out of the sea at dusk, and stray horses, goats, and mosquitoes. I played out this routine – swimming, lunch, swimming, sunbathing, supper – everyday, occasionally going into town for a change of pace. By the third day, I'd moved over the road and into a cattle shed of a room, which I loved.

The room had no light bulbs or air-con, and no locks, just twenty beds where everybody, guest, animal, or otherwise, invited or not, came and went as they pleased. Despite this, I was still able to leave my passport and flight tickets under my bed without any fear of them being stolen. Digital cameras, personal stereos and musical instruments were just some of the many valuables strewn around the place. Nobody cared; it was too hot. All I was paying for was somewhere to lie down at night as I was over at one of the other hotels for the most part, either dining or using their facilities, and nobody seemed to mind.

There was little need for a police presence either, so much so that the local holding cell consisted of a caravan moored on the edge of town. It was emblazoned with the word 'police' in blue letters along one side, such was the level of law enforcement required. The local supermarket was a Guantanamo Bay style compound, fenced off and guarded by a pack of ferocious dogs. You couldn't go in, instead you simply told the shopkeeper, or more often than not his ten-year-old son, what you wanted, and then passed him the money through a hole in the fence. Then he would go inside and invent a vastly inflated price for the goods before returning with none of the items you asked for. A trip into the town centre, around four miles away, was the best bet. When it bothered to turn up, you could catch a ramshackle bus, but only twice a day, that would take you to the main drag, consisting mainly of souvenir stores and restaurants. No sooner had I stepped off the bus than I was accosted by a persistent Indian shopkeeper who introduced himself as Praba and then pursued me all the way down the street whilst explaining to me the laws and customs of his home village in India.

Soon though, we ran out of road, the tourist area faded away, and I was unsure of my surroundings but sensing that I shouldn't have been there. The street ended with a left turn just at the edge of the known world, the only other options being the tourist information office across the road, or an unwelcoming alleyway. I immediately ruled out the tourist information office as there was a formidable man outside who turned out to be in cahoots with my new Indian friend. He seized my hand as I tried to keep calm and think of an excuse without appearing rude.

"My friend, you must come to my shop. It is only here," he insisted, gesturing towards the alleyway. "I make ornaments for you to buy."

We walked fifty yards or so down the alley then turned right, where, on the second floor of the building before us stood his much promised store, the generically named Fijian Handicrafts. Maybe I was being a bit paranoid in thinking he wanted to remove my kidneys and sell them on the Black Market. I was still apprehensive about the fact that we had to climb stairs to get to it though. A metal staircase on the outside of the building led us to a balcony, and eventually, the shop's outer office part. As I walked along the balcony, all I was thinking about was jumping the rail and landing on the roof of one of the parked cars beneath us, which looked to be something like a 30ft drop. The balcony was barely wide enough for two people to pass so when I saw three burly Fijians appear from the store, I knew I was in trouble. Praba introduced us all as we exchanged handshakes.

"He has come to hear the legend of the sleeping giant," Praba said to them, referring to me. They all nodded sagely before one of them muttered something in Fijian, at which the others all laughed. Praba then ushered me into the store, urging me to remove my shoes first. Praba sat cross-legged in the middle of the floor and produced a battered copy of the Fijian Lonely Planet. I sat opposite him as two of his cronies blocked the doorway. The other man went into the workshop and returned moments later with a hand-carved pick-axe that was sure to be embedded in my skull in the not too distant future. I was surprised then, when he handed it to me for inspection.

Now, I'm no expert on tools but I could see that it was a fine piece of work. Praba began to explain the process involved in its making. This included a demonstration of its submergence in a stew of black swamp water to strengthen it. In true Blue Peter fashion, he reached into the murky water and produced one he'd made earlier. I still had the original one in my hand and was ready to start swinging should the need arise. It would have been quite a way to go: a fight to the death with hand carved pick-axes in a Fijian souvenir store. I quite liked the idea but it didn't come to that. The two 'doormen' entered the shop, leaving my only escape route open as the third man suggested I go with him to another part of the building to collect his business card. Praba was drinking Kava and it had started to take effect.

"You go with him and collect card," he managed to slur.

"I wait here," I said, pointing at the floor, but the man insisted.

"It is just in here. You come."

"No. I will wait right here," I said firmly.

He entered the room alone and I'm sure just stood behind the door for a minute or so before returning empty handed. I was pulling on my shoes as he explained that the business card was locked in the draw. Could I come through and wait while he opened it? Could I fuck. He was twice the size of me but turned out to be half as fast so when he seized my left arm and tried to pull me into the other room, I was able to quickly angle towards him and give him what Rocky Marciano called his 'Suzie Q', a right hook that stone laid his opponents out. The impact was so great, it felt as though my arm had sheared off at the elbow but he was a bit tougher than most of the Brockton Blockbuster's opponents. We spun through the doorway like Torville and Dean, accompanied by a shit storm of handcrafted Fijian crockery. It was still corkscrewing around the floor as I grabbed a fistful of brown earlobe and pulled the gargoyle head attached to it fast towards me. I was about to meet it halfway with the sort of impact only previously seen in the Hadron Collider when someone grabbed the back of my collar and tried to yank me up. I managed to finish the head butt but the mystery guest had clean ripped the collar off my t-shirt. When I turned round, he was just staring at the piece of material in his hand. He looked amazed at first, then suddenly remembered we were supposed to be having a fight and I'd just nutted his mate through the floor. I gave my head a swift shake but the new boy was dragging me backwards with both hands under my chin. I gave the first man a quick kick in the baby maker as I slid back through the door, only to be greeted by a good old fashioned boot in the ribs. I let him have that one, I'd earned it, but I made sure I kicked over the bowl of water. This prompted Praba to jump up like a jack-in-the-box. Having been previously unconcerned about the destruction of the shop, he was now fretting about the water on the floor.

"Oh my friend," he said pleadingly, "this is becoming a disaster."

Becoming a disaster?

The other two men outside just laughed heartily at the whole thing, as one should after a good fight. So we were all mates now it seemed. Praba was busying himself with a mop like a stoned clucking housewife and the numb nuts next door was still prostate but showing signs of life. I wheezed as I got up, holding my ribcage.

"What about my fucking shirt?" I shouted, pulling at the remains of the collar. I was still squinting a bit from the head butt when Praba grabbed the collar out of the man's hand and handed it back to me apologetically.

I looked around stunned at all the ornaments. Why hadn't I used the axe?

"I'm not fucking buying anything after that," I said, then I broke into laughter.

It was like the end of an episode of some awful American sitcom, where they all stand around laughing, except the unconscious one on the floor in the next room.

"He okay," said Praba, dismissing him. "He always fighting." Then he extended a handshake.

"You need to work on your customer service skills big time, mate," I said.

"Oh, this very unusual in Fiji, my friend. It never happen before. Very strange."

I let out one more exasperated expletive and picked up the axe for a last look.

"You like?" Praba asked, in a final attempt at a sale.

I laid down the axe and backed out of the door – as the two goons on the balcony comically recreated scenes from the fight – making an excuse about having to meet a friend.

"Where, what time?" enquired Praba, standing up unsteadily.

"Er, down on the street. I must go." I was halfway along the balcony by now, promising I would return, with Praba following me. I crossed the road and entered the tourist information office as the coast seemed clear now that Praba's mate had gone.

Praba crossed the road too but waited outside. Once inside, I told the old woman at the desk I just wanted some leaflets on the island tours.

"Oh but you must sit here," she insisted, pulling out a chair for me.

"Just gimme the leaflets and I'm off," I said. I was really pissed off by now. Just then a big arm fell onto the desk in front of me. It belonged to the suspicious-looking man who'd been hanging around earlier. He began to bark what seemed to be abuse, in Fijian, at the woman. She stood up and waved her arms, as if to shoo him from the office.

Then he spoke in English. "She is a liar. She will charge you the most. She knows nothing. You come with me. Come."

Now I was beginning to understand. He 'saves' me from this old hag, who is probably his mother, or more likely his in-law judging by the way he spoke to her, then lures me to a grisly end, or worse, steals my wallet. I glanced over my shoulder to see that Praba was still outside.

An old Indian man came from the back office to see what was going on. He seemed to be trying to calm the woman but simply laughed and returned to the office at the rear.

"Come with me, my friend. My prices are better and more also."

I think by that he meant there was more variety in the island trips he was offering that I was supposedly looking for, but his 'shop' was even further away. I brushed him aside and crossed the street, again followed by Praba, but I soon faded away, into the crowds, something I'd learnt to do in Thailand if I thought I was being followed.

"You come back with your friend now, English," I heard Praba call. Back at the resort, two newlyweds from Adelaide, Dan and Liz, told me that they had found themselves in the same situation a few days previous but, like myself, had managed to worm their way out of trouble.

In much safer circumstances one evening, and by safer I mean by the pool with a bottle of rum, we were joined by a young couple that had recently arrived. Manu and Sarah were trying to drum up interest in a cruise around some of Fiji's 322 islands, dependent on getting a certain amount of people to go. So far they had had little success as everyone they asked was either short of cash, couldn't be bothered, or both.

Manu's childhood was spent in Zimbabwe and he'd retained the colonial accent that came with it, despite spending a lot of his time in England as a food photographer for various high street stores. He said it was an interesting enough job that led to all kinds of ribbing from anyone he explained it to. One fine example of his accent came one day when I asked if he knew where my roommate Barbara was.

"She's sourcing seamstresses," he chimed.

Sarah was a Bermudan anthropology student and like all American women – yes, I know Bermuda's a UK colony but you know what I mean – she could really talk. She spoke passionately about the subject, which led to us discussing Thor Heyerdahl's Kon-Tiki expedition at great length one evening but arriving at no discernable conclusion, other than that his boat was shit, but that's rum for you. Manu was constantly at pains to point out that he and Sarah were not an item, a subject that came up time and time again because they looked like the perfect couple, as if they'd stepped out of a holiday brochure: both of them fair haired, blue-eyed and equally charming.

"Hey," Sarah shouted one day, even though I was sitting next to her on the bus, "you guys wanna go party with some dignitaries tonight?"

"Y'wha?"

"There's a big political envoy of some sort visiting Suva today. I feel like partying with some dignitaries, don't you?"

She was twirling the frangipani in her hair as the bus belched thick smoke through the windows and into everyone's faces.

I pictured us all bowling into the Friendly Isles' conference room with a head full of rum each and causing a major diplomatic incident that would have our respective embassies running for cover.

"What about the dress code?" I asked, looking as I did at the time, like Dude Lebowski.

"Oh, gee, well I guess… er, hmmm. I don't know," she mused.

"Plus I don't have much pull in the field of South Sea politics," I added.

"Oh well. Maybe I'll still go."

Only someone with such a sunny disposition would come up with such a proposition. It was hard not to get taken away with it but I never did find out if they managed to make the boat trip as they were still chipping away at people when we left for Rarotonga.

Everyone seemed to be heading the same way, onto the States or maybe Tahiti first, from Fiji, and then making their way across to New York from LA, and always via Las Vegas. At Hollywood's Globe Hostel weeks later, Failem, who we'd previously bumped into in New Zealand and Fiji, showed up again, after a trip up from Tijuana, but my most amazing chance encounter involved Manu. A fortnight after we left Fiji, we flew into LA. One Saturday afternoon, I was heading north up West Hollywood's La Brea Avenue. Waiting at the crossroads at Santa Monica Boulevard, I was almost speechless to see him walking west to east at the lights. He was one of two people, the other being Tank, in a city with a population of fifteen million, that I knew, and there he was, right in front of me. He was as shocked as I was.

"You've caught me with one foot off the sidewalk here," he said, mixing his colloquialisms.

A broad "fuckin' hell" was all I could manage by way of a greeting.

"I'm on my way to a volleyball game if you fancy it," he said wearily "but I'm a bit worse for wear." This was the most preposterous invite I'd ever received.

"I'm hung over as well. I think I'll give it a miss," I said. Earlier I'd vomited into a plastic bag, well, some of it went into the bag, on the corner of Spaulding and Willoughby, in full view of passing motorists and disinterested dog walkers. Not one of them gave me a second look; it was, after all, Hollywood. On leaving Fiji, Manu had moved in with a girl somewhere off Santa Monica and Sarah had gone on to Samoa. Manu continued along Santa Monica and I along La Brea, slightly incredulous.

Five weeks after leaving Fiji, the government was overthrown for the fourth time in less than twenty years, this time by Commander Frank Bainimarama. Just before the coup took place, I was sitting at a bus stop in Arorangi, Rarotonga, discussing it with an Indian girl who worked in the hotel industry. You know how it is, you're at the bus stop one morning and that old chestnut, the Fijian coup d' etat comes up.

"It is just spear-shaking," she said, unconcerned.

"But you have family still in Fiji, right?"

"Yes. Sometimes I worry for them but the militia will just smash up a few shops maybe and then nothing until the next coup perhaps. It happens all the time."

Tank gave her a 'lucky' coin to protect her from harm, something you could get away with in that part of the world, South Sea islanders being no strangers to superstition.

Fiji's independence from Britain was established on October 10th 1970, but without its UK colonisation, which began in 1874, we probably wouldn't have had that conversation at the bus stop. It was the English who began the influx of Indian inhabitants when they 'recruited' them for cheap labour, most of them going on to make Fiji their home. Now it attracts 500,000 tourists a year to its many surrounding islands, like the Yasawas off the northwest coast of Viti Levu, a chain of giant stepping stones leading you astray into the South Pacific, where Tank caught a fish using a hand line. I include it here as it's his favourite man-versus-nature story.

CHAPTER 14:
THE COOK ISLANDS TO TAHITI

Jungle fever takes hold, George Lucas almost gets run over,
and the good people of France pick up my bar tab.

"Rarotongan mosquitoes are utter bastards
but compared to Tahitian ones are really quite friendly."

In flying to Rarotonga, we crossed the international date-line, which
meant we got to live Saturday all over again; or something like that.

My journal entry for October 27th reads, and it makes even less
sense now than it did at the time: 'I already wrote today's entry two
days ago! And I will have written tomorrow's yesterday. I think'. In
a nutshell: I think I'd gone back in time, which only added to the
mystique of the South Pacific. Giant mosquitoes, hallucinogenic
drinks, triangular coins, time travel; it's all there.

I didn't notice any of this during the flight as Tank and I
were laughing like small children at the in-flight entertainment,
particularly Peter Cook's piano-accompanied account of saving a
man's life by encouraging him to "jump into this 'ere blanket wot
we are holding". Luckily for the easily offended, it was being played
through our headsets. On landing, we moved from one Cook to
another.

Rarotonga is the capital of the fifteen Cook Islands, which
collectively were formerly known as the Hervey Islands. They were
renamed for Cook much later by a Russian party, led by Johann
Von Krusenstem in the 1820s, in order to commemorate the great
man. Cook himself would never have done anything as extravagant
as naming an island after himself. He is not thought to have come
ashore here, choosing instead to land briefly at Palmerston Atoll,
where all the current inhabitants are descended from one William
Marsters. It was the Tahitian, Iro, who tagged it Rarotonga, 'Raro'
meaning down and 'tonga' meaning south, in the language of his

tribe. Its discovery, as is the case with many of the South Sea Islands, is open to debate. Originally thought to have been inhabited around five thousand years ago, this theory was jeopardised in 1997 when a Japanese archaeological team found what turned out to be a marae – an area comprising a small stone monolith used for religious ceremonies – which was said to be 1,500 years old.

Of course the marae could quite plausibly be older than 1,500 years. The mythological story of its origins lie at the feet of a chap by the name of Maui Potiki. He supposedly hooked the island out of the sea one day after casually casting out his fishing line, although I think this theory can be disproved by science. It was however, similar to the New Zealand legend that states how the fish-shaped North Island was pulled from the sea by someone in the 'boat' of the South Island, using Stewart Island as a sort of choc to gain more leverage.

At one point, the Cook Islands was the only territory outside of the US and former Soviet Union, where space flights have returned to earth, this because of its latitude: 6'-23' longitude, 156'-167' latitude, that saw various space forays of the 1960s ending in the Pacific Ocean. Also down there, still to this day, is the wreck of a 1916 ship that struck coral two hundred yards off shore, taking its cargo of Model T-Fords down with it. A piece of the wreck is still clearly visible, rising from the surf like a black ghost, a time capsule of the South Pacific.

We stowed ourselves away in Arorangi, towards the southwest of the island's mere 32km circumference. It was the smallest piece of occupied land I'd set foot on in my life but still pulled in just short of 100,000 visitors annually.

"Kia orana," said the bus driver, handing me a ticket that had a little note on the bottom reminding all passengers to smile. What's not to like about a public transport system that reminds its patrons to smile? Two buses circled the island continuously, clockwise and anti-clockwise, but always seemed to have the same driver. Twins perhaps? When questioned he, or they, always grinned conspiratorially. Instead of riding into town then returning the same way, everyone on board paid a little extra to travel the whole way round to see what they were missing on the other side of the island, but it was equally perfect wherever you went.

It was small enough to up sticks and decamp to another part at a moment's notice though, and travellers on the bus could often be overheard whispering about moving to a whiter beach, or a bluer sea. Our location included a bottle green sea that broke violently off the coral reef around one hundred yards from the beach. The only protection from the sun was beneath the palm trees that lined the entire coast. It was exactly as it could have been thousands of years ago. That's without considering the effects of the new rock'n'roll that is global warming of course. Set back from the beach was the Raemaru track which I sweated my way up one day. A 350 metre yomp to its peak provides panoramic views of almost the entire coastline and nothing but sea and sky beyond that, giving it the impression of being the only place on earth. No matter where you are though, you are never far from home in one form or another; an Australian man walking his dog on the same route wanted to know if Mark Viduka would still be a Middlesbrough player at the end of the season.

The hostel was tucked away in the jungle. At night, the surrounding area was completely silent; probably most people were left speechless after watching the amazing orange and black sunsets from the balcony. The building itself was nothing more than a huge wooden hut on legs, with winged dormitories to its right and left. The centrepiece was the all-in-one kitchen/communal area that overlooked the pool. Soon enough, the place became our own, as the day after we arrived the previous 'long-stayers' had returned to England, leaving just San Franciscan Ben behind. Ben became the elder statesman of the group, otherwise made up of Mancunians Jimmy, Harvey and Dave, another Dave from London, and his girlfriend, and then a handful of others who came and went and only seemed to stay for one day at a time.

Ben also acted as the gopher as he owned a mountain bike so anytime we needed anything he would hop on and roll down the hill, either to the local store or to Tumeke's DVD rental place. By the time we arrived, Ben had amassed a collection of unreturned DVDs bigger than anything Tumeke could offer, the majority of which belonged to Tumeke's. After browning in the sun all day and watching dragonflies bounce off the surface of the pool, we would all limber up for a game of darts on the balcony, which along with chess became one of the two popular pastimes of our stay. When I wasn't playing darts, I was being strategically destroyed across the chessboard by anyone who I played against, usually Ben. The place had all the creature comforts of Fiji, and I mean creature literally: goats in the laundry, lizards in the toilet and winged-frogs – well that's what they looked like – on the balcony. The lizards appeared in droves when the indoor light was switched on at night, thus attracting moths and flies, which were soon made a meal of by the crafty lizards hiding behind picture frames and cupboards. Outside, they would spring from the walls onto the freshly picked banana bunches hung from the awning and nibble away, in the process making them totally inedible to humans as dengue fever-dispensing mosquitoes completed the scene.

Rarotongan mosquitoes are utter bastards but compared to Tahitian ones are really quite friendly. The Tahitian version is said to not so much bite you but instead gnaw you into a state of mild hysteria. I couldn't wait to get there. We decided to use our visit to Papeete, Tahiti's capital, as a stopover on the way to Los Angeles as we found it nigh on impossible to book any accommodation, at a reasonable rate anyway. Trawling the Internet for suggestions, I came across one place that instructed me, should we arrive after hours, which we would do, to head to the house opposite and raise hell in order to disturb the proprietress, a big French Polynesian woman called Mamy. You couldn't gain access until you'd done this apparently, as she was the only person who could check you in. On top of all that, there was the cost of the place to think about too. We eventually extended our stay in Rarotonga, so taken with the place and its people were we. In addition, we didn't want to miss another minute of the island's riveting news bulletins. I soon saw why Tumeke's DVD store was doing such great business. There seemed to be no TV coverage at all until 6pm, which began with the news and weather, followed by either a debate show of some sort and a made-for-TV movie, after which would be a recap of the island's big news.

On a particularly slow day, we learnt that one unfortunate resident had a bilge pump stolen from his garden shed. In other news, some children had attended a school and one man had even gone swimming! In sport, the Fijian woman's rugby sevens team were in town to take on their Rarotongan counterparts. Cue footage of a training session in which two unlikely-looking women in civilian clothing half-heartedly threw a ball around a car park. Then came the weather; according to the Ceefax graphics, a giant marshmallow with a yellow stalk was about to descend upon the island and unleash a torrent of Morse code onto us. Well, that's what it looked like to me. Eventually jungle fever took hold; I was living on a diet of Weetabix and vodka and Tank announced that on returning to England he would be applying online for a lordship. Then Phil returned.

An ex-resident, he'd left to move in with the Venezuelan CEO of a Swiss bank. They seemed an unlikely pairing. Phil was from the blue side of Manchester, and a nice enough bloke, and she was from South America.

"It's great," he told us, for the sixth time that day. "She won't let me lift a finger. Just wants me to save my energy, know what I mean?"

"She fuckin' loco, ey?" I said, in a Spanish accent. "Loco," I repeated, jabbing a finger at the side of my head. "Crazy. All Hispanic women are fuckin' wild, mate. Everyone knows that. Even madder than Mancs."

"Not her, mate," he defended, shovelling reconstituted fish guts in coconut oil into his mouth.

"If she's South American, she's probably worth the hassle though, right?"

"Fuck yeah," he said, nodding deliriously.

Two days later he was lumping his bags up the wooden steps to the balcony.

"I hope that settee's comfortable," he said.

So now there were four Mancunians. Jimmy, Harvey, and Dave were like identikit versions of the friends you have back home. Jimmy was de facto leader: "Sometimes I have to clap my hands to get their attention," he said one day, explaining Harvey and Dave's indecisiveness. Harvey and Dave deliberately wound Jimmy up to entertain themselves. Harvey was originally from Stoke and had met Jimmy and Dave at university, the three of them eventually deciding they were sick of the global young person's staple of the daily grind of dull office jobs, followed by a weekend of partying, before starting again on Monday morning.

Dave had travelled in Australia a few years earlier but seemed to have forgotten everything that might have been useful a second time round, making it a completely new experience of sorts. They'd arrived from San Francisco and were heading the opposite way to us so we filled their heads with all kinds of stories about Australia: man-eating kangaroos, that kind of thing, and like everyone we met who was going to Brisbane, we suggested they stay at Moreton Bay. The three are currently lost in the Outback.

Recklessness on motorbikes turned out to be their speciality, making a mockery of the island's impossible-to-fail motorcycle proficiency test. Rarotongans are some of the friendliest people on earth and have no interest whatsoever in fleecing naïve tourists, as happens elsewhere, so, at the insanely low cost of £7 to rent a moped and £5 to sit the test, they try to make it as easy as possible for you to pass first time. They had their work cut out with Jimmy, Harvey and Dave though. The 'test' consisted of steering said moped in a straight line for roughly three hundred yards before finishing with the devilishly difficult task of riding around a building; so far so easy then. Straight out of the starting gate, Dave swung a sharp left, the absolute opposite of the direction instructed a whole thirty seconds earlier. By the time he caught up with the others, Harvey had fallen victim to what Jimmy later called "a slight bend in the road", resulting in him being trapped under the bike and minus a wing mirror.

He eventually hobbled away with the legendary schoolyard injuries of grazed knees and elbows. Only Jimmy came away with any credibility.

"It's the first time I've been on anything so powerful," added Dave in his defence.

The following day Harvey went head first over the handlebars of Ben's bike.

Looking at our itinerary for the first time in six months, I noticed we were supposed to fly to Tahiti in six hours time, instead of the following day as thought. We rushed to the Air New Zealand office at the airport and were able to extend our stay another three days. We packed and checked out on the Monday afternoon, just before Tank checked the itinerary once more.

"It says 'ere we leave tomorrow. Something to do with the time difference," he informed me.

The time difference was fast becoming the 'fucking van' of the South Pacific. We had messed up again but this time we had nowhere to stay. After a few phone calls, I managed to secure my old bed, Tank saying he would sleep on the settee and pay only half the fee. The landlady agreed but after everyone had gone to bed, he sneaked into one of the many unlocked luxury apartments on the adjoining land.

The following evening we said our goodbyes to everyone for what would be the last time. We wouldn't stay anywhere in the US long enough to get cosy, which was just as I hoped, as we had a lot of ground to cover.

Waiting for our taxi that night, I talked to Ben about living in San Francisco.

"It's so great I moved to Suva in Fiji," he joked. "Used to see a lot of celebrities though. One time I almost ran down George Lucas in my car. He wasn't happy, then in the exact same spot years later I almost hit Jerry Garcia."

When he wasn't trying to wipe out some of America's most creative minds, he was hanging around the recording studio he used to work at, bothering the likes of Sammy Hagar and Grace Slick. Ben had the unmistakable sun-bleached look of a Californian, which was always topped off with an equally bright Bermuda shirt, but he wasn't the typically brash American I'd come to expect at all. I was about to meet plenty of those.

At Papeete's Fa'aa Airport, I could almost taste the heat. With a few hours to kill before our connecting flight, I wandered upstairs to relax, lying down and using my bag as a cushion beneath a model of a Pacific Blue Marlin that was caught nearby in 1986 by Francis Bonnet and Andre Tavarae. It weighed in at a rod-snapping 709 kg (1563 lbs). Unintentionally perhaps, the airport staff had painstakingly recreated the smell of the Marlin in the gents' toilets.

Minding my own business and marvelling at the Marlin, I couldn't help noticing a constant stream of well-dressed, mainly middle-aged travellers filing through what I thought was a fire exit at the far end of the lounge. From where I lay, I couldn't see where it led to. There was only one way to find out. As a small crowd bustled through, I tagged on to the end noticing they were all carrying their flight tickets. I wasn't as I'd left mine with Tank downstairs. Nor was I dressed for the occasion: Converse, three-quarter length trousers, enormous black sunglasses and a filthy slept in, flown in, t-shirt. No matter, I'd struck a blow for skint, hungry, backpackers everywhere. I'd sneaked into the business class lounge. I ghosted past the crowd of people at the front desk as they fished around for passports and tickets, and in the process obscured the receptionist's view of me.

I grabbed a copy of Newsweek and walked into the oak-panel walled treasure trove of the self-serve bar and buffet, hardly believing my luck. I calmly stocked my rucksack with fruit and water for the journey to LA before preparing a platter of some of the finest pastries known to mankind. These I washed down with a broad selection of aperitifs, all at the expense of the French government. I said au revoir to martini, cognac and vodka before a final beer to settle my stomach; c'est la vie. Then I put my feet up and read the A-Z by place name of America's news stories, a good three-quarters of which involved someone breaking the law.

PART V: THE USA

CHAPTER 15:
LOS ANGELES

House hunting with Mickey Zee, shooting hoops, and guns (almost) with the Rollin' 50s gang, and hanging out at Melrose Place.

"Penelope Pitstop was coasting along in the next lane in a pink Camaro."

We walked out of LAX Airport and onto the world's biggest film set. I felt like I'd been shoved on stage from the wings and told to do something entertaining. We drove to the hostel on the corner of Melrose and Fairfax, under what the American Lung Association deemed to be the country's most polluted sky in 2006, passing Pamm's Diner on the way. Samuel L Jackson and John Travolta were nowhere to be seen however and my attention turned back to the nicotine yellow skyline that loomed heavy over the city's twenty-seven freeways.

Now I was in America, I could do what Americans did and in no time I was pacing around impatiently waiting for the squawking Cyndi Lauper lookalike to get off the hostel phone.

"Hey lady, move it along a little, huh. I gotta call a guy in Vegas already."

Everyone at the hostel kept themselves to themselves and comprised of two groups: backpackers, and people on the fringes of the film industry, or so it seemed, the latter being so self-absorbed and hell-bent on superstardom that they had little interest in anything but themselves.

"There's a guy from the West Hollywood area. I think he's one of those wannabe actor types or something. He organises tours and all that," I'd overheard Dave's girlfriend say, back in Rarotonga. She was correct on all three counts. As he kept on reminding us in his rapid-fire Jewish delivery, Mickey Zee had worked with 125 bands, including Slayer and Dishwallah, in his thirty year career, mainly as lighting director for their stage shows through his company First Phase. When he wasn't illuminating rock stars, he worked as a gopher for various film studios – James Cameron is very fussy about his egg whites apparently – and did voiceover work on something called The Recyclers.

"It was big over in Japan and kinda cool," he claimed. Isn't everything big over in Japan? Like everyone in Hollywood, he had a story about Dustin Diamond – "Jerk pulled a knife on me one time but we're still buddies" – and talked a mile a minute, which was useful for an LA tour guide as there's so much to see. Occasionally he would get distracted from the job in hand. On a busy freeway passing the Staples Centre, he carved up traffic in his people carrier whenever he could.

"Hey fuck you, asshole. So you're driving a Chevy, who gives a fuck, you fucking jackass," he bawled once, before drowning himself out by thumping the horn, the soundtrack to American driving.

"Woah, take it easy, man," I suggested, using a bit of the local vernacular.

"I lived here for forty years, man. I drive however the fuck I… Hey guys, look, there's the Staples Centre right over there. Lemme tell you right now, Andrew Bynum's gonna fuckin' destroy teams that come here. Hottest property in the NBA, you guys." He took a swig on his $1 soda. "This'll last you all day, lemme tell you. A buck for a can this size. Can you believe that, huh? I fuckin' love this city."

Thundering down Cahuenga Boulevard, he stuck his head out of the window.

"Hey lady," he shouted down from the cab into the polluted wind.

Penelope Pitstop was coasting along in the next lane in a pink Camaro. She looked up.

"Hey lady, you gotta trim off your front tyre missing," Mickey pointed out.

"Yeah, I know, honey," she shouted.

"I know a place on Gregory and Vine. Right by Paramount y'know. Good deals for a chick like you. Fix that right up."

"Yeah? I'll check it out. Thanks."

Mickey turned his attention back to the road ahead and the woman tore off down Santa Monica Boulevard.

"People say a bunch of stuff about this place," said Mickey as we drove along West and Slauson, South Central, a stone's throw – no pun intended – from the spot where Rodney King was beaten senseless by the LAPD in 1992, triggering the riots. "But if you think places like Inglewood are bad, you should go to St Louis. Man, that's the roughest city in the whole goddamn country, lemme tell you guys. One time I scored some weed out there. I was feeling pretty damn good about it too. I opened the bag though, lemme tell ya, fucking pencil shavings. Jeez, can you believe that, huh?"

"You still smoked 'em tho, right?" I asked.

"Yeah, sure I did, I fuckin' paid for 'em, didn't I? Hey yous guys, now's a good time to score weed, right here in South Central. I know a guy, Eddie Love, runs with the Rollin' 50s gang. I'm just about the only white guy in this whole damn city who can drive through this neighbourhood so it'll be cool. The place ain't so bad, check out Budlong Avenue," he said, waving an arm out of a dangerously low window.

Despite Mickey's reassurance, Compton was proclaimed the fourth most dangerous city in the US in 2006 and is home to 22,000 Latino gang members. On the flip side, the affluent Ladera Heights district is one of the wealthiest African - American neighbourhoods in the country. I stared down Budlong Avenue to see a long street lined with enormous palm trees that sprouted from the tarmac on either side, creating its symmetrical appearance. Moving along, I saw the occasional pair of eyes following us from the porches of the houses. We must have stood out, Jewish Mickey driving an SUV full of white backpackers. He stopped soon after and summoned two youths. He had to stop as the two boys were playing basketball in the road. He seemed to know them. Despite him calling them to the vehicle, they didn't move from the pavement, instead folding their arms defensively.

"Hey you guys," Mickey shouted, "where's ma man, E-Love?"

He was referring to Mr Edward Love of the Rolling 50s.

"Where you think, man?" one of them shouted.

"He's inside?" Mickey guessed.

"Yuh."

"Ah jeez. You guy's are cool tho', huh?"

"Yuh," said one of them, breaking into a smile as the other made a gun shape with each hand, pointed them at us, and grinned. Mickey leaned over his driver's seat.

"Hey, you guys wanna play some basketball with these guys right now?" he asked. We all looked at each other then swung our heads left to right at the same time.

Mickey cracked a toothy grin.

"Hey guys, it's cool," he insisted, then swinging out of the window again, "Hey, these guys can play ball, right?" he asked, pointing at us.

"Yuh," said the gun-handed pair. Still no takers. The ball boys hadn't moved since we arrived. They just stood silently, looking at us with their heads, and probably their concealed weapons, cocked, as they fiddled with the hems of their Lakers vests.

"Okay guys, let's roll," said Mickey.

In 1886, Desmond and Daeida Wilcox purchased 160 acres of land just west of the Cahuenga Pass in the Hollywood hills for the sole purpose of growing oranges. In the fifty years that followed, Hollywood as we now know it, the epicentre of the film industry, was spawned. In 1903, the first of what came to be known as 'nickelodeons', the Electric cinema, opened. Soon after, filmmakers descended upon this land of milk and honey and in no time, the 'big five' – MGM, Paramount, Fox, Warners and RKO – were household names. Previously, the popular silent films of Laurel and Hardy and Mack Sennett were produced in the city's Echo Park district but they got wise to where the action was and ran for the hills.

When people like Chaplin, DW Griffiths, and Douglas Fairbanks Jnr arrived, things really took off. By the time Cecil B DeMille showed up, the seeds of the star system were sown. The famous sign on Mount Cahuenga, which until 1949 read 'HOLLYWOODLAND' in 30ft wide and 50ft high letters, became one of the world's most famous landmarks, and the Hollywoodland Real Estate Group office that brokered the deal for the land still stands in the Cahuenga foothills. And what stories those hills could tell. Failed Welsh actress Peg Entwhistle jumping to her death from the letter 'H' in 1932. Jim Morrison and James Dean racing up and down Laurel Canyon. Errol Flynn injecting his oranges with vodka to see him through his tennis games. Jack Nicholson's sedate little tea parties. Mick and Keith stumbling out of the single most partied-at place on the west coast – according to Mickey – the Rainbow Bar and Grill. The late suppers at Hef's mansion, and the opulence of the Coconut Grove club on Wilshire Boulevard, with its crystal chandelier-lined pavements.

Every last inch of the city screamed celebrity and there's hardly a square yard of land that doesn't have some sort of connection with the entertainment industry. Its history makes it a hideous place though, attracting hustlers, chancers, wannabees, could-have-beens, should-have-beens, failures, junkies, beggars, vagrants, buskers, barkers, gamblers, fakes, phoneys, fuck-ups and femme fatales, every one of them on the make.

There was an interesting contrast of the showbiz world when I visited Hollywood Boulevard, the old guard and the new within yards of each other. Tony Bennett was in town, singing and swinging at the Kodak Theatre to celebrate his birthday. Next door at Grauman's, Jack Black was premiering his long-awaited Tenacious D film, In The Pick Of Destiny. I sniffed around the Kodak, Bennett's show was of course sold out, before shuffling across the street to talk to some Hispanic girls queuing for tickets to Jimmy Kimmel Live, the latest noise in America's late night talk show battle.

"We sit here for all the night and then we get tickets for tomorrow's show," said the motherly leader. All the others giggled and then chattered away in Spanish.

"Who's on?" I asked.

"P Diddy and Aaron Carter."

On hearing this, the girls became hysterical.

"You can wait with us," one of them offered, amidst the laughter.

I left them to it and approached the doorman.

"How'd I get tickets for the show mate?"

"Call the number on the poster outside," he said abruptly.

It was one of those stupid phone numbers that Americans are so fond of: 666-JIMMY-TIX. I turned round to a man waving a hissing python in my face.

"You want photo my friend?" he enquired.

I brushed him away and joined a hub of people all cooing over something I couldn't yet make out. It was the world's smallest dog, a tea-cup Chihuahua. A man tried to sell me his latest CD, his clever sales pitch being to rap indecipherably into my face. This remains the best thing Tank has ever seen. The CD was simply a compilation of songs that he happened to like, and therefore blatant piracy. I declined and escaped into the Capitan theatre. Another of the Boulevard's stalwart cinemas, it was revamped by Disney in the late 1980s but still maintained that old school look you could still find examples of around town. I took some of Mickey Zee's advice and ducked into the Pig and Whistle for something to eat.

"A lot of the British music industry guys eat there when they're in town. Kind of an English-themed place, y'know? Hey, you guys really call your bars things like the Pig and Whistle, huh?"

Fucking ay Mickey.

It didn't strike me as being English-themed inside. Apart from the name, there was little to differentiate it from any other of the themed pubs out there. I ate a head-sized burger, tipped a dollar – "One lousy buck," I imagined the waitress squawking – and turned left-back towards the crowds, stopping at 1700 North Mcfadden Place, opposite Fredericks Of Hollywood, for a gawp at Al Jolson's walk of fame star. Jolson was an absolute colossus of showbusiness throughout his career and this slab of concrete beneath me only served to highlight just how legendary some of the 'old Hollywood' really are. Names like Gene Autry, the only person to have five stars on the walk of fame for his work in various fields, and one of four men to have the unusual distinction, along with Kirk Douglas, Gregory Peck and James Stewart, to have had their stars stolen. Since its inception on February 9th 1960, which saw the unveiling of Joanne Woodward's star, the Oliver Weismuller-designed attraction now boasts almost 2,500 names. These include two different Harrison Fords, several animals, and even a special commemoration to the Apollo astronauts.

Under the mountains of tinsel, celluloid, and plastic of Hollywood Boulevard though there was little to sustain my interest. For me, Sunset Strip was where the real juice was. We'd covered it briefly on Mickey's tour but only in a point and gawp kind of way. I wanted to get right up close to it so I conducted a walking tour that took me all the way from Vine, at its eastern end, down to Holloway Drive.

The Strip was the centre of the rock'n'roll world of the late 1960s and early 1970s. Already known for its decadence thanks to clubs like The Garden Of Allah in the 1920s, it would be another forty years or so before the musical revolution that had taken London by storm did the same here. Billy Wilder's Sunset Boulevard had already immortalised places like Schwab's Drugstore, a popular hangout for the likes of James Dean and Sal Mineo, when bands like The Doors, Love and Iron Butterfly came to prominence, playing residencies at a number of clubs in the area. Clubs like Elmer Valentine's Whisky-a-Go-Go, the red edifice that even today can still claim Jim Morrison's former band mates as its house band. I was disappointed to learn that we'd missed by just one day the remaining band members playing a low-key gig there. Elmer later opened the Roxy, a nightclub that flourished along with the Rainbow and the long-forgotten London Fog. It was a Sunday afternoon when I passed them so there was little activity but even by night you did well to get anywhere near the excitement of forty years ago. The bar had been raised too high by people like John Belushi, who famously died at the world's most intriguing hotel, the Chateau Marmont, and Depeche Mode's Dave Gahan, who is still barred from the Sunset Marquis for dying there once. Yes, you read that right: Dave Gahan, currently into his fourth decade as Depeche Mode lead singer, died there, which is about as rock'n'roll as you can get. Most people's knowledge of the area's nightclub scene starts and ends with the now infamous Viper Room though, right across the street from the Whisky, thanks to another famous death, that of River Phoenix. I stood outside the little black box of a place on the spot where he died of a drugs overdose in the arms of brother Joaquin and girlfriend Samantha Mathis, on Halloween 1993.

Nonplussed by its legend, apart from the fact that under the tutelage of Rick Rubin, Johnny Cash had previewed his American Legend album inside in almost complete darkness, I walked on. In the unlikely event of any of these people needing a bed for the night, they more often than not stayed at the Hyatt House Hotel. Somewhere in there was Room 1015, possibly still missing its television after Keith Richards threw it out of the window.

The House Of Blues opposite is the brainchild of Dan Aykroyd, also the man behind the Hard Rock Café chain. If you removed its surroundings – the hotels, bars and car parks – it could have been the Deep South juke joint it was supposed to be. Inside was a little too gift-shop orientated for my liking, but in a little enclosed seating area just outside, there stood an amazing piece of musical heritage. A monument to Robert Johnson was framed with the actual metal from the signpost at the crossroads junction of Highway 61 and Highway 49 of Clarksdale, by the Mississippi river, where Johnson is alleged to have sold his soul to the devil in exchange for his extraordinary guitar playing prowess.

As musical mythology goes, it is probably the most famous story of all and has given rise to modern tales of a non-musical bent, the selling of one's soul to the devil, the Faustian pact ensuing that Old Nick can 'call you downstairs' anytime he/she/it likes. If the story is true, Satan didn't wait long to summon Johnson after their meeting at Dockery's Plantation. He was dead at twenty-seven from alleged gin poisoning, thus setting the trend for countless music legend deaths at a young age that continues right up to the present day, (insert name of latest dead rock star here). As exciting as the devil yarn is, his ability came from playing with other Blues legends like Lonnie Johnson, Son House and Ike Zinnemann, and his extraordinarily long fingers, caused quite possibly by what would nowadays be diagnosed as Marfan's syndrome.

I'd absorbed as much of the strip's musical history as I could for one day when I left the House Of Blues but I still breezed past Doug Weston's Troubadour club, the west coast's folk-rock hub of the 1970s where Gram Parsons and CSNY carved up the nightlife alongside the Eagles, all presided over by David Geffen. Finally, I squeezed in a stop at Larry Flynt's Hustler Hollywood, which was effectively a supermarket for pornography. "Relax. It's just sex," announced a provocative sounding voice over the pa system. Right outside the door, not to be outdone by the mainstream, the ever-enterprising Flynt had arranged for the great and the good of the porn industry to have their handprints, and other body parts, set in the concrete floor. Jenna Jameson, Ron Jeremy, Ginger Lynn and Larry himself had all left their mark.

If you're wondering where most of these people live then you might want to head to Beverley Hills. If it's good enough for Frank Sinatra, it's good enough for anyone. And where else can you find Christopher Walken waving politely at Mike Myers as he collects the morning papers? Doheny Drive was home to Sammy Davis Jnr at one point and now boasts the postcodes of David Spade and Dana Carvey, (whaddaya mean, "who are they?"). Robert Blake might have nipped next door to Gene Simmons' place to borrow a tea bag if he needed to. All of the houses were big, especially on Mapleton Drive, where Magic Johnson has a great view of the pool at the Playboy Mansion, but none were bigger than 594 South Mapleton Drive, by floor space at least. At 56,000 sq. ft. and $85,000,000 at last sale – to Petra Eccelstone – it was built by Aaron Spelling on land once owned by Bing Crosby. The Manor, as it's referred to, is the biggest pile on the west coast and we saw more than most as we passed when the enormous automated gates slid open, ready to receive a delivery. A mosaic driveway led around the obligatory fountain towards what looked to be security cordons and then onto its 123 rooms, at last count, as staff scurried around the place. Spelling had made his fortune from TV shows like Charlie's Angels, Dynasty, Peyton Place and of course, Beverly Hills 90210, which cemented the area's reputation as a place of beautiful people and ugly personalities, and where the sun always shined. They all shopped at Rodeo Drive, lunched at the Beverly Wilshire and had breast augmentation at Cedars Sinai as the smell of credit cards hung heavy in the air.

It was like being in a pop-up edition of Heat magazine.

There was nobody pumping iron when we arrived at Muscle Beach Venice, to give it its full name, and I wasn't about to start. Instead, I sat in the bleachers and watched Tank shoot three pointers against the backdrop of the Pacific Ocean. At the other end of the court, where scenes for American History X and White Men Can't Jump were filmed, a game of four-on-four was in full flow. Everywhere looked to be a shadow of its former self, of the image that was presented to the rest of the world by TV and film, and this summed up the west coast for me. I'd wanted the Los Angelean ideology of everything being great because it looked great confirmed but I knew this wasn't possible.

Too much of the place was ugly when you scratched through the glitter. Skid Row didn't look good and that's why you hardly see it. Whole families live in the gutter, all of their possessions stuffed into a shopping trolley, as the fog of crack cocaine squeezes everything out of them.

For a less gloomy time, the next day I headed south to the Farmers' Market at Fairfax and 3rd St. It was a celebrity hangout of sorts thanks to its proximity to the CBS studios and had attracted the likes of Britney Spears and Goldie Hawn in recent days.

It was located in a giant undercover courtyard that specialised mainly in food, particularly fruit and vegetables. Beyond the stalls was the obligatory multiplex cinema and a collection of gift stores and tourist attractions. I ate at Deano's, where from the corner of my eye, I noticed that the bar next door, EB's, sold English lagers, namely Fosters – Australian I know but where do you think Australians come from; you were paying attention earlier right? – and Newcastle Brown Ale (spit!).

I watched Neil Young Unplugged from behind my $2.50 Peroni and overheard some laughably American conversations, choice lines being, "I'm really into bananas at the moment," and this, from an overly dramatic middle-aged liberal seated behind me who even rose to her feet to emphasise her point, "Guys… this is post 9/11 we're talking about here."

I stole an orange from a nearby fruit stall and walked back to the hostel where Boogie, the effervescently-chirpy Balinese entertainments manager had laid on a keg of beer for anyone who invested $5. By 11pm, I'd drunk my $30 worth and was looking for somewhere to go. After a ten minute walk, I was sitting at the bar of Canters Deli on Fairfax having my drinks bought by a woman called Francis from Yuma. Canters became my favourite spot in LA for a number of reasons. You could get a reasonably priced beer and a seat at the bar, a la Bukowski, without hassle, and see good live bands like The New West, who were presumably hoping to follow in the footsteps of another Canters house band, The Wallflowers, who broke out of the local scene in the 1990s. After listening to the man next to me drunkenly bemoaning the lack of nipple tassels on modern day strippers, I took a look around and learnt more about its heritage. It started out as Canters Deli, which was now situated next door to the bar in an adjoining room and still had people queuing out into the street on a regular basis. As a result, the bar was now a separate area, more commonly known as the Kibbutz Room, and attracted music fans every day of the week and LA barflys of all kinds.

Like the rest of the town, it boomed in the 1950s and 1960s and boasted Brando and Pacino as regulars. Dylan was known to pop in whenever he was in town to sample its Jewish cuisine and photos on every wall showed him and various other rock stars, mostly 1980s hair-metallers like WASP and Van Halen, hanging around, and sometimes even performing. Anyone who could play could turn up any time and get a gig and that's what happened when The New West packed up. The stage was taken by one of the barmen and a band of musicians he'd plucked from nowhere and they lurched into a polished cover of Spinal Tap's Pink Torpedo.

"The bigger the cuuushion the harder the puuushing, or so it is said," roared the singer as everyone erupted.

I rolled back up Fairfax at 3am, already hung over.

Feeling ropey, I spent my final day in Hollywood unsuccessfully trying to arrange accommodation in Las Vegas, naively opting to stay in the seedy downtown area.

"I just came from there," said the Australian girl in my room. "Somebody was shot on Fremont Street last week."

So what, I used to work near Exchange Square in Middlesbrough on a Saturday night.

She continued, "I stayed in a $300-a-night place just to be on the safe side."

You can't put a price on not dying I suppose but I didn't have this luxury. Instead I had a fallback in the shape of the Sahara resort at the northern end of the strip, where Tank and I had arranged to meet a friend from home. Like so many of Vegas's visitors, all I had was a Greyhound ticket.

CHAPTER 16:
LAS VEGAS

Ant arrives, Tank talks turkey, and Jeremy ends up in a wheelchair.

"Dial '0' for a ho."

Nelson's voice was as flat as the desert beneath us.

"Ladies and gentlemen, I will not repeat what I am about to say. My name is Nelson and I will be your driver for the journey to Las Vegas. Passengers are reminded that any drinks may only be brought on board in a sealed container. The same applies to all foodstuffs. Anyone found leaving any refuse will be removed from the bus. We will be making three very brief stops on the way. Should you find yourself returning to the bus one second after the given departure times then you will be wasting your time as I will not be there. You do not want to be left behind in the desert come nightfall, trust me on that one. All cell phones will be switched to silent for the duration of the journey. And remember, what happens in Vegas…" Everyone chorused at the same time, "…stays in Vegas."

He wasn't wrong about being left behind. The last place you wanted to spend the night was in Barstow. To stretch my legs, I strolled over to the shopping precinct that inside resembled the set of one of the Dawn Of The Dead films, a seemingly abandoned mall with just two shops trading: one a discount tat outlet, the other a music store. As I turned to look at the former, the zombie cashier reached for the shutter then paused, daring me to enter. I inched forward to test him and his arm stretched nearer the shutter. I retreated slightly and so did the arm. I went to the music store opposite but a sign in the window ordered me to return in five minutes. I couldn't help thinking about the trade they were missing out on by taking a break at such a busy time. I didn't delve much further into the bowels of the place for fear of being savaged by the guardians of the afterlife. I stepped into the deserted car park and looked up into the clear blue sky from which, according to a spectacularly intoxicated Hunter S Thompson in his book, Fear And Loathing In Las Vegas, a flock of manic bats descended upon his car. From the same sky in 1997, a manacled, handcuffed and caged magician was thrown from an aeroplane just 18,000ft from the ground. He somehow escaped and deployed his parachute five seconds before impact at 1,200ft, to set a world record for the lowest death-dive escape.

There were no manic bats or falling magicians today though. There was nothing. I returned to the bus five minutes early, so as not to incur the wrath of Nelson, and we moved off northeast through the Mojave Desert. I hadn't seen landscapes like this since Australia: arid, scorched, snake-riddled dustpans, punctuated by spinifex, tumbleweed and the occasional truck stop.

"If you go to Vegas by road, you can see the lights from twenty-one miles away," somebody told me.

Somebody else said, "Dial '0' for a ho."

"They use computers to control the weather," said another.

In a town where nothing is real, all of these things turned out to be true.

The Greyhound station in Las Vegas is slammed right in the downtown area that was once, before the advent of the Strip, the heartbeat of Las Vegas. I shoved past the crowd of bums and junkies in the doorway and set about searching for an address of what seemed to be the only hostel in the whole of Nevada. I couldn't find it so I walked through the night, almost two miles, without knowing the area at all, past countless seedy motels, bail bond brokers, brothels, strip joints, pawn shops, and porn shops, until I saw the lights of the Strip.

To use one of Rusty's terms, the Strip is 'deceptive' to say the least. You can see the towering fronts of the casinos that loom over you, making them appear much closer than they are, but out of view are the enormous parking lots and the maze of walkways designed to drag you in, like a resort, within a resort, within a resort. I was relieved to reach the front entrance of the Stratosphere that night.

Over the crossroads of Sahara Avenue stood the Sahara itself, my emergency option should I have nowhere to stay.

When it comes to holidays, Ant isn't one for lounging around on sandy beaches. More likely, he'll spend around seventy hours of the one-hundred-and-sixty-eight that make up a week on the gaming floors of various casinos. I know this because he dragged Tank and I along for the ride in Las Vegas, not that we needed persuading.

I interrogated everyone I met on the backpacking circuit who had been to Las Vegas about the best places to stay and the best ways to bleed the place dry. I knew, like everyone else, about the complimentary food and drinks and discounted, or even free, room rates for frequent players but the one thing everyone suggested was to book a room for one, or maybe two people, and then stuff as many people as you want in there to split the cost. In Auckland, my Brazilian roommate Fernando told me he'd rocked up to the reception desk of Bally's, booked the most expensive room available, then piled in nine of his mates. We were then, extremely grateful to Ant for putting up with us in room 1129.

"I was coming anyway," he said, stuffing $6,000 into his trouser pocket.

I reached the Sahara completely exhausted by the bus journey and from having to drag my backpack along Carson Avenue but was totally revitalised when I saw Ant and Tank sitting in the casino's sports book.

Ant's was the only familiar face we had seen from home since we left and we were looking forward to hearing about what, if anything, had been going on back in Middlesbrough. He'd forgotten everything of course, understandable as he'd been awake for almost twenty-four hours and on a plane for twelve of them. True to form, he'd gone on a bender in Manchester the night before his flight and managed to wheedle out a late night lock-in at a bar in someone's house. From there, he boarded the flight and was dispatched at McCarron airport half a day later. Within half an hour he'd checked in, changed, and was holed up in the Sahara poker room with a cigar hanging from his lip, flanked by myself and Tank.

The Sahara became the sixth hotel on the strip when it was opened in 1952. Under the guidance of its first proprietor, Milton Prell, it had become, by 1954, home to the most popular cabaret show in town, that of jazz shouter Louis Prima's residency, alongside his wife Keeley Smith, and sax man Sam Buttera.

Today, pictures of the three of them adorn the walls of the building, next to black and white shots of the Beatles, Rory Calhoun lounging by the pool, and Elvis Presley. Come the boom era of Vegas in the early 1960s, Del Webb had taken over from Prell, and the resort became famous for Jerry Lewis's telethons for years after. Now it boasted the likes of Amazing Jonathan, the Platters, the Drifters and the Coasters, all featuring none of the original line-ups. Its main attraction now though was the NASCAR exhibit. Americans love NASCAR.

It's big, noisy, expensive, smelly, fast, and the perfect excuse for the spectators to sit down and eat large portions of food. The exhibit was concerned mainly with the exploits of the late Dale Earnhardt, the undisputed king of NASCAR, who dominated the sport throughout the late 1980s and 1990s, and contained a number of his trophies and autographed apparel, but the big draw in the casino was one of his actual cars.

The exhibit was surrounded by every conceivable arcade game known to man, all blazing away at 5,000 decibels. Directly above it was the all-you-can-eat-buffet, another classic Las Vegas tradition. I soon made up for six months of meagre rationing and poor food by eating my way through the city, all free of charge, thanks to the fistful of coupons I'd armed myself with on arrival. I was eating so much in one sitting that it sustained me for a full twenty-four hours, until the next day's meal. Normally I couldn't justify consuming steak, pork, fried chicken, roast beef, pasta, spaghetti bolognese, pizza, onion rings, potato wedges, apple pie, ice cream, chocolate cake, strawberry gateaux, meringue, jelly, muffins, apples, oranges, bananas and a litre of orange juice in one sitting but, in my defence, I was on holiday.

One day I ate so much that I lost all feeling in my left arm. There followed a shooting pain in my upper right arm that lasted around half an hour. I think the food was beginning to crush my heart. It was all I could do to finish my dessert. I rose unsteadily with a pocket full of fruit and biscuits – for supper – and found that I'd almost blinded myself through eating.

I came to a couple of hours later, vowing not to eat so much next time.

In 1931, twenty-six years after it was officially established with the development of the red light area of Block 16, Las Vegas received one of the first six gaming licenses to be issued in the state of Nevada. It was awarded to the Pair-O-Dice club on Fremont Street, making it the city's first official and legally recognised casino. Ten years later on 3rd April El Rancho became the first hotel on what is now known as the Strip, or Las Vegas Boulevard, as it's officially named, which runs from the Sahara to the Mandalay Bay resort at the southern end. As a result, the area was moderately successful as a tourist destination but in 1946 something far-reaching happened with the arrival of gangster Benjamin 'Bugsy' Siegel, who came to oversee the development of the Flamingo. Siegel didn't last long though and by the summer of 1947 was being fitted for a wooden suit courtesy of the Mafia's head tailor after the Flamingo's construction budget soared to six times its expected cost. Siegel was shot dead at his home in Beverly Hills and the Flamingo still carries a memorial to him.

The Mob had a strong foothold by now and as of 1951, eight of the ten existing Las Vegas casinos were controlled by them alone. In the wider area of the Nevada basin, the US government had cottoned on to the notion that still exists today as far as they are concerned, of activating unfeasibly large explosions in the desert. Over the next eleven years, they would detonate 126 nuclear devices around the city.

The Sahara poker room, still as it was for the opening night, had covered all the demographics as far as the contestants were concerned: wily eastern European gangsters, mouthy yanks and conservative Brits. I sat back for the most part until my two pairs were scrubbed away by the Serb's higher two pairs. I occupied myself at various blackjack and roulette tables, never playing more than three hands or spins at one table so as not to get too comfortable, which seemed to do the trick, and I made small gains all week. When I wasn't gambling, I was standing in on the craps games trying to learn what I could about the game which had always captivated me: the randomness of the red dice on the green baize, the massive array of available bets, and the excitement of the players, but most of all the terminology used. Terms like box man – one of the croupiers, shooter – the player throwing the dice, big red – the number seven, and snake eyes – a pair of ones thrown, all fascinated me, as did all other gambling phrases. It was a language on its own – gamblese.

"Early start in the morning," announced Ant.

"What for?"

"Craps lessons, half ten downstairs."

We didn't make it. We'd lost all concept of time and we hadn't even left the Sahara yet. I knew enough about craps already, despite never having played before, to be able to hold my own but I only ever bet the hard ways; any pair, usually after roughly every eight throws, and this kept me going, but I was just happy soaking up the atmosphere. There was lots of dice kissing and whooping it up going on, some of it from me, but I never threw.

"Hey kid. You shooting?" barked the horn man. The horn is the rake-like stick used to retrieve the dice after each throw.

I couldn't respond with a typically appropriate response, something like, "Hey buddy, I'm passing on them there devil's cubes yessirree." Instead I went for the blustering Englishman's response of, "What me? Er... no."

He pushed the dice towards the next man and we all braced ourselves for the 'come out roll'. The shooter throws the 'come out roll' in order to 'make his point', in this case a six and a three. From thereon, players can make a series of bets that includes the field, which is any number from 2, 3, 4, 9, 10, 11 or 12, the self-explanatory odd or even, the 'hard ways' which is any pair, or that the shooter will throw a seven – sometimes called a natural – and 'crap out', signalling the end of the game. At this point, the dice change hands and a new shooter starts the next game. The above are just a brief selection of the available bets that casinos are constantly developing in order to tempt punters. For more information, simply switch on the TV in your hotel room and watch the gambling lessons channel, where every single bet appears to win, such is the magic of television.

Las Vegas has a strong tradition of live shows, most of which feature spectacular conjuring tricks, none more spectacular than those of Siegfried and Roy at the Mirage, probably the most famous Vegas show ever after the legendary 'Sands summits'. Siegfried and Roy's animal extravaganza was the most expensive magic show ever produced when it opened in February 1990 at an incomprehensible cost of \$28,000,000, most of which was spent on cat food, but it did run for 5,750 shows until Roy seriously pissed off Manticore.

The Mirage's current attraction was George Martin's Beatles-based musical Love, directed by the extravagantly-named Dominic Champagne, but the resort still acknowledges its heritage with its white tiger habitat. Animals in casinos were popular in Las Vegas. The MGM Grand was home to a pride of lions that prowled around the place, much to the astonishment of the public, and a hungry Mike Tyson had fought there on several occasions, most famously against Evander Holyfield. With the possible exception of Madison Square Garden, Vegas is the home of the big fight and the credentials of the Grand are second to none: Tommy Hearns, Marvin Hagler, Roberto Duran and Sugar Ray Leonard had punched themselves to a standstill there in the 1980s and Frank Bruno had come unstuck in the same ring against Iron Mike. During my stay, Phillipino powerhouse Manny Pacquaio was about to go toe-to-toe with Erik Morales for the third time in recent years, the series tied at one win apiece, much to the excitement of the Mexican family I sat next to on the monorail one evening.

"MORALES, MORALES, MORALES!" they chanted, over and over, with fists raised. The father of the family told me he'd wagered $300 on 'El Terrible' Morales to win. Later that night, in front of 18,000 people at the Thomas and Mack Centre, Morales went down and stayed there, along with the old man's $300 bet; another Vegas punt straight in the bookie's satchel.

I wasn't doing too badly as it happened. After three days in town, I was somehow still on my original $100 dollars and eating like a man with two mouths. I considered the excesses of the place nevermore than when in Caesar's Palace, one of the most opulent resorts in the whole of Nevada. As its name suggests, it's a throwback to the days of ancient Rome and was the brainchild of Jay Sarno. Sarno was one of the highest of high rollers, once winning $100,000 and then losing $200,000 in the same day, but will be more likely remembered as one of the men, along with Steve Wynn and Kirk Kerkorian, who made Las Vegas the family friendly tourist attraction it is today.

I stood at a craps table in the lobby of Caesar's, the very lobby where on New Year's Eve 1969 one Robert 'Evel' Kneivel laid down a losing $100 dollar bet on a blackjack table, threw down a glass of Wild Turkey at the adjacent bar, and then strolled out of the main doors I'd just walked in through. An hour later, he took to the skies on his motorbike and jumped the famous fountains in the courtyard, resulting in a remarkable list of injuries. As a result, he was in a coma for twenty-nine days, but the important thing was another Las Vegas legend had been cemented forevermore.

At the craps table, I couldn't resist a hard eight. In the middle of a forest of mobile phones, a voice drifted out.

"Okay, here we go," it said, "whaddaya'll need here?"

"Just the fours," I shouted.

The shooter glanced up from under his familiar black hat.

He looked puzzled.

"Hard eight," I shouted.

He smiled and primed his throwing arm, a muscular, tattooed limb, that determined the destiny of the dice. His entourage noisily hustled him and jostled for position around the table. I would love to tell people that when I was in Las Vegas, Kid Rock threw me a winning bet, and sometimes I do, but he didn't. He threw a seven, thus crapping out, much to the entire foyer's dismay. We all "ooohhed" at exactly the same time: Kid Rock, his cronies, the croupiers, the box man, the bar staff and the crowd. Even the dice looked apologetic.

The total cost of flights for the trip came to £1,200. A flight from the UK to Nevada's McCarron airport would have cost around £400, but you could fly straight there and still see some of the world's most recognised landmarks, albeit slightly condensed versions. Along the four miles that make up Las Vegas Boulevard, you can experience the South-East Asian orientated Mandalay Bay, or the adjoining Luxor resort, should you want a taste of ancient Egypt. The Excalibur provides a window to the world of Olde England and looks like something straight from the pencil of Fantasia-era Disney. Cross Tropicana Avenue and the Statue Of Liberty looms large as the frontispiece of New York, New York, except this Big Apple is entangled in a rollercoaster. The Tropicana itself sits at the opposite apex of the crossroads. Then comes the Monte Carlo, but for a bigger dose of French culture, they'll always have Paris. Just look for the 540ft high, half scale replica of the Eiffel Tower out front. Inside you might as well be strolling down the Champs Elysees in the shadow of the Arc De Triomphe, day or night, they've recreated both, and any kind of weather you might fancy. Over the garden fence from the Monte Carlo is the Bellagio and its incredible musical fountain show out front. 1,000 nozzles and 250ft high jets of water dance to various tunes at half hour intervals; you don't get that at Lake Como. Out on the fringes of the strip are the Rio, Tahiti Village, the Orleans and Tuscany. Back on the Strip, there's China's Imperial Palace, Barbary Coast, the opulence of the Venetian, with its Sistine Chapel frescos, and then furthest north, the Sahara and the Stratosphere. By contrast, the Fremont Street casinos still carry the traditional names one would associate with the Wild West: names like the Golden Nugget, the Horseshoe and the Gold Spike, that evoke images of gold diggers, prostitutes and gunslingers. Other less obviously themed resorts on the Strip included Bally's, the MGM Grand and Wynn. Billionaire Steve Wynn can be considered the father of modern Las Vegas thanks to his development of resorts like the Mirage and the aforementioned Wynn. Alongside MGM Grand boss Kirk Kerkorian, the pair have had a hand in making this tiny strip of parched earth home to twenty of the thirty biggest hotels in America. The MGM Grand alone contains 5,034 rooms. Kerkorian's head was screwed on tight.

"If economists were any good at business, they would be rich men, instead of advisers to rich men," he once said.

The big hotel though, attracted a big score in 1993 when $2.9 million dollars was stolen from a Loomis armoured car that was waiting to collect from inside. The following year, the gang had their melons all in a row again when they hijacked another Loomis delivery in the Circus Circus parking lot, this time bagging over $3 million dollars. The driver was never seen again, prompting the authorities to suggest that the heist was an inside job, although I wouldn't have hung around with that sort of wedge in my pocket.

I'd entered the diamond ring prize draw at the Sahara but had inadvertently put my entry form into the bi-hourly butterball turkey draw, much to the amusement of Tank and Ant. It didn't make me eligible for both, or either, as I later found out when my entry was drawn out! It was drawn again and this time Tank's entry was selected.

He was in the middle of a blackjack marathon at the time and so skipped a few hands to collect his voucher.

What possible use did we have for a raw turkey in a casino? Luckily, the prize was in voucher form for the time being but over a few more hands of blackjack, Tank used it to wangle a Thanksgiving Day invite to someone's house.

"You can have the turkey," he said to the persistent woman playing next to him, adding, ever enterprisingly, "for $20."

"Give me it and you can come to mine and eat it," she haggled.

"Where do you live?"

"Florida."

He still has the handwritten address on a piece of paper. Maybe next year. It wasn't the only piece of Thanksgiving hospitality we were offered in Las Vegas.

We wandered around the New York, New York complex, in particular Central Park, and a fibreglass replica of the East Village. Ant had insisted on a "couple of daiquiris, just for something to hold onto as we're walking about". You can't fault the logic of a man who uses daiquiris as a walking aid. They weren't any old 'daqs' either, served up as they were in what looked like a luminous plastic elephant gun that was so unwieldy you were given a safety harness. We sat down and tipped them into our mouths. Once our brain freezes had thawed, we played Sic Bo, a Chinese variation of craps in which three dice are tossed around in a canary cage for a bit, Caribbean stud poker, and of course more blackjack. In the first hand of blackjack, I drew five cards without going bust.

Reverting to roulette, the bizarre occurrences continued. On two consecutive spins, the ball left the table, and then later on the ball simply refused to drop into the number trap. It jumped off the wall of death and hovered disbelievingly in the no-man's land between its starting point and the number wheel, rolling left to right over a distance of about six inches. We all watched it for maybe thirty seconds before the croupier summoned the floor manager and a respin was made.

"We all win, right," said one man optimistically.

We all lost.

We'd walked around the Strip for too long one Saturday night before settling on Aladdin, having spent most of it in New York, New York as practice for the real thing a few days later. It had just about the right balance between madness and sanity, which is always welcome when you've just stepped out of the Coyote Ugly bar.

It was just around midnight then, when we arrived at Aladdin and got comfortable at the bar with almost the whole place to ourselves. We familiarised ourselves with the bar staff, Andy and Sammy, and the video poker machines immediately, in order to procure ourselves free drinks. This was an instant success and soon after, Jeremy and Rachel, the only other customers, joined us after some back and forth banter about English drinking habits.

"I am tricking you guys out," announced Jeremy, as we attached ourselves to the bar like limpets. They were from Echo Park, Los Angeles, and regulars in Vegas, especially at the Aladdin, so much so that Jeremy was looking to max out his comps card and was happy to share it with us.

After the initial introductions, we set about the cocktail menu in spectacular fashion until first light. Jeremy was a film editor and had just finished work on Rocky VI. I asked him what his first project was.

"Truman Show," he said, before going on to say he was hoping to get out of the film industry.

"It's tough to avoid it if you live in Los Angeles. It's everything and everywhere," he said ruefully. "I'm working on a script though," he added.

A man approached the bar and walked away with a glass full of the colour pink.

"What's the barman's name again?" whispered Ant, for about the eighteenth time that night.

"It's still Andy," I replied, straightening out a greenback for the poker machine.

"Hey Andy," Ant said, "what were those drinks that man just bought?"

"Miami Vices."

"Three Miami Vices, please."

As he poured them, Andy listed the ingredients: grenadine, orange juice, soup and plasticine – all topped off with bubble bath – delicious, as you'd expect. Jeremy was lining up the Sambucas as we finished the Miami Vices, burping bubbles in the process.

"You guys are alright by me. I love you English guys," he was saying, before toasting our health, a pointless gesture after those cocktails.

"What's a smart guy like Tony Blair doing hanging out with George Bush?" asked Rachel. The political debate was on in earnest. I kept out of it as I was talking to Andy about Dirk Nowitzki but by the time the others turned their attention back to us, Jeremy and I had almost come to blows over a much more important issue: Hendrix or Clapton? Fingers were pointed – as Ant constantly reminds me – brows were furrowed and accusations were bandied about, all in the name of rock'n'roll.

We all managed to compose ourselves though and turned our energies back to the bar.

I'd moved onto the Manhattans by now, whiskey, vermouth and bitters, in homage to another Las Vegas legend, Frank Sinatra.

The Rat Pack breezed into town in 1960 on the pretence of making a film, Ocean's Eleven, but that was just to give them all something to do through the day. By night, they were tearing holes in the Strip with their now almost mythological 'Sands summits', held in the Copa Room, now the site of the Venetian. After the show, they'd head elsewhere and disrupt somebody else's show, Frank famously heckling Eddie Cantor on one occasion. They'd hang around with a broad on each arm and a drink and a smoke in each hand. First thing on a morning, they'd splash their faces with cold water as a substitute for a night's sleep and would be back on set for that day's shambolic filming. The effect they had on the place is indelible, hence Dean Martin Drive that runs along the west side of the Strip. I think a nice statue would be a good memorial to a couple of Vegas legends in particular. How about a Vegas Vic-sized solid gold casting of Elvis and Ol' Blue Eyes in the middle of a duet? Nothing too tasteless, this is Vegas we're talking about here.

Vegas Vic is the giant cowboy with the shit-eating grin that once stood on Fremont Street, or Glitter Gulch, as it was sometimes known, outside the Pioneer Club. He was erected in 1951 by the Electric Sign Company and every twenty minutes for the next fifteen years greeted everyone with a "howdy pardner" or some equally cowboyish phrase. Bizarrely, Vic's voice box was removed in 1966 when Lee Marvin complained about it during a stay at the Mint. According to local legend, Vic was 'shotgun married' to

Vegas Vicky, or Sassy Sally, as she's also known, and now it is she who overlooks Fremont Street.

By the end of the night at the Aladdin, or rather by daybreak, Jeremy was so drunk he had to be taken away in a wheelchair by security guards and an apologetic Rachel.

"Come to ours for Thanksgiving," she said, as she left.

Jeremy was replaced by Jay, an alarmingly young real estate broker from Philadelphia, in town for a stag weekend. He'd overheard the political rants from earlier in the night and had come to offer his views.

"I fucking love you English guys," was his opening line, delivered as he chewed on an expensive cigar.

"Crown Seven, please Andy," he said, leaning cockily against the bar. "Say what you like about the Republicans but they sure know how to make money," he informed us. Every statement was followed by that most American of gestures, the air jab of a fat cigar. "I'm twenty-one and I'm comfortably wealthy, only because I was lucky enough to have been born into the right family." His father and grandfather had made a big success of the family business. Jay had been in Las Vegas for three days and claimed to have spent a baulk-inducing $5,000 in that time. With this revelation, he immediately lost my attention but Ant was happily up to his neck in Democratic manifestos with nothing to hide behind but a caramapple Martini.

The first light of a Sunday morning shattered us as we flagged down a cab to return us to the Sahara. By now, the daylight was the only pointer as to what time of the day it was, somewhere between 6am and 6pm probably. At the Caravan Café, I ate a traditional Vegas breakfast of steak and eggs with toast and hash browns, all for a measly $2.50. I thought I might never leave. I did though, two days later, but spent the last night downtown. I wasn't leaving without visiting the Horseshoe.

Better known as Binion's, after Vegas godfather Benny Binion – the casino was the first to lay carpets – it is the original home of the World Series Of Poker, and is still the only casino on the planet that has a no-limit rule on all bets. In other words, they'll happily accept any bet you can think of, however large, provided it is your first on the premises on that day; Binion certainly knew the value of publicity. It was old school Vegas, as I was reminded when I looked at the Hall Of Fame entrants displayed on the wall: Doyle 'Texas Dolly' Brunson, Jack 'Treetop' Strauss - the man responsible for the much quoted poker phrase 'a chip and a chair', the biggest loser - Nick 'the Greek' Dandalos, the remarkable Stuey Unger - himself the finest gin rummy player that ever lived, Felton McCorquodale - the unknown soldier of Texas Hold-Em, and many more, all gazed down from the wall, alongside Benny.

For all its tradition and legend, the Horseshoe could just as easily have been in Blackpool, with its drab interior and 'older' crowd, as could most of the downtown casinos on Fremont Street. Today Las Vegas is the Strip and no mistake. As a result, there can be no more Sinatras, Knievels, or Binions, all of them not merely gamblers, but opportunists, stuntmen and folk heroes. Now the tables produce careerist card players instead.

I walked through the lobby of the Sahara for the last time, stopping only to throw down my last Federal Reserve note on the wheel of fortune. In such a futile situation, I should have bet on the outcome with the longest odds, 40-1 shot, the joker, but instead opted for a wise 10-1 punt. I pondered this as a green around the gills George Washington looked up at me from the table. It was no laughing matter when the joker came up.

I boarded the Deuce under the strict gaze of another of America's hard-line bus drivers and managed to block every single walkway with my now even tighter-jammed backpack thanks to the fragrant mountain of soap and shampoo I'd awarded myself, and Ant's absentmindedness. He'd left behind a pair of his shoes and a jacket, the same jacket that he'd previously left on his chair at the Let It Ride table that had yet another pair of my sunglasses in the pocket, which soon disappeared. Then he lost his safe key, resulting in arrangements being made to have someone drill their way to his cash. The bus took me literally to Paradise, the actual name of the district in Clark County that houses most of Las Vegas and its main airport, McCarron, out in the dust.

I was flying at one of the busiest times of the year, two days before Thanksgiving. This would be an experience, especially considering America's current obsession with national security. In a brilliant move in the name of homeland security, the boarding gates were opened just thirty minutes before the departure time. It took over forty minutes to pass through the security checks, what with the retina scan, having to remove my socks and shoes, and have my palms read by the anti-terror palmist. The area was a mess of discarded shoes, belts, and toiletries, all casualties of the war on terror. People were running past me, a trail of luggage in their wake, as they barged their way onto the monorail that would take them to their departure gate. I felt like I should probably be moving a bit faster by now, just because everyone else was, my thinking being that most of them would be flying to New York on the same flight as me so the plane wouldn't leave without us. I strolled along and turned the corner to the desk to discover that it would. The digital clock above it read 16.16.

"Mr Nett?" enquired the attendant.

I nodded.

"Sir, the doors for this flight closed at 4.15pm."

For the first time in my life, I'd missed my flight. It felt like an achievement.

"You may board the next available flight, at 11.35pm, if you wish."

It was a blessing in disguise. My original arrival time at JFK Airport was to have been around midnight local time so I planned to spend the night in the airport anyway. Now I would be flying overnight. With time to kill, I plonked myself in front of a slot machine and made a tidy profit in no time.

CHAPTER 17:
NEW YORK

I attend the Thanksgiving Parade, give a ticket tout a nervous breakdown, and meet the man who wrote Puff the Magic Dragon.

"I'd really arrived now, being called a 'cracker' by a New Yorker."

The travelling was taking its toll once more. By the time I reached the hostel in New York, I'd been awake for twenty-two hours, flown through a time zone during my four hour flight, and eaten just an apple, a cookie and a bar of chocolate. From JFK, I'd blindly winged it in finding my way to the Upper West Side during the morning commute but again I'd made it, the last real test, and I knew it, although at that point I hadn't reckoned on passing through London during the morning rush hour.

I might as well have been blindfolded during the commute from the airport to Manhattan as I had no real idea where I was going for most of the journey. A helpful woman at the train station managed to get me on to a train that she insisted would take me to exactly where I wanted to go, provided I knew where that was of course. I was looking for Central Park Backpackers on 103rd Street but first the train rumbled west through the harsh surrounds of Brooklyn, then across the Williamsburg Bridge and into Manhattan. When I boarded, the carriage was almost empty, but I still sat down next to a tramp, waking him up in the process.

I must have been particularly bedraggled by then as he looked me up and down before getting off at the next stop. I had the seat to myself for all of a minute until commuters flooded on from every direction; rabbis, office workers, couriers and more tramps made up the numbers and soon I couldn't move, which didn't matter as I didn't know where to get off. I deduced that when most of the office workers departed, we were somewhere near the financial district, towards the south of the island I thought, and that the low to high numbered streets ran from south to north, meaning that 103rd Street was still some distance away. I couldn't hear any of the pa announcements either because of the noise of the carriages being buffeted along the tracks. The last thing I wanted to do was overshoot my station and fetch up in the middle of Harlem so I impulsively jumped up and strode off, clearly emitting the air of someone who knew exactly what they were doing. Far from it. I was directly underneath West 49th Street with just another fifty-four blocks to go. I hopped onto the next train, without paying – Fuck You Mayor Bloomberg! – as there was no-one around to collect fares. I spotted a map and it was plain sailing from there onwards. I was relieved to see, as soon as I climbed the steps that deposited me onto the street, Central Park Backpackers, in amongst a row of Brownstones, my second choice of accommodation after I heard a rumour, later confirmed, that my first choice had became infested with lice.

The hostel, the last I would stay in, was without the tightly knit vibe I'd been used to elsewhere but this was New York, where everybody has got somewhere to be and no time to be holding open doors for people and exchanging pleasantries. The guests consisted mainly of Australian and Europeans but I was one of only two Englishmen. The other was Glenn, an even tamer version of Rusty, if such a thing exists. How he'd survived a stay in New York I still haven't worked out. A friend from home had drummed into me years earlier that, "Nobody called Glenn is interesting or exciting, they are almost always firemen and/or health and safety officials." Fortunately for all who met him, Glenn was no health and safety chief and god forbid that he should ever be responsible for putting out a fire.

He insisted on calling me William, and always in that simpering tone of voice he used, the only one he had as far as I could make out, to talk about the most mundane of subjects. I returned to the room one day to find him explaining to a Mexican guest how to make cheese on toast. I was crestfallen to discover that it is as easy as putting some cheese on some bread and toasting it. Christ, Glenn, where have you been for the last six months while I've been starving to death?! I await the release of his first cookbook.

On noticing my presence, he turned to his usual line of questioning.

"So, er, William, is it true that in Thailand you can go into a pub and girls will be sitting on stools at the bar, William?" Note repetition of my name at either end of the sentence. Yes, Glenn, in Thailand they have bars with girls in them.

"Is it true some of them are..." Long pause followed by lowering of voice. "...man girls?"

Man girls? Yes, Glenn, but the common term is usually ladyboys.

"Ooh I wouldn't like any of that," he said, followed by, "Will they let you buy them a drink, William?"

Yes Glenn, and they will do things with a ping-pong ball that you wouldn't believe, as long as the price is right.

"Will I meet girls in Bali, William?"

Yes Glenn.

"Will they talk to me?"

Probably not Glenn.

By now, his head had started to slowly implode but still he continued.

"Will I find girls on the street?"

I expect they do leave the house from time to time, yes, Glenn, but how about making them sound less like post boxes or dog turds? Then a swerve ball of a subject change from him.

"Someone's taken the Jeremy Clarkson book from downstairs, William. That's a shame."

No, it's not, Glenn; now we won't have to look at it.

"I perhaps might have thought about quite possibly reading it at some point," he informed me, somewhat indecisively, I thought.

Goodbye Glenn.

I spent most of my first day in the Big Apple in bed sleeping off jet lag and avoiding Glenn but managed to drag myself down to the lounge that evening where I met Gail, a Texan woman who seemed to be living at the hostel long term. She was old enough to know plenty about the place and had a wealth of interesting anecdotes that ranged from the aforementioned Jim Morrison story, and that of the Hollywood shagger she'd lived below in her Texas apartment – I wasn't surprised when she told me who it was – to a breakdown of the city's recent history.

"New York owes a lot to Rudy Giuliani for clearing up a lot of the crime that it was known for," she said. "Fifteen or twenty years ago you couldn't go anywhere without the threat of at least a mugging, or worse, especially on the subway. I think 42nd Street has really lost its character since it was cleared of all the pimps and hookers that helped make it so colourful. It's safer now, yes, much more attractive for tourists, but it lacks something."

And what of his successor, Michael Bloomberg?

"He's taken up where Giuliani left off, for better or worse, but it's too early to say at the moment."

"And do you know what you learn if you're a New Yorker?" Lauren Bacall once said, "…the world doesn't owe you a damn thing."

After walking around Manhattan for six hours, I knew what she meant and have yet to hear it summed up more succinctly. New Yorkers were hard in every sense of the word. They worked hard, played hard, talked hard and looked hard. You could throw anything at them and still they would come, no weather could deter them, no wars could fatigue them, and nothing could stop them. Come the end of the world, Manhattanites will still be shoving around mobile bagel stands, honking away in taxis, shouting at the Knicks, and shovelling snow, and all of its majestic buildings will still be standing because it simply refuses to lie down, as history has shown, in the face of any adversity. London is the same, that indomitable pride of its people that keeps it going forever, but London's strength comes from its well-drilled efficiency and organisation (most of the time). New York has an unbreakable toughness that you can see, hear, and smell.

I didn't use any public transport whilst in New York, except when leaving and arriving, instead opting for the cardinal American sin of walking, and lots of it. Every day, I set out from the hostel and most times walked as far south as the Lower East Side. By the fourth day, I'd covered most of Manhattan and could hardly walk another step as my feet were in such pain but I kept going in order to see as much as possible. That first day I'd told myself not to go too far, not knowing the area so well, maybe just around Central Park, but soon enough I'd been sucked in by the goings on around the Rockerfeller Centre on 6th Avenue.

Central Park was alive with joggers, power walkers, cyclists, and the kind of women you only see in adverts for tampons. You know the ones; they're always being pulled along on roller skates by an understandably knackered pack of dogs. It was a few weeks until Christmas and Manhattan was being readied for the holidays. Lights and decorations were being strung up anywhere there was room and a few places where there wasn't, but before Christmas came the equally celebrated Thanksgiving parade, which was taking place the following day.

"For a secret little New York experience for not so tourist-orientated people like yourself, you should check out the blowing up of the inflatables for the parade on Columbus Avenue," suggested Gail. Even though there were hundreds of other people there, it still felt like a well-kept secret, as though the balloons were being blown up very quietly away from the main street of 8th Avenue in order to surprise everyone the next day.

So there I was, on a cold winter's night in one of the most famous cities in the modern world, watching a 20ft high SpongeBob SquarePants being corralled and cajoled by a group of burly roadies. Whenever I think of the Thanksgiving Day Parade, or giant inflatable cats, I always think of Felix The Cat, for me the most instantly recognisable of the balloons, and I think Kathleen Caronna would agree with me, as far as cat-shaped air balloons are concerned.

During the 1997 parade, the mischievous moggy ploughed into a lamp-post which in turn sent debris from a nearby building crashing down on Caronna's head, fracturing her skull. She settled out of court for an undisclosed fee. So far so 'only in America'. A month or so before I arrived in Manhattan another bizarre episode unfolded. A light aircraft flown by New York Yankees pitcher, Cory Liddle, crashed into the 41st floor of the Belaire Apartments on East 72nd St, depositing its engine onto the bed of none other than... ta-daaa, Kathleen Caronna! Luckily, she wasn't home at the time. Not so lucky were Liddle and his co-pilot, who both died instantly.

There were no such catastrophes on this occasion as thousands of New Yorkers crammed into the triangular Times Square and onto the bleachers that lined 8th Avenue. The rain didn't douse the enthusiasm though as the parade made its way through Manhattan. In the lowest temperatures I'd experienced since leaving England, I stood at the corner of 7th Avenue and 42nd Street surrounded by rampant consumerism. Big screen adverts for jewellery, perfume, hip-hop albums, TV shows and theatre tickets burnt up millions of watts of electricity right before my eyes as the faces of tourists gawped skywards. It rains mass marketing and the promotion of celebrity twenty-four hours a day in Times Square and plonked right in the middle is a small police station, swathed in neon, that looks just like a TV studio. It wasn't always like this, of course. Formerly called Longacre Square, it was once a boon for pickpockets but soon became the hub of the city's Theatre District once Oscar Hammerstein had opened the Republic and the Victoria in 1899, the latter attracting the attention of Gypsy Rose Lee before becoming the better known Minsky's. The 'Times' moniker was added in 1904 after the nearby New York Times tower. This also gave rise to the incredibly stupid New Year's Eve celebration that consists of a ball falling down a stick or something.

It's easy to forget that indefatigable Manhattan is an island, and I'd visited plenty on my journey, but none as fascinating as this. None that were home to 1.5 million people, none with Greek revival architecture, and none that could boast over sixty museums. At times, it can be as hot as anywhere else I'd been, or as cold as the English winter I would soon be returning to. It was everything at once.

New York itself is home to more than seven million people and covers an area of just in excess of 300sq miles. Within that, up to eighty different languages and dialects can be heard, from the Harlem and El Barrio (Spanish Harlem) districts of upper Manhattan, all the way south to the Teutonic settlement of Yorkville, the Irish of Hell's Kitchen in Midtown, and further on, Chinatown, the 'Littles' of Italy, India, Korea, Ukraine and the Jewish community centred around Rivington Street on the Lower East Side. Manhattan has always welcomed its immigrants, usually through the gates of Ellis Island. The immigration depot on the island, now a museum, closed in 1954 but by then some of the biggest names in entertainment had arrived and thrived, most notably Irving Berlin, Jolson, Samuel Goldwyn and Rudolph Valentino, who all arrived over a twenty year period between 1893 and 1913 and went on to become absolute titans in their respective fields. In later years, Harry Houdini lived on West 113th Street. Andrew Carnegie, the Scottish philanthropist who funded Middlesbrough's Central Library where much of this book was researched, resided at East 91st Street, and, arguably New York's most famous ex-pat resident of recent times, John Lennon, lived and died at the Dakota Building.

It was also, more interestingly for me personally, the old stamping ground of one Robert Zimmerman, particularly the Greenwich Village area. I could see what attracted young Robert, later Bob Dylan, to the still bohemian part of Manhattan as I sat in Washington Square Park with Stanford White's 1895-built marble arch to my left. I read on the plaque beside it that in 1916, a group of 'creatives' led by Dadaist pioneer Marcel Duchamp climbed to the top and declared the square an independent republic, as part of the new state of 'New Bohemia'. This was all very well, although he should really have been spending his time more productively, fighting in the First World War for example, but I couldn't work out how they'd gotten up there. Months later, I read in the New York edition of the consistently brilliant Eyewitness Travel Guides that the right hand pillar of the tower contains a staircase. Like the rest of America at first glance then, the arch wasn't as it seemed. Until September 11th 2001, the view directly through the arch was of the

World Trade Centre, depending on which side you stood, as seen in just about every film made in New York before that fateful day. Looking west from where I sat was a statue of Guiseppe Garibaldi, the famous biscuit pioneer. He was exiled on Staten Island in the 1800s before returning to Italy to resume the fight for unification. It was also in Washington Square Park that Samuel Morse had first demonstrated the code that would carry his name for long after, but enough of such trifling achievements. I needed to find the house of the man who wrote A Hard Rains-a-Gonna Fall.

Dylan had lived a short walk away from Washington Square Park, at the corner of Jones and West 45th Streets, in the early 1960s, with Suze Rotolo, the two of them and the snow-capped house later immortalised on the cover of Bob's Freewheelin' album. Alongside Dave Van Ronk, and a host of other folk singers, one of whom I would later meet, Dylan gigged around the bars and clubs of Macdougall Street, eking out a living at places like the Gaslight and Café Wha? The latter, still running Dylan notices on the wall outside, was closed when I arrived. I'd previously only seen black and white footage of Macdougall Street but here it was in glorious Technicolor.

The musicians of the day had taken their cue from literary giants like Jack Kerouac, who could regularly be seen at Le Figaro, the coffee bar further on up the road at the crossroads of Bleecker Street. I contemplated all of this creative history as I ate at Pizzeria, about half way down the street, and opposite a bar where moments later I accidentally spent $6 on a bottle of beer, despite a $1 per bottle offer that was on. I was so enraged with myself at the time that I've forgotten how it happened.

I calmed myself down with a visit to what was once Dylan's local, the White Horse Tavern, which seemed to have an almost supernatural air to it as I looked at it from across Hudson Street. It was in the White Horse that poet Dylan Thomas supposedly took his last sip in 1953, before Bob borrowed his name at the turn of the decade. Thomas actually died at the Chelsea Hotel on West 23rd Street. Reading Time Out New York at the bar, I saw that

Peter Yarrow, an old friend of Dylan's, and the first third of Peter, Paul And Mary, was playing a free gig at the Church Of Latter Day Saints up on Columbus, as part of the festivities that marked the turning on of the city's Christmas lights.

I inadvertently came across another fragment, well two actually, of popular culture that day, that I'd never previously heard of, as I was nosing around Manny's Music Store on West 48th Street. It was there I discovered the fable of 'Old Yellow', according to the display 'the world's most played musical instrument'. In a glass case hung a decrepit yellow Fender electrical guitar, or at least it was yellow at one time. By now, the paint had faded or had been scratched off to reveal the wood beneath. The head had been broken off but was still on display. The story goes that in the 1960s, it was Manny's policy that potential customers wishing to purchase an amplifier must use 'Old Yellow', rather than their own guitar, which they always brought along anyway, therefore the sound quality was determined by the amplifier rather than anyone's modified guitar.

Consider then, the amount of people who passed through the store every day, some just there to jam and not necessarily buy anything but who still had to use 'Old Yellow'. Manny wouldn't budge on policy, even when regulars George Harrison, Jimi Hendrix and Eric Clapton turned up at one time or another insisting that they use their own guitars. They all played 'Old Yellow'. Hendrix grew to like it though, and made Manny a handsome offer for it. Manny refused, as he did years later when John Lennon offered $200 for it. Still it remains, unplayable now, the guitar that one day saw a queue consisting of Joe Cocker, Jerry Garcia and Bob Dylan, all waiting to play it.

'The Village', as Greenwich Village is often called, began to develop in 1822 when city folk fleeing the Yellow Fever epidemic of the greater area came here to seek refuge. The area's confusing design of angular streets and identical-looking houses is at odds with the rest of Manhattan's simply numbered patchwork layout, and reflects its residents' non-conformist nature. Its key areas are Washington

Square Park and Sheridan Square, the latter the site of the draft riots of 1863, and in 1969, the Stonewall Inn riots. It was then, a place for rebellion, but anyone brought to task for such a thing may well have found themselves, up until 1945 at least, at Jefferson Market Courthouse. 'Old Jeff', named after one time president Thomas Jefferson, was also the site of what the New York Times called 'the trial of the century'.

It concerned the murder of architect Stanford White by millionaire Harry K Thaw. White's contribution to New York can't be overestimated. As well as Washington Square Park's marble arch, and the Players Club in Gramercy Park, which could boast Mark Twain and Winston Churchill among its members, he also remodelled the Castle Clinton Monument at Battery Park into the aquarium that exists today, as part of Mckim, Mead and White, the city's most famous architectural company. His best-known work though, is the second development of Madison Square Garden that he oversaw during the late 1880s. It soon became the place to be seen for the high society Broadway crowd and it was on the rooftop terrace, during a performance of Mam'zelle Champagne, that he was shot dead by Thaw, jealous of White's relationship with his former lover, showgirl Evelyn Nesbit. The ensuing trial revealed to a gripped public the decadence and excess of Manhattan's elite as never before.

Walking back up 8th Avenue from the Village that day, I saw a man blasted 10ft in the air when a Durango people carrier charged through the crossroads at West 22nd Street. As with most men involved in such incidents, he simply dusted himself off, through severely gritted teeth, and immediately checked to see if his bike was alright. By now the bike was the least alright thing I'd ever seen, having been reduced rather neatly to exactly a quarter of its original size. The man continued his textbook 'bloke in an accident' drill by becoming increasingly agitated by the crowd's insistence that they call an ambulance. This being New York, eyewitnesses were on the scene within minutes and I overheard two delivery men unloading a van informing someone that the man had been thrown, "twenty… no wait… forty feet in the air, maaan."

On the Saturday night of my stay, I went down to Madison Square Garden with $30 in my pocket in order to hustle a ticket for the New York Knicks v Chicago Bulls basketball game. Wishful thinking perhaps, but at the hostel I'd been told that a good way to get a cheap ticket was to turn up at the cashier's window just before the start of the game, when you might pay as low as $20. I did this and was informed that only two single seats were left, at a cost of $230, which even now I still think I misheard, but not before I'd haggled a man almost to the point of a nervous breakdown on 7th Avenue. There was no shortage of touts around Penn Station, all chorusing the same thing, "Got Knick's tix." I was wary of buying from a tout because of the risk of buying a fake ticket, rather than paying over the odds. There was no chance of that, but one tout had me marked as a soft touch. I was in no mood to be messed around and when I merely enquired as to the going rate one guy snapped, "Hey, you wanna buy 'em or not?" ushering me off the street.

"How much first?" I said, manoeuvring away from him. He wanted me to say I would buy before he told me the price.

"How much?" I repeated.

He was offended that we were not doing it on his terms.

"Hey, come on buddy," he tried.

"How much? Gimme something to work with," I said.

He tried to usher me again, away from the middle of the street. Then his accomplice arrived.

"No price. No money," I barked, and walked on.

I overheard him saying, "Fuck him, let that cracker walk a few blocks."

I'd really arrived now, being called a 'cracker' by a New Yorker. I smiled and turned away. I didn't need a ticket as badly as he needed to sell one. I walked the few blocks, as he suggested, then, as I reached the Garment District, I felt a hand on my shoulder. I turned sharply. It was the accomplice.

"Alright mate?" I said.

"Okay, okay," he started, "these cost $168 but you can have one for a straight $100," producing two tickets from his pocket. They looked authentic enough, although I'd never seen a basketball ticket before in my life.

"Forget it, mate," I replied, and again turned to leave.

He tried again. "$75?"

I was still walking.

"$60?"

Faster now, and grinning as his false economy collapsed before my eyes. Now he was selling a ticket that he claimed was worth $168, for $60!

A block from Penn Station, the first guy came running over to break the stalemate.

"Hey, hey, buddy." Now I was his buddy, "...what do you want to pay?"

Now I was naming the price.

"$30," I said, through an enormous smile.

He knew it was game over. "$40," he pleaded.

I felt sorry for him by now.

"$30." I wasn't budging.

"Aww maan," he whined, screwing his face up, "I can't go lower than $40. I just can't."

I knew he couldn't sell for less than that and still make a profit. I'd crippled him. I stared at him for a few seconds, to give the impression I was thinking about it, but I wasn't. He hopped excitedly from foot to foot. $40 for a Knicks v Bulls ticket is pretty good, I thought, but I could take it or leave it. I had to leave it as I only had $30 in my pocket. I looked across the street.

"Hey, that's Macy's department store, right?" I asked.

"Yuh. Why?"

"I gotta see that place. I only ever saw it on the telly, you see." With that, I drifted between the yellow cabs and bagel stands, leaving behind a broken man with an immovable basketball ticket.

At the corner of 56th and Madison, I watched a hopelessly-staged card game, played entirely for my benefit. The basic premise was to watch your card as it was turned face down and then moved around rapidly along with two others, a variation on the cups and balls game, before selecting 'your' card. Firstly, a woman who 'doesn't know how to play', her own words, had an astonishing run of beginner's luck that the dealer laid on so thick that even she seemed taken aback, although the ruse was punctured slightly when he refused to pay her. It went downhill from there. By now, I was the 'mark', the 'limey' about to be fleeced by the brash 'yankee'. Not quite. Another challenger appeared.

"Gimme five goes," he demanded excitedly. In a stunning display of method acting, he actually handed over some money to the dealer. Then the dealer thrust $100 into my hand and said I could keep it, as long as I had twenty goes at $5 each. I handed the money to the woman who was supposed to be 'player one', confusing her so much that she panicked and immediately returned it to the dealer, who she now somehow knew the name of.

The above are just two examples of the fine American traditions of haggling and hustling that Manhattan was founded on, thanks to the shrewd bartering of Dutchman Peter Minuit, who in 1626 bought the island from the Algonquin Indians for the measly sum of $24 worth of trinkets. The Dutch had arrived in 1621 to set up a fur trading post after hearing of explorer Giovanni da Verrazzano's sighting of the harbour years earlier. The Dutch landing was a success and the area began to prosper in what they called New Amsterdam. True to form, in 1664, the English showed up and made it their own, rechristening it New York and running it successfully, until the American War Of Independence in 1783.

It wasn't until 1898 that New York came to consist of the five boroughs we now know, comprising Brooklyn, the largest of the five, Queens, connected since 1909 to Manhattan by the Queensboro Bridge, Staten Island, The Bronx, and of course, Manhattan. Even after what would now be called the 'Americanisation' of New York, it still maintains much of its Dutch heritage, especially in its place names. Broadway comes from the Dutch name Breede Wegh. The Bed-Stuy housing project that remains today is named after hard-line Dutch governor Peter Stuyvesant, and the city's many museums carry artefacts such as the earliest known European relic, timber from a Dutch vessel called the Tiger that dates back to 1613. Under English rule, the city was fortified, most significantly in 1693 when ninety-two cannons were installed in an area that became referred to as the Battery, on the current site of Battery Park. In the first quarter of the 1700s, the cross-dressing Lord Cornbury was appointed governor, a slave market was established, and the city's first newspaper launched. Fifty years later, and as with most of the British colonies at one time or another, the locals began to get annoyed, eventually deciding there was only one thing for it: a rebellion. In an economically sound move, the statue of King George III was torn down and melted to make ammunition.

Then one fellow up the road in Boston had a brainwave. In protest at high taxes imposed by the British, he and his merry band threw imported tea into the harbour, hence the Boston Tea Party. The group knew then that if you really want to get up the nose of an Englishman, you couldn't do much worse than destroy his supply of tea. Without tea, the English troops refused to start work every morning and spent most of the day sitting around in the van reading the New York Gazette. Order was restored in 1783 with the signing of the Treaty of Paris that saw the defeated British forces flee the city. Six years later at Federal Hall and George Washington was sworn in as the country's first president.

Apart from the children, and grandchildren, of most of the audience, I was by the far the youngest person at the Peter Yarrow concert. The festivities for the switching on of the Christmas lights continued outside as the New Orleans Pinstripe Jazz Band got the crowds swinging, assisted by a group of break-dancing street punks from Philadelphia. A circle was formed and onlookers took it in turns to cut loose on the pavement. Inside, in a conference room at the Church Of Latter Day Saints on Columbus Avenue, as advertised, stood Peter Yarrow, accompanied on stage by his daughter Beth and stand-up bass genius Rufus Cappadoccio, "one of the most talented musicians I've ever worked with," said Peter.

Praise indeed from a man who performed regularly alongside Dylan down in the bars of Macdougall Street. The audience were much too mature to demand that he 'play the hits' but when he started in on Leaving On A Jet Plane, which he dedicated to former bandmate Mary Travers, everyone went "oooaahhh", at the same time and the woman next to me began to cry.

With two days proper left before I returned to England, I couldn't think of a more appropriate song. He ended with two anthems of the oppressed, Woody Guthrie's This Land Is Your Land, and We Shall Overcome.

"You don't know who Peter Yarrow is, right?" the woman wrongly assumed. An unavoidable assumption I suppose, because of the age difference.

"Yes I do, but I can't claim to have been there in the early sixties. How was it?" I asked. Only my English accent and the fact that we were in God's house saved me from a clip round the ear.

With one full day left, I needed to cram in the Brooklyn Bridge, Ground Zero and what Mickey Zee called, "the big Green bitch", but most of the world recognises as the Statue Of Liberty. And the Guggenheim Museum, the Flatiron, Chrysler and Empire State buildings, and Grand Central Station. I made an early start, walking for the last time through Central Park and onto 'museum mile' on the Upper East Side. I didn't want to go inside the Guggenheim, I just wanted to have a look at its unusual design from the outside. This plan was scuppered though when I arrived and found that it was currently undergoing renovations, and as a result was completely obscured by advertising hoardings and scaffolding. Either that or it was some kind of exhibit. I stayed on 5th Avenue all the way past Trump Tower and Rockerfeller Plaza, where yet more Christmas lights were being turned on, this time by Christina Aguilera, according to an advert I'd seen on TV, and through Midtown, before stopping at the crossroads of East 34th Street, the site of New York's highest structure, the Empire State Building.

It's usually this, and the World Trade Centre, that garner the attention of tourists, as far as big buildings go, the latter for nonarchitectural reasons, but the city is home to many eye-popping feats of construction, that are lesser known to many.

Take for example, the Art Deco General Electric Building on Lexington Avenue, or the Gothic threat of St Patrick's Cathedral at the corner of 5th Avenue and 50th Street. The former, being Art Deco, is similar to its bigger, shinier brother, the Chrysler Building, and was designed to compliment St Bartholomew's Church next door. It succeeded in totally overshadowing the church, although viewed from the right angle they seem to get along. St Patrick's Cathedral on the other hand, stood alone and looked every inch the most interesting building in the city, inside and out. Looking at James Renwick's 2,500 seater from across 5th Avenue reminded me immediately of Edinburgh's Scott Monument, its soaring white towers guarding its 20,000lb bronze doors. Force your way through these and inside you'll find, among other exhibits, sculptor William O Partridge's Pieta and the shrine of Elizabeth Ann Seton, the first Native American to be made a saint. St Patrick's is the largest Catholic cathedral in the country and was first conceived by Archbishop John Hughes in 1850, but not completed until 1878, its cloud-tickling spires finished ten years later.

There's little I can say here about the events of September 11th 2001 that hasn't already been said and I was unsure what to expect as I approached Ground Zero via Vesey Street. My mind soon drifted as I considered the narrow enclosed streets that surround the immediate area. There was little room to manoeuvre at the best of times, what with delivery men going about their business, and pavement cafes doing the same, as commuters came and went, so I could hardly imagine the hysteria of being in such an enclosed area as 110 storeys of death, dust and debris rained down on Lower Manhattan. I then passed the fenced off building site that could have been anywhere in the world, were it not for the poignant memorial at the Liberty Plaza side.

It showed a timeline of events from the day, mounted on the metal fence, and a gallery of photos from in and around the building taken during, and shortly after the attacks, one of which said more about the events of the day than anything I've ever seen or read on the subject. I won't waste words on such a thing here, other than to say that if you ever visit the exhibition, you should check out the work of photographer Steve Simon.

In the middle of this emotional scene of hundreds of visitors paying their respects, a woman ranted and raved at the top of her voice, which took the edge off the whole thing. Her accent was so thick I couldn't work out what she was saying or what she was on. She was either anti-American or pro-shouting. Either way she needed a good kick in the teeth. Everyone seemed to ignore her, just another one of New York's diverse cultural orators.

Brooklyn Bridge is a short walk from Liberty Plaza, along Park Row, and I made it my next stop as a damp mist approached from the Lower East Side. As a result, visibility was low as I stared through the Brooklyn tower portal, another fine example of Gothic architecture and the gateway to Brooklyn, or Manhattan, depending on which side you were on. As the Bayonne Ferry passed beneath me, I thought of German engineer John Roebling, who in the 1860s found himself surrounded by the ice of the frozen river during a ferry crossing and gradually came to develop the idea of a bridge connecting one side to the other. In 1883, his dream was realised when the 1,091metre suspension span was opened. Roebling wasn't around to see it however. In 1869, just as construction was about to begin, he was crushed by a ferry when his foot was caught against the landing dock.

He died soon after and it was left to his son to oversee completion of the project. He wouldn't survive either, eventually contracting caisson's disease, later diagnosed as the 'bends', caused by the water pressure increasing as workers dug lower and lower into the river bed from inside the caissons, that left him paralysed (a caisson is the enclosed chamber beneath the bridge's towers that enabled the men to work beneath the water's surface). His wife then took over under his bed-ridden direction. Thereafter, the bridge was plagued by a series of self-perpetuated, bizarre accidents. During its first year of existence, a woman tripped over on the bridge. Moments later, twelve people had been crushed to death by the crowd of 20,000 people present in the ensuing hysteria. Others escaped by jumping into the river. How such tragedy evolved from such an innocuous occurrence is still uncertain. They were not the only ones jumping into the river though. Almost two years to the day later, Robert Odlum, in order to win a bet, did the very same and died from internal bleeding, his winnings still unclaimed to this day.

Today the bridge has the same weather beaten hue of the Statue of Liberty and looks as formidable. It had to be, this was New York.

My trip was coming to an end and what better way to finish it off than with a stroll into Harlem to do some laundry. I was unsure of the protocol when it came to washing dirty underwear in one of America's largest African-American communities and the colour issue made me feel slightly uncomfortable. The colour issue I refer to of course alludes to the fact that I was wearing purple socks, the only pair I had left having lost the others, and the perfect complement to the milk white skin of my ankles that were highlighted regularly by my too-short trousers. The homeless congregated around the stoops of the adjoining buildings as others shuffled around with shopping trolleys full of clothes and junk. They had few possessions but for the bundles of clothes they dragged around with them. I was exactly the same but I had a home to go to.

CHAPTER 18:
NORTH

To London, where I cement my reputation as a true Yorkshireman by complaining about the prices and leaving in a huff.

"How I yearned for the days of the $3 a night hostel."

I'd been warned about 're-entry syndrome' before and during the trip and now I was having to prepare for it. I needed to condense the story of a year long trip into the time it took to drink ten free pints. Even now there still comes the constant barrage of questioning to which I respond on autopilot: "Where was the best place you went?", "Weren't you scared?", "Are there really no clocks in Las Vegas?", "Didn't you want to kill each other?", "Haven't you seen Wolf Creek?", "Is Rusty really that incompetent?", etc, etc. Incidentally, the answers to the above are as follows: New York, although this changes on a regular basis; Nah, but really I was at least once and as a result, I will never sail on a boat made of lolly sticks again; No, but at any one time it's either day or night and that's enough to get you through the night. Or day. Or whatever it is; Yes; Yes, but not until I'd returned to England and finally yes, I've never been more certain of anything in my whole life.

I arrived back in the 'Old Country' at 8.26am on a bright November morning. By 8.27am, I was ready to leave again. I couldn't though. I'd spent the national debt of Greece on a train ticket to Leeds.

"If you are returning to King's Cross within thirty days, you can do so for just one extra pound, sir," the clerk informed me, counting the seventy she'd just prised from my iron fist.

Needless to say, I wasn't. I shared the journey to Leeds with a Geordie fantasy role-play enthusiast, listening in as he told his sidekick, and the rest of the carriage, that actually, "Even tho' ah divn't look 'ard like, ah've given wor kid a good kickin' down the

Bigg market an' it took four bobbies to pull me off." By 'pulling him off', I assume he meant during the fight.

I reintegrated myself back into Blighty society by spending a few days with friends in Leeds, then Wakefield, thinking I would gradually downsize as far as cities went, before returning to Middlesbrough, which would eventually seem like a sleepy little satellite town by the time I got back.

I was looking forward to not having to stay in squalid accommodation any more. That would have to wait as instead I crashed at the student house of a good friend of mine in Headingley. How I yearned for the days of the $3 a night hostel. It took me half an hour to get an answer at the door because, "We thought you were the landlord", but once inside I was permitted to sit on a throne of beer cans. I should have done this before I went away in order to prepare for the horrors that were to come. The following day, I went for a drink with two secondary school teacher friends, both of whom have instructed me not to name them, suffice to say both are old enough to know better, and looked on as one of them almost got into a fight with a Manchester United fan over a highly debatable penalty awarded against Middlesbrough.

I know what you're thinking: 'Manchester United awarded a highly debatable penalty against Middlesbrough, or anyone for that matter? Surely not?' The other verbally abused members of the public from the comfort of a double-decker bus. Then I fell over in the pub, one of the sure signs of jet lag. I'd changed but nothing else had.